Law of the Sea and Maritime Delimitation

The law of maritime delimitation has been shaped by the interpretation of certain provisions of the United Nations Convention on the Law of the Sea, which has led to State practice being neglected in current scholarship. This book presents an overview of the under-examined question of the impact of State practice in Latin America and the Caribbean on the development of the law of maritime delimitation.

Examining the status of maritime boundaries in Latin America and the Caribbean, this book also ponders the impact of State practice and case law on the law of maritime delimitation. It outlines the historical framework of the establishment of maritime jurisdiction during colonial times and assesses the evolution of maritime delimitation and the contribution of Latin America and the Caribbean to the modern law of the sea. It discusses the law of maritime delimitation and, through jurisprudence, the development of the three-stage methodology to describe and explain maritime delimitation agreements in Latin America and the Caribbean according to the method or methods of delimitation employed. It reviews maritime boundaries in Latin America and the Caribbean that were submitted to third-party adjudication as well as provisional arrangements, considering the role of State practice in Latin America and the Caribbean on the development of the law of maritime delimitation.

With a renewed focus on maritime delimitation, and increasing litigation focused on Latin America and the Caribbean, the book will be of interest to students, academics and practitioners in the fields of international law, law of the sea, and State practice.

Angel V. Horna is a lawyer and career diplomat. He is currently Counsellor at the Permanent Mission of Peru to the International Organizations in Geneva. Prior to that, he was an Adviser to the Cabinet of Peru's Foreign Minister. He was also the Legal Adviser of the Permanent Mission of Peru to the United Nations in New York (2014–2019), including during Peru's last term on the UN Security Council (2018–2019). He was also the Vice-Chair of the Sixth Committee of the General Assembly in the 72nd session. He worked at the Peruvian Advisory Office for the Law of the Sea, during which time he took part in the preparation of Peru's participation in the oral proceedings of the Maritime Dispute (*Peru* v. *Chile*) before the International Court of Justice. He was also part of the first training programme on dispute settlement established by the International Tribunal for the Law of the Sea.

He attained a PhD in international law at the Graduate Institute of International and Development Studies (IHEID) in Switzerland, trained for a senior civil service career at École nationale d'administration (ENA) in France, and earned a summa cum laude law degree from the University of Lima (UL) in Peru. He has held teaching positions at the University of Lima, the Peruvian University of Applied Sciences, and the University of San Ignacio de Loyola.

Routledge Research on the Law of the Sea

Available titles in this series include:

The International Court of Justice in Maritime Disputes
The Case of Chile and Peru
Julio Faundez

Freedoms of Navigation in the Asia-Pacific Region
Strategic, Political and Legal Factors
Sam Bateman

Maritime Claims and Boundary Delimitation
Tensions and Trends in the Eastern Mediterranean Sea
Nicholas A. Ioannides

Freedom of Navigation and the Law of the Sea
Warships, States and the Use of Force
Cameron Moore

Due Diligence and the High Seas
Tony Cabus

The Law of the Sea
Normative Context and Interactions With Other Legal Regimes
Edited by Nele Matz-Lück, Øystein Jensen and Elise Johansen

Law of the Sea and Maritime Delimitation
State Practice and Case Law in Latin America and the Caribbean
Angel V. Horna

Law of the Sea and Maritime Delimitation

State Practice and Case Law in Latin America and the Caribbean

Angel V. Horna

Routledge
Taylor & Francis Group
LONDON AND NEW YORK

First published 2023
by Routledge
4 Park Square, Milton Park, Abingdon, Oxon OX14 4RN

and by Routledge
605 Third Avenue, New York, NY 10158

Routledge is an imprint of the Taylor & Francis Group, an informa business

British Library Cataloguing-in-Publication Data
A catalogue record for this book is available from the British Library

ISBN: 978-1-032-26906-1 (hbk)
ISBN: 978-1-032-26907-8 (pbk)
ISBN: 978-1-003-29045-2 (ebk)

DOI: 10.4324/9781003290452

Typeset in Times New Roman
by Apex CoVantage, LLC

To Mia and Barbara

Contents

Foreword

The literature on international law in the field of maritime delimitation is quite voluminous. Good texts analysing the question from a general perspective, or from a particular aspect of its intricate process of adoption, are not scarce. However, the analysis of regional perspectives, although existent, is not entirely covered by doctrine. One must congratulate Dr Angel V. Horna for having filled a gap in this regard. His book is an important contribution to the knowledge, understanding and analysis of the input provided by the Latin American and Caribbean States in this field. Indeed, this volume even goes back to the period of independence achieved by those States in the nineteenth and twentieth centuries. For the first time, the practice during the expansion of colonialism in the so-called New World, as far back as the eighteenth century, is also scrutinised and its scope is determined.

It is true that other studies have also attempted to shed light on certain subregions of Latin America, attempting in particular to reveal the possible existence of regional customary rules for the establishment of maritime delimited areas. Dr Horna's book goes beyond this objective. It passes under review the Latin American and Caribbean practice from a broad perspective. The author rightly gives the notion of "practice" a comprehensive meaning. Thus, the positions adopted by States during the United Nations Conferences on the Law of the Sea, the individual and collective statements, the agreements proposed or concluded among them and with extra-continental States, and the positions defended during proceedings are all presented to the reader.

At this stage, there is no need to insist on the key role played by Latin America in the extension of the outer limits of the territorial sea and the emergence of the exclusive economic zone. A similar comment can also be made on Latin American practice in the field of the existence and extension of the continental shelf, although US President Harry Truman is generally recognised as its "father".

Latin American and Caribbean countries have also been good "clients" of the International Court of Justice and international tribunals in general and in the field of maritime delimitation in particular. The geographical and historical particularities of these cases have given rise to a significant range of situations that have been discussed and settled. As a matter of course, these situations are not always exclusive to the region considered. As such, they allow examples and conclusions to be reached that can be extended and applied to other regions of the world.

In addition to all the judgments and awards delivered until 2021, the present volume examines 43 maritime delimitation or related treaties concluded between 1942 and 2021. They are considered in the temporal context, taking into account the status of the law of the sea existing at the time of their conclusion.

While primary sources have constituted the essential "raw material" of Dr Horna's research, the author has also taken into account the extensive literature existing in this field. One can commend his openness to the diversity of languages in which these academic contributions have been produced. The reader will also be grateful for the very useful tables annexed to the text.

In sum, whether or not one agrees with all or part of Dr Horna's analysis, this book will no doubt be very welcome to both scholars and practitioners from all regions of the world and will constitute a useful tool for all of them.

Prof. Marcelo Kohen
Professor of International Law, Geneva Graduate Institute
Geneva, 22 May 2022

Acknowledgements

I should first like to thank Professor Marcelo Kohen, whose support and guidance as PhD supervisor allowed me to carry out this project. I am also most grateful to other international law professors that I have had over the years, including Professor Lucius Caflisch, whose inspirational instruction allowed me to discover the Law of the Sea during his last seminar at HEI (present-day Graduate Institute) in 2005–2006; Professor Tullio Treves, who played a significant role in my further specialisation in the Law of the Sea; and Professor Pierre-Marie Dupuy. Other international law professors provided me with valuable insights on previous versions of this work, including Professor Tullio Scovazzi, Professor Alex Oude Elferink and Professor Mathias Forteau. Special mention also goes to Sir Michael Wood and Mr Eduardo Valencia Ospina. To all of them I offer my deepest gratitude.

I should also like to acknowledge the direct or indirect support given to my academic pursuits by a number of distinguished figures of the Peruvian Foreign Service, including former foreign ministers, Ambassador Allan Wagner, Ambassador Manuel Rodríguez Cuadros, Ambassador Oscar Maúrtua de Romaña and Ambassador Gustavo Meza-Cuadra; as well as Ambassador Francisco Tenya, Ambassador Paul Duclos and Professor Juan José Ruda Santolaria. In the same vein, I should also like to thank Mrs Edwige Belliard and Mr Olivier Guyonvarch at the French Ministry of Foreign Affairs for their support during my traineeship at the Quai d'Orsay.

Similarly, I would like to express my gratitude to several institutions that, in one way or another, have supported my education and research, in particular the Swiss Confederation (Commission fédérale des bourses pour étudiants étrangers – CFBE de la Confédération Suisse); the Nippon Foundation, which funded the training programme that I undertook at the International Tribunal for the Law of the Sea in Hamburg; the Center for Oceans Law and Policy – University of Virginia School of Law, which funded my participation in the Rhodes Academy of Oceans Law and Policy (Thirteenth Session); the Ministry of Foreign Affairs of Peru and the Academia Diplomática del Perú in Lima; the Max-Planck-Institut für ausländisches öffentliches Recht und Völkerrecht in Heidelberg; the International Hydrographic Organization in Monaco; and the Ministry of Foreign Affairs of

France (Sous-direction du droit de la mer, du droit fluvial et des pôles), as well as Campus France.

Special thanks go to those who, at some point over the years, inspired, helped or encouraged me, including Ramón Huapaya, José Marín, Sarah Grimmer, Pablo Sandonato de León, Heidi Hardt, Luis García Corrochano, Wagner Menezes, Mosammat Shahanara Monica, Leyla Aslanova, José Antonio Saavedra, Alexandre Piquet and Marirene Muniz. I would also like to recognise the inspirational roles played in general by my colleagues, legal advisers from Permanent Missions to the United Nations in New York and Geneva, as well as colleagues working at different levels of the United Nations Secretariat, civil society and academia. Moreover, I would like to thank Karen Tucker, Daniel Stewart and Charlotte Beauclerk.

I should also like to thank my beloved mother, Alicia; my father, Dr José Horna Torres, a law professor holding two PhDs; and my brothers, José, Douglas Enrique, David and Pierre Martín.

Last but by no means least, my gratitude beyond measure to Barbara and our daughter Mia, for their love and inspiration; not to mention Mia's advice on the design of the cover.

Abbreviations

ABLOS	Advisory Board on Law of the Sea
AFDI	Annuaire français de droit international
AJIL	American Journal of International Law
ASIL	American Society of International Law
BFSP	British Foreign and State Papers
BYIL	British Yearbook of International Law
CACJ	Central American Court of Justice
CCS	Convention on the Continental Shelf
CFCLR	Convention on Fishing and Conservation of the Living Resources of the High Seas
CHS	Convention on the High Seas
CTS	Convention on the Territorial Sea and the Contiguous Zone
DOALOS	Division for Ocean Affairs and the Law of the Sea
EEZ	Exclusive economic zone
EXTRAPLAC	Programme français d'extension du plateau continental
ICJ	International Court of Justice
ICLQ	International Comparative Law Quarterly
IJMCL	International Journal of Marine and Coastal Law
ILA	International Law Association
ILC	International Law Commission
ILM	International Legal Materials
ILR	International Law Reports
IMO	International Maritime Organization
ITLOS	International Tribunal for the Law of the Sea
LNTS	League of Nations Treaty Series
NAD	North American Datum
PCA	Permanent Court of Arbitration
PCIJ	Permanent Court of International Justice
RGDIP	Revue générale de droit international public
RIAA	Reports of International Arbitral Awards
RPDI	Revista Peruana de Derecho Internacional
OAS	Organization of American States
OAU	Organization of African Unity

UNCLOS	United Nations Convention on the Law of the Sea
UNCLOS I	First UN Conference on the Law of the Sea
UNCLOS III	Third UN Conference on the Law of the Sea
UNLS	United Nations Legislative Series
UNTS	United Nations Treaty Series

Glossary

This glossary includes certain useful definitions, such as the main categories of methods of maritime delimitation, namely, (1) the equidistance method, (2) methods derived from equidistance and (3) other methods.

As for the first category, it is subdivided into (a) simplified equidistance and (b) modified equidistance. The second category, in turn, is subdivided into (a) partial effect, (b) coastal length comparison, (c) perpendicular to the general direction of the coast and (d) bisector. Finally, the third category is subdivided into (a) parallels and meridians, (b) prolongation of the land boundary, (c) enclaving and (d) the thalweg concept.

Method of maritime delimitation

A mathematical application of the relationship between the length of the coastal fronts of States (with opposite or adjacent coasts), which is employed to divide their overlapping maritime jurisdictions.

Methods of maritime delimitation are different than techniques aimed at measuring the outer limits of maritime zones. Whereas the latter include the *tracé parallèle* on the one hand and the "arcs-of-circles" techniques on the other, the former refers to a number of mathematical applications of the relationship between the length of the coastal fronts of States, aimed at dividing overlapping maritime jurisdictions between opposite or adjacent coasts. They are divided into three main categories: equidistance method, methods derived from equidistance and other methods.

Equidistance method

The equidistance method consists of constructing a line "every point of which is equidistant from the nearest points on the baselines from which the breadth of the territorial seas of each of the two States is measured" (UNCLOS, Art. 15). According to technical experts, the equidistance method constitutes a useful start because, pursuant to UNCLOS Article 15, it is the method that has to be employed in the absence of agreement, historic title or other special circumstances. The other good reason to use it is because "it is a well defined geometric method", easy to apply provided the baselines are clearly determined.

Technical considerations aside, equidistance theoretically has three variations, namely, strict equidistance, simplified equidistance and modified equidistance. Yet in practice, the first case, that of strict equidistance – as defined by the 1958 CST and the 1982 Convention – is rather rare, since geographical reality does not allow a line to remain equidistant from the relevant coasts for long. Indeed, a strict equidistance line, comprising a large number of turning points joined by geodesics or other curves, brings about a "rather convoluted line" with all its inconvenient consequences. That is why only simplified and modified equidistance will be tackled below.

Simplified equidistance

This type of line is resorted to when a strict equidistance line brings about a complicated line. It consists therefore of adapting the equidistance line so as to " 'straighten' sections of it", hence reducing the number of turning points. The final result is the so-called area compensated line. The *Manual on Technical Aspects of UNCLOS* defines it as a line that "should consist of the smallest practicable number of elements which still maintain the general course of the original line. The turning points should all be linked by 'straight lines'", resulting in a situation where the "area gained or lost by the States is essentially zero."

Modified equidistance

This variation of the equidistance method seems to be necessary in the case of "outstanding geographical features". While in the case of maritime delimitations between States with opposite coasts, such outstanding features are usually offshore islands, in the case of lateral delimitation such features are commonly promontories in the vicinity of the land boundary terminus, although they could also include islands close to the coast.

In this scenario, the usual solution consists of applying the equidistance line, as a starting step, and then adjusting it by either selecting or discontinuing certain base points or by according a reduced effect to them. The outcome of a modified equidistance, unlike the simplified one, is a greater alteration of the result, which implies an unequal distribution of the maritime space at stake.

In a 1993 work by Legault and Hankey, the authors discussed four types of modified equidistance: selection of base points, partial effect, bisection of angles representing coastal fronts, and ad hoc modifications. Yet in the present research, only the "selection of base points" criteria is considered as the case of a modified equidistance, while some of the others are deemed to be better placed under the following category of "methods derived from equidistance", since as pointed out by Legault and Hankey themselves when referring to their view of modified equidistance, "the resulting modifications can be so substantial that the final boundary may bear only a tenuous relationship to the notion of equidistance."

Methods derived from equidistance

In this second category, one can find the following methods: the partial effect method; the coastal length comparison method; methods related to the "general direction" of the coastline, that is, perpendicular to the general direction of the coast; and the bisector method, which could be said to be a variant of the perpendicular.

Partial effect

As for the partial effect method, it is used when a particular baseline feature, many times an island, has a disproportionate effect on the course of the projected line. This distortion is therefore to be corrected by allocating partial (reduced) effect, no effect at all, or even a ratio of relevant coasts to said feature. Sometimes the solution is to assign it half effect, that is, exactly between a full effect line and a no-effect line. In other circumstances, some smaller features have been given a more reduced effect, such as being accorded only a territorial sea of 12 nautical miles.

Coastal length comparison

The coastal length comparison, referred to on several occasions by case law, consists of ascertaining relevant parts of the coast and then measuring its length. Once this is done, for which technical experts employ several techniques, a comparison between them should follow. If there is a marked difference in coastal lengths, the line might need an adjustment, normally a shifting of the median line towards the shorter coast, so as to achieve an equitable result. Furthermore, if the concerned States manage to agree on the relevant area, which is often difficult to achieve, it is possible to then use modern systems to establish the division of the maritime areas according to the ratio projected from the coastal fronts.

Perpendicular to the general direction of the coast

This constitutes a special form of equidistance, because it consists of drawing a perpendicular to the general direction of the coast. The problem here is how to determine, on an objective basis, what the general direction of a certain coast is. Possible answers to this question include (1) determining a limited length of coastline at either side of the land terminus, (2) taking as a reference the whole of the coasts of both States and (3) taking into account the general direction of the whole landmass spanning several States. The other question is how to draw the straight line that constitutes the "general direction" of a certain coast. It could be a loxodrome, or it could be a line determined by geodetic computation. In any case, it seems possible to say that "[t]he perpendicular method has merit to the extent that, in appropriate circumstances, it produces a simplified equidistance line." Yet, one problem that may arise in this situation is that the starting point of the maritime boundary begins at some distance out at sea, as was decided by the International Court of Justice (ICJ) in its 2007 judgment in the *Nicaragua* v. *Honduras* case.

Bisector

The bisector method is one of the so-called *méthodes de lissage*, and it consists of bisecting "the angle created by lines representing the relevant mainland coast". It is a variant of the perpendicular and "an approximation of the equidistance method". In order to construct the bisector, the general direction of the coasts or parts of the coasts of the incumbent States (adjacent or opposite) have to be determined beforehand. Once it is done, the delimitation line is formed by bisecting the angle formed by the two lines representing the relevant mainland coast. This is to be carried out on the basis of the "macro-geography of a coastline" while taking care not to refashion nature.

Other methods

Parallels and meridians

Also referred to as "arbitrary lines" by the *Manual on Technical Aspects of UNCLOS*, these are the lines that for historical or political reasons are constituted by simple geodesics or loxodromes such as a parallel of latitude, a meridian, parallel lines forming a corridor and the like. They tend to be equitable when the continental coastline follows the same general direction, for instance, west-east or north-south. In that situation, these lines would tend to produce an equitable solution.

However, a widespread use of lines of latitude or longitude in maritime delimitation around the world has been argued by Honduras before the ICJ so as to demonstrate that its claimed "traditional line" has its roots in State practice. Such widespread use includes boundaries in North America, Central America and South America. The method of using a parallel of latitude is even thought to have been employed so as to construct the neutrality zone established in the 1939 Declaration of Panama.

A small number of authors consider the case of "parallel lines", also called the "corridor method", in this category, such as in the 1984 maritime boundary agreement between France and Monaco or the 1987 Dominica and France treaty. By the same token, it appears possible to claim that some portions of the composite lines established by the 2012 *Nicaragua* v. *Colombia* judgment were inspired by this method.

Prolongation of land boundaries

This is one of the methods already considered for codification since the 1930s. It seemed to be a practical method at a time when most States did not claim any space beyond three nautical miles. However, this method may produce an inequitable result where a land boundary does not reach the coast at a right angle, that is to say it does not have at least a last section that is perpendicular to the general direction of the coast. The other shortcoming of the method is that as soon as there are important variations in the macro-geography of the coastline, the projected boundary can rapidly turn inequitable.

Enclaving

This method is usually applied to islands lying at a considerable geographical distance from the coastal State or the rest of an archipelago, which is why it is said that they are located on the "wrong side" of the equidistance line. The application of this method results in a reduced area of maritime space for the island enclaved.

Thalweg concept

The thalweg concept, according to the Institut de droit international, is defined as "the median line of the channel" in the case of the boundary of States separated by a river. Yet that concept, borrowed from the practice concerning river delimitation, does not seem to have a uniform understanding in the law of maritime delimitation. For some, a thalweg is no more than a navigable channel. Others claim it is the median line of the navigable channel, whereas a third group considers it the deepest water line or the centre of the deep water channel (i.e. the line of maximum depth along a river channel or lake) but could exist in any coastal channel. In any case, State practice in maritime delimitation has not made use of this method, despite some authors' advocacy as being applicable to the case of straits.

Loxodrome

Loxodrome, also called a rhumb line or spherical helix, is a curve cutting the meridians of a sphere at a constant nonright angle. Thus, it may be seen as the path of a ship sailing always oblique to the meridian and directed always to the same point of the compass.

Introduction

This book examines the present status of maritime boundaries in Latin America and the Caribbean and discusses the impact of State practice and case law in that region on the law of maritime delimitation. It argues that it was in Latin America and the Caribbean that coastal States put forward the most significant claims concerning the extension of sovereignty, sovereign rights and jurisdiction over the sea. In fact, the extension of fisheries jurisdiction and economic zones to 200 nautical miles was the primary trigger for the need for clearly defined maritime boundaries across all regions in the world.

The law of maritime delimitation has been shaped, to a large extent, by international judges and arbitrators' interpretation and application of international law as reflected in the United Nations Convention on the Law of the Sea (UNCLOS), which is why some have described it as "judge-made" law. Hence case law has helped to reduce subjectivity and uncertainty in this field, which may explain why the focus of most international legal scholarship has been on case law, rather than on State practice.

Exploring the under-examined matter of the impact of State practice in Latin America and the Caribbean on the development of the law of maritime delimitation is thus one of the drivers for this work. It entails an analysis of the practice of States as reflected in 43 maritime boundary agreements currently in force in Latin America and the Caribbean, as well as relevant case law. Based on this analysis, it has been possible to identify and clarify the contribution of the region to this particular branch of the law of the sea.

Other questions addressed in this work include the methods of maritime delimitation in Latin America and the Caribbean, the relationship between State practice in that region and the formation of a general rule of customary international law concerning maritime delimitation, and the ways in which States engage with rules of international law as reflected in maritime delimitation case law.

The initial idea for this research occurred to me while studying the views advanced by both Nicaragua and Honduras on the question of the methods of maritime delimitation, in their *Territorial and Maritime Dispute* before the International Court of Justice (ICJ). That idea turned into researching whether there are peculiar methods of maritime delimitation in the region. In order to do so,

DOI: 10.4324/9781003290452-1

I undertook an examination of those methods in every agreement concluded in the region. Similarly, I looked into relevant judicial decisions and arbitral awards.

Through this exercise I was able to identify the relevance of the relationship between State practice and the law of maritime delimitation. It was hence possible, on the one hand, to determine a number of meaningful developments and key actors in State practice on maritime delimitation in the region; and, on the other, to explore the impact State practice has had on this field of the law. More broadly, I have also attempted to contribute to the field of the law of maritime delimitation, because clearly defined maritime boundaries are essential for good international relations and effective ocean management.

In this context, the working proposition has been that States of Latin America and the Caribbean have made significant contributions to the law of maritime delimitation. To that end I argue that State practice in Latin America and the Caribbean, during the Third United Nations Conference on the Law of the Sea (UNCLOS III), carried great weight in the formulation of the UNCLOS provisions on maritime delimitation; that State practice in Latin America and the Caribbean (before and after UNCLOS III) appears to have been taken into consideration by international courts and tribunals when settling maritime delimitation disputes; and finally, that the need for clearly established maritime boundaries, utilising rules on delimitation, is a result of State practice in Latin America and the Caribbean.

The scope of this book spans a rather large time frame of almost 80 years, that is, between 1942 and 2021. However, it does not aim to look at every aspect pertaining to maritime delimitation during those years. It studies methods of maritime delimitation and only those employed in a specific region, Latin America and the Caribbean. This book similarly sheds light on the wider contribution of the region to the law of the sea more generally, which was the object of a vast literature during the 1970s and 1980s.

In order to achieve this, the book is organised into two main parts. Part I, "Maritime Jurisdiction in Latin America and the Caribbean throughout the Years", includes a chapter briefly presenting Latin America and the Caribbean as a region and covers, from a historical perspective, questions of maritime jurisdiction established *between* and *within* colonial powers in that region. It shows that the former situation was not common but that the latter was even pleaded before international courts and tribunals. Part I also discusses the evolution of the law of maritime delimitation, as well as efforts of codification and progressive development, leading to the conventional framework now in force, in particular the manner in which the three-stage methodology has been attained.

Part II ponders the "Impact of State Practice and Case Law" on the law of maritime delimitation, and is divided into four chapters. The first reviews all maritime delimitation agreements concerning Latin America and the Caribbean, offering a chronological perspective. The second chapter examines the relevant case law on maritime delimitation. It sets out the cases submitted to third-party adjudication and the method(s) of maritime delimitation employed by international courts and tribunals. The next chapter contains references to provisional arrangements of a practical nature, signed but non-ratified maritime delimitation treaties, and outstanding maritime boundaries. Finally, in the chapter "Impact of State Practice on the Law of Maritime Delimitation", I look into the practice mentioned above and conduct an exegesis to identify key developments and key actors. I then proceed to examine the questions surrounding the relationship between State practice and the law of maritime delimitation in the region.

The book concludes that in the almost 80 years that elapsed between 1942 and 2021, a direct relationship appears to have developed between the practice of Latin American and Caribbean States concerning maritime boundary delimitation and the applicable international law. This law, the first version of which was codified in the late 1950s, developed during UNCLOS III and was enshrined, albeit open-endedly, in the 1982 Law of the Sea Convention. Ever since, it has been clarified by maritime boundary case law which has, in turn, reduced elements of subjectivity and uncertainty. The progressive development of the law has benefited a great deal from the practice of States, among which the practice, be it unilateral or bilateral, of Latin American and Caribbean coastal States has carried a great weight.

Part I

Maritime Jurisdiction in Latin America and the Caribbean Throughout the Years

1 Geographical Scope

Latin America refers to all regions of America in which, in the period after Columbus' "discovery", Latin-based languages have been spoken (i.e. Romance languages derived from Latin), such as Spanish (Castilian), Portuguese and French.[1] According to one author, the term "Latin America" was first coined in France during the 1860s.[2] Some even claim that it was taken by the French Empire of Napoleon III during (and in the aftermath of) the French invasion of Mexico (1862–1867) with the aim of positioning France, in the American continent, against Spain, the UK and the US.[3] Different interpretations of the term include (1) as a synonym of *Hispanoamérica* (Spanish America), restricting the term to Spanish-speaking areas; (2) as a synonym of *Iberoamérica*, which includes the Portuguese-speaking regions (i.e. Brazil); and (3) signifying all of the former plus French dependencies of the Americas,[4] particularly in the Caribbean, including Haiti, Martinique and Guadeloupe, as well as French Guyana. Be it as it may, it seems that in no case is the term applied to countries in South America that speak non-Latin-based languages, such as Guyana and Suriname; to several English- and Dutch-speaking islands in the Caribbean; or to Belize in Central America, which has taken English as its official language.[5]

Latin America comprises South America,[6] Central America and other Hispanic territories, including Mexico, Cuba and the Dominican Republic, as well as Haiti.[7] During its independent life, South America has been considered to be among the most stable regions in the world. It has had, comparatively, fewer inter-State wars than any other region of the world.[8] In that context, it has been claimed that because of the territorial transfers involved, out of all the wars that took place in South America, the War of the Pacific brought about the most important modification to the political map.[9] South America extends south and east of the Isthmus of Panama and occupies the southern portion of the American landmass. Although this could be geopolitically contested, in geographical terms it includes nearby islands, such as Aruba, Bonaire and Curaçao (former Dutch Antilles) and Trinidad and Tobago, which are considered to be part of South America's continental shelf. Conversely, the San Andrés Archipelago and Aves Island are part of Colombia and Venezuela, respectively, although not part of South America. Other insular features considered to be part of South America include the Galápagos Archipelago (Ecuador); the Falkland Islands (Malvinas); South Georgia and the South

DOI: 10.4324/9781003290452-3

Sandwich Islands;[10] the Trindade and Martim Vaz Archipelago; and the Fernando de Noronha Archipelago (Brazil).

Generally speaking, Central America extends from the northern borders of Belize and Guatemala to the Isthmus of Panama where it connects with South America. In strict geographical terms, Central America is considered to comprise all mainland regions between the Isthmus of Tehuantepec in Mexico and the Isthmus of Panama.[11] It is bordered to the west by the Pacific Ocean, to the east by the Caribbean Sea and to the north by the Gulf of Mexico. Central America's isthmian configuration and consequent potential as a route connecting two oceans has marked its political destiny, especially that of Nicaragua and Panama.[12] One of the key geographical features on the Pacific coast of Central America is the Gulf of Fonseca, a relatively small bay with a complicated coastline in its inner part. From a legal standpoint it is all the more particular due to its being shared by three coastal States, namely, El Salvador, Honduras and Nicaragua.

The term "Caribbean" refers in turn to a region essentially comprising islands, islets, reefs and cays, yet three mainland States are said to be part of the Caribbean for historical and cultural reasons, although one is located in Central America and two in South America. Those countries are Belize (formerly British Honduras), Guyana (formerly British Guyana), and Suriname. Most of the territories of the Caribbean are English-speaking as they were or are still part of the Commonwealth Caribbean.[13] Some Caribbean States were formerly under French rule, as was the case of Haiti; and some, like Cuba, the eastern half of Hispaniola (i.e. the Dominican Republic) and Puerto Rico used to be under Spanish rule. Within the Caribbean, it is possible to distinguish between the Greater Antilles, comprising the islands of Cuba, Hispaniola (Dominican Republic and Haiti), Puerto Rico and Jamaica, and the Lesser Antilles, mainly composed of English-speaking nations.[14] The Lesser Antilles are, in turn, subdivided into the Windward Islands and the Leeward Islands.[15] Finally, the so-called Northern Islands, namely, the Bahamas and Turks and Caicos Islands (also known as the Lucayan Archipelago), together with the Cayman Islands, are considered part of the Caribbean.

To sum up, for present purposes the expression "Latin American and the Caribbean" is treated as a whole and consists of all territories of the Western Hemisphere including all of Spanish America, Brazil, and all French, Dutch and English-speaking territories south of the US.[16] As regards the waters surrounding these areas, they are located in the Pacific Ocean and Atlantic Ocean, and include, more specifically, the South-East Pacific Ocean, the South-West Atlantic Ocean, the Caribbean Sea and the Gulf of Mexico.

Notes

1 Chaunu, Pierre (1949), *Histoire de l'Amérique Latine*, Paris: Presses universitaires de France, pp. 3 *et seq.*, and Barton, Jonathan R. (1997), *A Political Geography of Latin America*, London and New York: Routledge, p. 5.

2 Barton (1997), *ibid.*, and Dabène, Olivier (2012), *Atlas de l'Amérique latine. Le continent de toutes les révolutions*, Paris: Autrement, p. 7.

3 Bancroft, F. (1896), "The French in Mexico and the Monroe Doctrine", *Political Science Quarterly*, No. 11. Also see: Allain, Jean-Claude; Guillen, Pierre; Soutou, Georges-Henri; Theis, Laurent and Maurice Vaïsse (2005), *Histoire de la diplomatie française. II. De 1815 à nos jours*, Paris: Perrin, pp. 116–119; Rémy, Pierre-Jean (2001), *Trésors et secrets du Quai d'Orsay. Une histoire inédite de la diplomatie française*, Paris: JC Lattès, pp. 567–581; and more recently: Couffignal, Georges (2012), "La politique étrangère de la France vis-à-vis de l'Amérique Latine", in: Couffignal, Georges (ed.), *Amérique latine. L'Amérique latine est bien partie*, Paris: IHEAL, pp. 60–61.

4 Note that the case of Clipperton (also known as *Isla de la Pasión* or *Isla de Médanos*), lying at around 900 km from the closest coast, in Mexico, is special, because it is not clear whether it is part of America. See, however: Remiro Brotóns, Antonio (1993), "Problemas de fronteras en Iberoamérica: la delimitación de espacios marinos", in: Mangas, A. (ed.), *La Escuela de Salamanca y el Derecho Internacional en América: del pasado al futuro*, Salamanca, p. 123. See also: *Arbitral Award on the Subject of the Difference Relative to the Sovereignty over Clipperton Island, Decision Rendered at Rome, 28 January 1931, AJIL*, Vol. 26, pp. 390–394.

5 About the "locational reference to Latin America", Barton (1997) *ibid.*, p. 5, there seems to exist an element of "ethnocentricity" that reflects that the word "America" has been "linguistically usurped" to reinforce US hegemony in Central and South America; see: Barton (1997), *ibid.*; see also: Quijano, Anibal and Immanuel Wallerstein (1992), "Americanity as a concept, or the Americas in the Modern World-System", *International Journal of Social Sciences,* No. 134, p. 549.

6 Argentina, Bolivia, Brazil, Chile, Colombia, Ecuador, Guyana, Paraguay, Peru, Suriname, Uruguay, and Venezuela.

7 Belize (although for some it is rather a Caribbean State), Costa Rica, El Salvador, Guatemala, Honduras, Nicaragua and Panama. A French author described Central America as "seven independent States that share a territory that is smaller than Metropolitan France"; see: Carré, Frédéric and André de Séguin (1998), *Mexique, Golfe, Caraïbes: une méditerranée américaine*, Paris: PUF, pp. 151–175.

8 Buzan, Barry and Ole Waever (2003), *Regions and Powers: The Structure of International Security*, Cambridge: Cambridge University Press, 564 pp. Those wars included: the Cisplatine War between Brazil and Argentina (1825–1828), also known as *Guerra del Brasil* which led to the independence of present-day Uruguay; the War of the Confederation (1836–1839), a conflict between the Peru-Bolivian Confederation and, on the other side, Chile and Argentina; the War (of Peru and Chile) against Spain (1864); the War of the Triple Alliance (1865–1870), also known as Paraguayan War; the War of the Pacific between Chile against the joint forces of Peru and Bolivia (1879–1883); the Chaco War between Bolivia and Paraguay (1932–1935); the Leticia War between Colombia and Peru (1932–1933); the War between Ecuador and Peru (1940–1941), the Cenepa Conflict (1995), also between Ecuador and Peru; and the Falkland Islands (Malvinas) War (1982).

9 The War of the Pacific (1879–1883) was fought between Chile, on the one side, and Bolivia and Peru on the other. It is also known as the "Saltpeter War" due to its original cause, the control over huge quantities of high-quality nitrate deposits (guano and saltpetre) in the Atacama Desert; their fertilising properties; and their being a key ingredient for explosives that had been discovered during the 1840s. As a result of Chile's victory, Bolivia was left a landlocked country, giving to Chile the control of present-day Antofagasta region. Peru, in turn, lost Tarapacá and Arica. See, for general information: Ireland, G. (1938), *Boundaries, Possessions and Conflicts in South America*, Cambridge, MA: Harvard University Press, pp. 160–175; and Marchant, A. (1944), *Boundaries in the Latin American Republics*, Washington DC: US Government Printing Office, pp. 279–280. On 24 April 2013 Bolivia submitted to the International Court

of Justice an application instituting proceedings against Chile. The dispute concerned negotiations on Bolivia's sovereign access to the Pacific Ocean. Bolivia's application requested the Court to adjudge and declare, *inter alia*, that Chile has the obligation to negotiate with Bolivia in order to reach an agreement granting Bolivia a fully sovereign access to the Pacific Ocean, and that Chile must perform the said obligation in good faith, promptly, formally, within a reasonable time and effectively, to grant Bolivia a fully sovereign access to the Pacific Ocean; see: *Obligation to Negotiate Access to the Pacific Ocean* (*Bolivia v. Chile*), *Judgment, I.C.J. Reports 2018*, p. 507.

10 The question of the Falkland Islands (Malvinas) will not be tackled in the present research since there is a dispute about their sovereignty between the UK and Argentina.

11 "La stricte définition géographique de l'Amérique Centrale réserve cette dénomination à l'ensemble des régions comprises entre l'isthme de Tehuantepec et l'isthme de Panama . . ."; see: Carré and de Séguin (1998), *ibid.*, pp. 151–175.

12 Girot, Pascal O. (1994), "The Interoceanic canal and boundaries in Central America. The case of the San Juan River", in: Girot, Pascal O. (ed.), *World Boundaries. The Americas*, Vol. IV, London and New York: Routledge, 202 pp., at pp. 84–109.

13 This expression refers to independent English-speaking countries of the Caribbean region: Antigua and Barbuda, the Bahamas, Barbados, Belize, Dominica, Grenada, Guyana, Jamaica, Saint Kitts and Nevis, Saint Lucia, Saint Vincent and the Grenadines, and Trinidad and Tobago. Some of them formed also part of the Federation of the West Indies (1958–1962) and then became sovereign States. Another category is what is now called "British Overseas Territories" (formerly known as "British Dependent Territories"): Anguilla, Bermuda, British Virgin Islands, Cayman Islands, Montserrat, and Turks and Caicos Islands. See, for instance the Commonwealth website and the UK Border Agency website.

14 These are also members of the Caribbean Community (CARICOM), namely, Antigua and Barbuda, the Bahamas, Barbados, Belize, Dominica, Grenada, Guyana, Haiti, Jamaica, Montserrat, Saint Lucia, Saint Kitts and Nevis, Saint Vincent and the Grenadines, Suriname, and Trinidad and Tobago.

15 The Windward Islands include Dominica, Saint Lucia, Saint Vincent and the Grenadines, and Grenada; as well as the French département of Martinique; see: Le Monde (2000), *Atlas Universel*, Paris: Sélection du Reader's Digest, p. 112; and also *Encyclopaedia Britannica* (online). The Leeward Islands include Antigua and Barbuda, Saint Kitts and Nevis, French and Dutch Saint Martin/Sint Maarten, Saint Barthélemy, Saba, Sint Eustatius, the British Virgin Islands, the US Virgin Islands, Anguilla, and Montserrat; see: Le Monde (2000), *Atlas Universel*, Paris: Sélection du Reader's Digest, p. 112; and also *Encyclopaedia Britannica* (online).

16 It bears reminding that in this region, independent States coexist with non-self-governing territories (NSGTs); for a full list of NSGTs, see the United Nations and Decolonisation website. The list of NSGTs in the Atlantic and Caribbean area includes Anguilla, Bermuda, British Virgin Islands, Cayman Islands, Montserrat, Saint Helena, Turks and Caicos Islands, and the US Virgin Islands.

2 Maritime Jurisdiction Prior to Independence

Precursors of maritime delimitation can be traced back to colonial times and are reflected in two situations. One relates to the establishment of maritime jurisdiction *between* colonial powers, that is to say, international maritime jurisdiction which could have resulted in newly independent States acquiring maritime jurisdiction from two or several colonial powers. The second concerns maritime jurisdiction *within* colonial empires and will be examined in the following section. This could have led to a situation where States succeed to the maritime jurisdiction established administratively by one colonial power. Those two scenarios, in one way or another, touch upon the application of the principle of *uti possidetis juris* to maritime jurisdiction and delimitation (maritime *uti possidetis*). Indeed, the application of the principle of *uti possidetis juris* to the delimitation of maritime spaces was already discussed in 1917 by the Central American Court of Justice (CACJ), the first-ever standing international court.[1]

Between Colonial Powers

Although there is no doubt that maritime jurisdiction was established in connection with colonial possessions in Africa and Asia,[2] with regard to what is now called Latin America, prior to 1810 the main boundary line was between Spanish and Portuguese possessions.[3] The maritime relations between those two colonial powers may of course be traced back to the Treaty of Tordesillas of 7 June 1494 whereby the two States agreed upon a limit that was different from the line previously established by the papal bull Inter Caetera (Pope Alexander VI).[4] During the sixteenth century there were attempts by Spain and Portugal to establish a precise delimitation between their respective possessions, but they achieved no success in this endeavour. Only during the late seventeenth century and the eighteenth century were some treaties adopted.[5] They concerned especially the southern front, where the Portuguese founded *Colônia do Sacramento* on the left bank of the Río de la Plata (Gabriel Island). Among these treaties, the Treaty of San Ildefonso of 1 October 1777,[6] although not effecting any territorial sea delimitation, does deserve some attention.[7] It related to territorial disputes in South America and established the cession of territories by Spain to Portugal in the Amazon basin in

DOI: 10.4324/9781003290452-4

exchange for maintaining control over present-day Uruguay. Hence *Colônia do Sacramento* and *Misiones Orientales* remained under Spanish sovereignty.

In the Caribbean, where European struggles played a more important role, maritime relations between colonial powers were reflected in one landmark agreement, the Convention of London of 14 July 1786,[8] also known as the 1786 Anglo-Spanish Convention. It established the evacuation of all British settlements from the Mosquito Shore and adjacent islands, in return for which the King of Spain accepted to expand the territory available to British loggers in the Yucatan Peninsula, in an area between the Sibun River and what is now Belize.[9] Furthermore, in its Article 6 it stated that

> the English may fish freely and undisturbed on the coast of the land assigned to them by the last peace treaty [they refer here to the 1783 Treaty of Paris] and the land added by this convention; but without exceeding their boundaries, and limited to the distances specified in the previous article [this referred to the distances of eight leagues from Wallis River, seven from Cay-Casina and three from Sibun River].

Another example of a treaty between Great Britain and Spain during colonial times that concerned their maritime relations was the 1790 Nootka Sound Convention,[10] although it referred mainly, but not exclusively, to their possessions in North America. The treaty prohibited Britain from navigating or conducting fishing activities near Spanish territory on the American continent. In its Article 4 it read:

> His Britannic Majesty engages to employ the most effective measures to prevent the navigation and fishery of his subjects in the Pacific Ocean or in the South Seas from being made a pretext for illicit trade with the Spanish settlements; and with this in view it is moreover expressly stipulated that British subjects shall not navigate nor carry on their fishery in the said seas within the distance of 10 maritime leagues from any part of the coast already occupied by Spain.

In then follows that newly independent States in Latin America and the Caribbean, as would later be the case in Africa and Asia, could have inherited maritime jurisdiction in application of either customary rules related to State succession with regard to treaties, as reflected by the 1978 Vienna Convention on Succession of States in respect of Treaties, or the *uti possidetis juris* principle for maritime spaces.[11] It is to be recalled, in this line of inquiry, that while originally aimed at transforming administrative boundaries into international frontiers, *uti possidetis* was later upgraded to a principle of general applicability to decolonisation wherever it occurs, including the division of the borders of new independent States based on the borders established by former colonial powers.[12] In any case, in this situation, both principles (State succession and *uti possidetis juris*) would have had the same result.

Within Colonial Powers

By the time of independence (spanning from 1808 to 1826) no terra nullius existed in Latin America. Indeed, the principle of *uti possidetis juris* was the basis of Latin American public law.[13] On those grounds, the possibility of having some kind of jurisdictional divisions over the sea, in application of *uti possidetis juris* as originally conceived of, within colonial powers was envisaged and put under consideration of international adjudication.

One example was the case between Nicaragua and Honduras before the International Court of Justice,[14] where Honduras advanced that its title to the territorial sea and its seabed, as well as to the islands north of the 15th parallel, was the maritime *uti possidetis juris* principle.[15] Nicaragua, in turn, rejected that view, claiming that the Crown had not assigned jurisdiction over waters to provincial authorities but rather to higher authorities (i.e. Audiences, Captaincies General, Viceroyalties).[16] In assessing both claims the ICJ rejected Honduras' claim that there existed a separation of the respective maritime jurisdiction of the colonial provinces of Honduras and Nicaragua in the following terms:

> The Court thus cannot uphold Honduras's assertion that the *uti possidetis juris* principle provided for a maritime division along the 15th parallel "to at least six nautical miles from Cape Gracias a Dios" nor that the territorial sovereignty over the islands to the north of the 15th parallel on the basis of the *uti possidetis juris* principle "provides the traditional line which separates these Honduran islands from the Nicaraguan islands to the south".[17]

Another case in which contending Parties pleaded the existence of administrative divisions during colonial times was the dispute between Argentina and Chile concerning the Beagle Channel.[18] In it, Argentina's argument included an interpretation of Article III of the 1881 Treaty between Argentina and Chile,[19] whereby in application of the principle of *uti possidetis juris* it had received "in succession to the Spanish Crown a maritime jurisdiction over the whole of the littoral of the Atlantic Ocean from Río de la Plata as far as Cape Horn".[20] This was also referred to as the "Oceanic" principle, whereby the main emphasis of Argentina's claims was placed on the Atlantic seaboard and that of Chile's claims on the Pacific seaboard "in the southern regions where the Cordillera of the Andes died away and no longer provided a natural boundary". Stated in another way, according to that principle the Viceroyalty of Río de la Plata possessed jurisdiction over the waters of the Atlantic Ocean and the Captaincy General of Chile over the waters of the Pacific Ocean. The Arbitral tribunal did not uphold Argentina's contention.[21]

The ICJ, however, also in its 2007 *Nicaragua* v. *Honduras* judgment, observed that the *uti possidetis juris* principle "might in certain circumstances, such as in connection with historic bays and territorial seas, play a role in a maritime delimitation".[22] In this sense, one could refer for instance to the case of the waters of the Gulf of Fonseca, the legal nature of which was the object of a pronouncement in the early years of the twentieth century by the Central American Court of Justice

(CACJ) in a dispute between El Salvador and Nicaragua. In it, the CACJ decided that the three coastal States in the Gulf of Fonseca (El Salvador, Honduras and Nicaragua) had succeeded to the rights of the Spanish Crown over the "territorial waters" of the bay.[23] It stated that

> The historic origin of the right of exclusive ownership that has been exercised over the waters of the Gulf during the course of nearly four hundred years is incontrovertible, first, under the Spanish dominion – from 1522, when it was discovered and incorporated into the royal patrimony of the Crown of Castile, until 1821 – then under the Federal Republic of the Centre of America, which that year attained its independence and sovereignty until 1839; and, subsequently, on the dissolution of the Federation in that year, the States of El Salvador, Honduras and Nicaragua, in their character of autonomous nations and legitimate successors of Spain, incorporated in their respective territories, as a necessary dependency thereof for geographical reasons and purposes of common defense, both the Gulf and its archipelago, which nature had indented in that important part of the continent, in the form of a gullet.[24]

Similarly, the ICJ in its 1992 judgment on El Salvador/Honduras stated:

> [t]he legal situation of the waters of the Gulf of Fonseca is as follows: the Gulf of Fonseca is an historic bay the waters whereof, having previously to 1821 been under the single control of Spain, and from 1821 to 1839 of the Federal Republic of Central America, were thereafter succeeded to and held in sovereignty by the Republic of El Salvador, the Republic of Honduras, and the Republic of Nicaragua, jointly, and continue to be so held, as defined in the present Judgment, but excluding a belt, as at present established, extending 3 miles (1 marine league) from the littoral of each of the three States, such belt being under the exclusive sovereignty of the coastal State, and subject to the delimitation between Honduras and Nicaragua effected in June 1900, and to the existing rights of innocent passage through the 3-mile belt and the waters held in sovereignty jointly.[25]

Although not a bay but a river,[26] the case of the Río de la Plata can also be utilised as an example of water area over which historic rights have been exercised since colonial times. Arbitrator Luis María Drago, in his *Grounds for the Dissent* to the *North Atlantic Coast Fisheries Award*, stated in regard to the historical character of certain bays:

> So it may be safely asserted that a certain class of bays, which might be properly called the historical bays such as Chesapeake Bay and Delaware Bay in North America and the great estuary of the River Plate in South America, form a class distinct and apart and undoubtedly belong to the littoral country, whatever be their depth of penetration and the width of their mouths, when such country has asserted its sovereignty over them, and particular

circumstances such as geographical configuration, immemorial usage and above all, the requirements of self-defense, justify such a pretension.[27]

To sum up, not only has the application of the *uti possidetis juris* principle been envisaged in cases of administrative divisions of waters in present-day Latin America and the Caribbean, it has indeed played a role in connection with the historic character of the waters of the Gulf of Fonseca. In other words, the application of the *uti possidetis juris* principle to maritime delimitation is possible both *between* and *within* colonial powers. When applied *between* colonial powers, it is done without prejudice of the rules of succession of States in respect of treaties that could also be applied and would have the same result.

Notes

1 See: *The Republic of El Salvador* v. *The Republic of Nicaragua* (*Opinion and Decision of the Central American Court of Justice, 9 March 1917*), *AJIL*, Vol. 11, p. 674. Similarly, ICJ Judges Ago and Jiménez de Aréchaga accepted the application of that principle to maritime delimitation; see their respective Separate Opinions attached to the 1982 *Tunisia/Libya* judgment: *Continental Shelf* (*Tunisia/Libyan Arab Jamahiriya*), *Judgment, I.C.J. Reports 1982, Separate Opinion of Judge Ago*, pp. 97–98, para. 5; and *Separate Opinion of Judge Jiménez de Aréchaga*, p. 132, para. 102. The principle was then applied in the *Guinea-Bissau/Senegal* arbitration; see: *Affaire de la délimitation de la frontière maritime entre la Guinée-Bissau et le Sénégal. Sentence du 31 juillet 1989, RIAA*, Vol. 20, p. 188, para. 88. *Cf.*: *Dissenting Opinion of Mohammed Bedjaoui, ibid.*, pp. 167–198, paras. 34–35. It was also pleaded before the ICJ by Nicaragua, see: *I.C.J. Pleadings, Maritime Delimitation between Nicaragua and Honduras in the Caribbean Sea* (*Nicaragua* v. *Honduras*). Nicaragua's first round of oral argument (Counsel: Antonio Remiro Brotóns), 7 March 2007 (CR 2007/03), pp. 33–35, paras. 72–83. See also: Bardonnet, Daniel (1989), "Frontières terrestres et frontières maritimes", *AFDI*, Vol. 35, pp. 1–64, especially at p. 61, but in general pp. 59–64; and Kohen, Marcelo (2009), "L'uti possidetis iuris et les espaces maritimes", *Liber amicorum Jean-Pierre Cot. Le procès international*, Brussels: Bruylant, pp. 157–159.

2 *Continental Shelf* (*Tunisia/Libyan Arab Jamahiriya*), *Judgment, I.C.J. Reports 1982*, p. 18; *Case concerning the delimitation of the Maritime Boundary between Guinea and Guinea-Bissau* (*Republic of Guinea* v. *Republic of Guinea-Bissau*), *ILR*, Vol. 77, p. 635; *Affaire de la délimitation de la frontière maritime entre la Guinée-Bissau et le Sénégal. Sentence du 31 juillet 1989, RIAA*, Vol. 20, p. 121. According to Marissa Wood, in: "An Examination of Africa's Maritime Boundaries", available at sovereignlimits.com (accessed on 1 March 2022), "The oldest established African maritime boundary is from 1913 between modern-day Cameroon and Nigeria. In 1913, the colonial powers of Germany and the United Kingdom, respectively, established a land boundary separating their African territories. The territorial frontier ends in the thalweg of the Akpa Yafe River, and the colonial powers agreed to extend this out to sea. In 1971, independent Cameroon and Nigeria formalized the colonial border". As for references pertaining to the Asian continent, it is possible to mention the cases of Malaysia, the Philippines and Brunei, the maritime limits of which date back to colonial times; see: *Affaire de la délimitation de la frontière maritime entre la Guinée-Bissau et le Sénégal. Sentence du 31 juillet 1989, ibid.*, para. 64.

3 This is the case, although colonial powers could have concluded maritime delimitation agreements in Latin America and the Caribbean. In that sense, in the *Guyana/Suriname* arbitration, Guyana stated: "The United Kingdom and the Netherlands, the

former colonial powers administering the territories of Guyana and Suriname, respectively, were not able to conclude a formal agreement on the delimitation of their adjacent maritime boundaries"; see: *Arbitral Tribunal Constituted Pursuant to Article 287, and in Accordance with Annex VII, of the United Nations Convention on the Law of the Sea in the Matter of an Arbitration Between Guyana and Suriname,* Memorial of the Republic of Guyana, 22 February 2005, para. 1.4. For an account on the relationship between law and geography in European empires see: Benton, Lauren (2010), *A Search for Sovereignty: Law and Geography in European Empires, 1400–1900*, New York: Cambridge University Press, 358 pp.

4 Kapoor, D.C. and Adam J. Kerr (1986), *A Guide to Maritime Boundary Delimitation*, Toronto (etc.): Carswell, p. 2. The authors stated that: "The first maritime delimitation was an outcome of the great discoveries made at the close of the fifteenth century by such famous navigators as Bartholomew Diaz, Christopher Columbus and Vasco da Gama. These discoveries made it necessary to define the exact limits of the contending claims of Portugal and Spain."

5 The treaties concluded were: Peace Treaty of Lisbon of 13 February 1668, in: Parry, Clive (1969), *The Consolidated Treaty Series*, Vol. 10, Dobbs Ferry: Ocean, p. 425; Provisional Treaty of Lisbon of 7 May 1681, in: Parry, *ibid.*, Vol. 16, p. 81; Peace Treaty of Utrecht of 6 February 1715, in: Parry, *ibid.*, Vol. 29, p. 201; Boundary Treaty of Madrid of 13 January 1750, in: Parry, *ibid.*, Vol. 38, p. 457. In the latter, see recapitulation of the whole history of Spanish-Portuguese territorial disputes since 1493. See also: Verzijl, J.H.W. (1973), *International Law in a Historical Perspective*, Martinus Nijhoff, 861 pp., at pp. 496–497.

6 Parry, *ibid.*, Vol. 46, p. 321.

7 Kohen (2009), *ibid.*, p. 159.

8 Parry, *ibid.*, Vol. 50, p. 47.

9 Dawson, Frank (1998), "The evacuation of the Mosquito Shore and the English who stayed behind, 1786–1800", *The Americas*, Vol. 55, pp. 63–89. Furthermore, the issue of sovereignty over Belize could have been the first case to be submitted to the ICJ, see: Kunz, Josef (1946), "Guatemala vs. Great Britain: in Re Belice", *AJIL*, Vol. 40, pp. 383–390.

10 Parry, *ibid.*, Vol. 51, p. 67. This agreement was negotiated by George Vancouver and his Spanish counterpart Juan Francisco de la Bodega y Quadra. For a historical account of the Nootka Sound controversy, see: Evans, Howard (1974), "The Nootka Sound Controversy in Anglo-French Diplomacy – 1790", *Journal of Modern History*, Vol. 46, pp. 609–640.

11 Kohen (2009), *ibid.*, p. 163. *Cf.* Sanchez-Rodriguez, Luis (2004), "*L'uti possidetis*: application à la délimitation maritime", in: Colloque international: *Le processus de délimitation maritime. Etude d'un cas fictif*, Paris: Pedone, pp. 303–315, at p. 305. When referring to the case of regions where several colonial powers coexisted, the author stated: "le recours au principe [*uti possidetis*] n'est pas indispensable, puisque l'on sait que l'on peut arriver à la même solution au fond par l'application des règles sur la succession d'Etats en matière de traités".

12 *Frontier Dispute, Judgment, I.C.J. Reports 1986*, p. 554, paras. 23–24.

13 In the 1922 Arbitral Award concerning the dispute between Colombia and Venezuela, reference is made to "South American public law", but there is no reason to restrict the statement to South America when it can also be applied to Latin America the way it is treated in the present research; see: *Affaires de frontières Colombo-vénézuéliennes (Colombie contre Vénézuéla), 24 March 1922, RIAA*, Vol. 1, pp. 223–298, at p. 228. Note also that, as opposed to *uti possidetis juris* principle, the notion of *uti possidetis de facto*, referred to effective possession, was put forward by Brazil in South America's decolonisation, claiming that the lands actually held at independence would determine the boundary; see for instance: Ratner, Steven (1996), "Drawing a better line: Uti

possidetis and the borders of new States", *AJIL*, Vol. 90, pp. 590–624, at p. 594. See also: Kohen, Marcelo (2009), "La contribution de l'Amérique latine au développement progressif du droit international en matière territoriale", *Relations internationales*, Paris, No. 139, pp. 13–29.

14 *Territorial and Maritime Dispute between Nicaragua and Honduras in the Caribbean Sea* (*Nicaragua* v. *Honduras*), *Judgment, I.C.J. Reports 2007*, p. 659.

15 Note that the allusion to the 15th parallel is made for the sake of simplicity, since the actual parallel is constituted by the coordinate 14°59.8′00″N; see: Counter-Memorial of the Republic of Honduras (HCM), 21 March 2002, Vol. I, p. 2. See also: HCM, p. 71 and p. 84, paras. 5.33–5.34; and *Territorial and Maritime Dispute between Nicaragua and Honduras in the Caribbean Sea* (*Nicaragua* v. *Honduras*), *Judgment, I.C.J. Reports 2007*, paras. 229–230.

16 Reply of the Government of Nicaragua, 13 January 2003, Vol. I, p. 66, para. 4.60; and *Territorial and Maritime Dispute between Nicaragua and Honduras in the Caribbean Sea* (*Nicaragua* v. *Honduras*), *Judgment, I.C.J. Reports 2007*, para. 231. It is worth distinguishing the application of this principle to insular territories from its application to the maritime spaces themselves. Applicability of *uti possidetis juris* to insular territories was particularly relevant, for instance, in: *Land, Island and Maritime Frontier Dispute* (*El Salvador/Honduras: Nicaragua intervening*), *I.C.J. Reports 1992*, p. 558, para. 333.

17 *Territorial and Maritime Dispute between Nicaragua and Honduras in the Caribbean Sea* (*Nicaragua* v. *Honduras*), *Judgment, I.C.J. Reports 2007*, para. 233.

18 *Dispute between Argentina and Chile concerning the Beagle Channel. 18 February 1977, RIAA*, Vol. 21, pp. 53–264.

19 De Martens, *Nouveau Recueil général de traités*, 2nd series, Vol. XII, p. 491.

20 *Dispute between Argentina and Chile concerning the Beagle Channel. 18 February 1977, RIAA*, Vol. 21, p. 90, para. 21. See also reference to the Memorial of the Argentine Republic in: Kohen (2009), *ibid.*, p. 163.

21 *Dispute between Argentina and Chile concerning the Beagle Channel. 18 February 1977, RIAA*, Vol. 21, p. 120, paras. 11 and 66.

22 *Territorial and Maritime Dispute between Nicaragua and Honduras in the Caribbean Sea* (*Nicaragua* v. *Honduras*), *Judgment, I.C.J. Reports 2007*, para. 232.

23 The term "territorial waters" at the time of the judgment was understood as what is now called "internal waters", see: *Land, Island and Maritime Frontier Dispute* (*El Salvador/Honduras: Nicaragua intervening*), *I.C.J. Reports 1992*, p. 592, para. 392.

24 *The Republic of El Salvador* v. *The Republic of Nicaragua* (*Opinion and Decision of the Central American Court of Justice, 9 March 1917*), *AJIL*, Vol. 11, p. 700.

25 *Land, Island and Maritime Frontier Dispute* (*El Salvador/Honduras: Nicaragua intervening*), *I.C.J. Reports 1992*, p. 616, para. 432.

26 Jiménez de Aréchaga (1962), "El Río de la Plata no es un estuario", in: *Marcha*, 14 December 1962, pp. 11–12; and also: Bouchez, Leo (1964), *The Regime of Bays in International Law*, Leiden: Sythoff, pp. 164 *et seq*.

27 *North Atlantic Coast Fisheries Case* (*Great Britain, United States*), *7 September 1910, Grounds for the Dissent to the Award on Question V by Dr Luis M. Drago, RIAA*, Vol. 21, pp. 167–226, at p. 206. For an appraisal, see: Bouchez, Leo (1964), *ibid.*, pp. 164–167.

3 Evolution of Maritime Delimitation

Before looking into the evolution of maritime delimitation per se, five points should be set out. First, a distinction should be made between two concepts: *methods* of maritime delimitation and *techniques* developed to measure the outer limits of maritime zones.[1] These are two different things. A method of maritime delimitation is a mathematical application of the relationship between the length of the coastal fronts of States (with opposite or adjacent coasts) that is employed to divide their overlapping maritime jurisdictions (see Glossary). As regards techniques used to determine the outer limit of a jurisdictional zone at sea (i.e. the seaward limit of the belt of the territorial sea), the question first arose at the beginning of the twentieth century in the framework of two international disputes, namely, the 1910 *North Atlantic Coast Fisheries Arbitration* and the 1917 *Gulf of Fonseca* case.[2] In both cases, the same idea (though worded differently) was put forward: the outer limit should be drawn "following the sinuosities of the coast" or simply following "the contours of the respective coasts". The *tracé parallèle* technique was hence introduced in the international legal arena,[3] in relation with the unilateral casting of the outer limit of the territorial sea, this being the only maritime zone in which the coastal State held sovereignty. Another technique of constructing the seaward limit was the "arcs-of-circles" technique, which consisted of drawing the outer limit following the envelope of all arcs of circles having a radius of a certain extension, originally three nautical miles.[4]

Second, a distinction will also be made between *methods* of maritime delimitation and a *principle* of maritime delimitation. Article 15 of UNCLOS, when dealing with territorial sea delimitation, refers explicitly to the equidistance *method*, whereas Article 74, paragraph 1 and Article 83, paragraph 1 of UNCLOS do not and refer instead to a vague formula aimed at achieving an equitable solution. Therefore, it can be stated that equidistance is the most important *method* and an equitable solution, the *principle*. The latter is clearly expressed in the following dictum:

> The delimitation process may begin with a line of equidistance but it does not necessarily end with one. Otherwise, one would fall into the trap of regarding equidistance as a principle of law, that is, a legally binding rule, and not simply a method.[5]

DOI: 10.4324/9781003290452-5

In connection with that, the expression "equitable principles" was first employed in the 1945 Truman Proclamation on the Continental Shelf[6] and later introduced into maritime delimitation case law in 1969 with the *North Sea Continental Shelf* judgment. It refers to the principles and rules which may be appropriate in order to achieve an equitable result. Two related issues ensue: first, the inconvenience of employing the same term, "equitable", to characterise both the result and the means to be applied to achieve that result;[7] and then, that the principles are subordinated to the goal. In other words, the main issue is to define the means whereby the delimitation can be carried out in such a way as to be recognised as equitable.[8]

Third, the title (entitlement) of a coastal State to a maritime space originates in the well-established principle "the land dominates the sea". The ICJ has referred to this ever since its above-mentioned decision on the *North Sea* cases. The principle has been continuously reaffirmed by the ICJ in a series of cases, such as the 1978 *Aegean Sea* (between Greece and Turkey), the 2001 *Qatar* v. *Bahrain*, the 2007 *Nicaragua* v. *Honduras*, the 2009 *Romania* v. *Ukraine*, and the 2012 *Nicaragua* v. *Colombia*. In those instances, the Court stated that "the land is the legal source of the power which a State may exercise over territorial extensions to seaward";[9] that "the coast of the territory of the State is the decisive factor for title to submarine areas adjacent to it";[10] and that "the title of a State to the continental shelf and to the exclusive economic zone is based on the principle that the land dominates the sea through the projection of the coasts or the coastal fronts".[11]

Fourth, the delimitation of maritime spaces cannot take place when there are no overlapping entitlements. This reflects the interrelation between these two concepts: entitlement and delimitation. The International Tribunal for the Law of the Sea, in that regard, made the following statement:

> Delimitation presupposes an area of overlapping entitlements. Therefore, the first step in any delimitation is to determine whether there are entitlements and whether they overlap.[12]

Fifth, there is a diverse use of terminology, both in case law and literature, concerning *method*, *methodology* and *approach* that appears to have been caused by the different use of words made by English and French versions of ICJ reports. While, for instance, the English version of a judgment refers to the "equidistance/special circumstances *approach*" (emphasis added), the French version reads "la *méthode* associant équidistance et circonstances spéciales" (emphasis added).[13]

"Lines in Water Areas" and Private Codification Efforts

Although it even seems possible to trace back to Roman times and before some notions of dividing lines at sea, the drawing of "lines in water areas"[14] started taking place in the nineteenth century and in the first decades of the twentieth century.[15] This, however, should take into account that those lines would hardly ever be precise enough for a cartographer to lay them down on charts,[16] a fact that according to Smith was explained because "neither sailors nor geographers" had adequately participated in the drafting of those instruments.[17] In this context, it would come as no surprise that in the early 1940s an international law professor could claim that "the law of territorial waters" was "one of the most unsatisfactory portions of international law".[18]

Against this backdrop, a codification process that took States' practice into account started in the late nineteenth century. One could note, in that regard, the "Règles sur la définition et le régime de la mer territoriale" adopted by the *Institut de droit international* in its 1894 Paris session,[19] and the 1895 formula adopted by the International Law Association (ILA) during its 17th conference, held in Brussels, which was reaffirmed in 1926 by means of the ILA's Draft Convention on the Law of Maritime Jurisdiction in Time of Peace.[20] Other efforts include the Japanese Association of International Law and the Research in International Law of Harvard Law School. The records of those codification projects show that there was a tendency towards the median line method of delimitation.[21]

In the framework of the 31st conference of the ILA, held in Buenos Aires in 1922, a proposal by Segundo Storni concerned the case of certain straits in which the application of the median line method could have a non-equitable result. In this case, what became known as "Storni's formula", advocated the idea that maritime delimitation should be effected only by agreement between the concerned States.[22] Contrary to this train of thought, Gilbert Gidel was in favour of the median line method being applicable as a general rule to all situations involving both opposite and lateral territorial sea delimitation.[23] In this sense, Gidel's formula consisted in maritime delimitation based on a median line method as the general rule. Some suggest that the difference of opinion between Storni and Gidel about the word "equitable" shaped the evolution of the future law of maritime delimitation.[24]

From The Hague Codification Conference to the Truman Proclamations

Under the auspices of the League of Nations, a Codification Conference on the Law of the Sea was called for and took place in The Hague in 1930 (hereinafter referred to as the "Hague Codification Conference, 1930" or the "1930 Hague Codification Conference"). In terms of the accomplishment of its main purpose, that is to say the agreement upon a Convention on territorial waters, the conference was considered a failure.[25]

There were, however, in the years prior to the conference and during its preparation, some instances where issues concerning the lateral delimitation of the territorial sea were touched upon.[26] The rapporteur of the sub-committee in charge of delimitation, Walther Schücking, while preparing the work on lateral delimitation, highlighted the importance of preferring an agreement between the States concerned, or even of resorting to arbitration, instead of setting down "an immutable principle".[27] Despite that, alternative approaches for establishing lateral limits in the territorial sea, as well as in the case of opposite coasts, were discussed. None of those approaches, however, was included in the final text of the so-called Basis of Discussion, as provided by the Preparatory Committee.[28]

The main concern of States attending the 1930 Conference was to agree upon a Convention on territorial waters, including an agreement on the breadth of the territorial sea. Failing that overarching agreement, it is understandable that any consideration of rules on maritime boundary delimitation – at the time a less compelling topic – had been left aside. Furthermore, apart from the main discussions on the breadth of the territorial sea, States in attendance were more concerned about how they would measure that breadth, whatever its extension, than about how they would delimit it.[29] Yet, this would be referred to – however mistakenly – as "territorial sea delimitation". Whittemore Boggs himself seems to have confused two concepts that are now clearly differentiated,[30] namely, delineating outer limits of territorial waters and delimiting them.

Some years later, on 28 September 1945, in what has come to be considered as a momentous expression of unilateral lawmaking, US President Harry Truman adopted two decisions, also known as proclamations, addressed to third States, in order to assert unilaterally the rights of the US over the marine resources adjacent to its coasts. This has been characterised by an author as "the territorial temptation [that] turn[ed] seaward",[31] and indeed is considered to have marked a turning point in the law of the sea in the twentieth century.[32]

However, it should also be noted that those two proclamations were different in nature. While the Truman Proclamation on fisheries[33] was limited to the regulation and control of fisheries resources in the high seas and hence was a rather toothless claim more in line with the traditional law of the sea,[34] the Truman Proclamation concerning the continental shelf[35] claimed that the natural resources of the subsoil and seabed appertained to the US.[36] In any case, unlike subsequent unilateral claims,[37] neither of the Truman Proclamations claimed jurisdiction over a specific distance beyond the territorial sea; they merely asserted the right of the US to exercise jurisdiction over a non-defined area for certain purposes.

On the other hand, the continental shelf proclamation made by Truman also remains relevant as an antecedent to the rules on maritime delimitation. It envisaged the possibility of a solution in case the shelf extended to the shores of another State, presumably due to the greater importance of the resources on the continental shelf (i.e. petroleum and gas) vis-à-vis those found in the water column adjacent to the coasts of the US. Accordingly, President Truman proclaimed, as a policy with respect to the natural resources of the subsoil and seabed of the continental shelf, that

> [t]he United States regards the natural resources of the subsoil and sea bed of the continental shelf beneath the high seas but contiguous to the coasts of the United States as appertaining to the United States, subject to its jurisdiction and control. In cases where the continental shelf extends to the shores of another State, or is shared with an adjacent State, the boundary shall be determined by the United States and the State concerned in accordance with *equitable principles* [emphasis added].

The most relevant part of the quoted text, for the purpose of this work, is the last part, where the proclamation considers the possibility of the US continental shelf encroaching upon the continental shelf of another State and the consequential manner in which the boundary shall be determined, that is "in accordance with equitable principles".

The connection between the Truman Proclamation on the continental shelf and an emerging notion of the law of maritime delimitation was stated by the ICJ, already in 1969, in its judgment concerning the *North Sea Continental Shelf* cases.[38]

The statement by the Court held that the 1945 Truman Proclamation came to be regarded as the "starting point" of the positive law and the doctrine on the continental shelf. After that, some years would need to elapse before the doctrine of the continental shelf assumed, in the words of Lord Asquith, "the hard lineaments or the definitive status of an established rule of international law",[39] which would happen in 1958.

The Geneva Conventions on the Law of the Sea

In 1949 the International Law Commission (ILC) included the regimes of the high seas and of territorial waters as a priority for the progressive development of international law and its codification.[40] The 1953 Report of the ILC to the United Nations General Assembly[41] was the result of a process that started in 1951, when the ILC decided to initiate work on the regime of the territorial waters and appointed Mr J.P.A. François as special rapporteur. At its fourth session, in 1952, the ILC decided to request Governments to furnish the Commission with information on their practice regarding the delimitation of the territorial sea of two adjacent States, and to submit any observations which they might wish to make in that respect.

Twelve Member States responded to the request and did furnish information to the ILC.[42] In their response, they considered, in addition to the median line, the following three methods: continuation in the seaward direction of the land frontier, a line perpendicular to the coast at the point where the land boundary reaches the coast, and a line perpendicular to the general direction of the coast.[43]

After assessing all information on State practice furnished by Member States, the Group of Experts of the ILC, while rejecting the method of the perpendicular to the general direction of the coast, adopted the equidistance method instead. It stated:

> The group of experts was unable to support (the perpendicular) method of drawing the boundary line. It agreed that it was often impracticable to establish any "general direction of the coast" and the result would depend on the "scale of the charts used for the purpose and . . . how much coast shall be utilized in attempting to determine any general direction whatever." Consequently, since the method of drawing a line at right angles to the general direction of the coastline is too vague for the purposes of the law, the best solution seems to be the median line which the Committee of Experts suggested.[44]

This leading document is thought to have been considered by the delegates to the 1958 Conference on the Law of the Sea which produced the Geneva Conventions on the Law of the Sea.

In 1957 the ILC put forward 73 draft articles on the law of the sea,[45] which included provisions on the question of delimitation as between adjacent States (this has been referred to as the first time that issue was "taken up seriously").[46] Those draft articles were based upon, *inter alia*, State practice, the works of the 1930 Hague Codification Conference, the work of institutions and distinguished academicians, international conventions, the emerging doctrine of the continental shelf, and three judgments of the ICJ.[47] They constituted the working document for the First United Nations Conference on the Law of the Sea (UNCLOS I) that took place in Geneva from 24 February to 27 April 1958.[48] As is well known, this conference resulted in the adoption of four separate conventions and an additional protocol on dispute settlement.[49]

Unlike the 1930 Hague Codification Conference that did not achieve its main purpose, the establishment of the breadth of the territorial sea, let alone any rules on maritime delimitation, the 1958 Geneva Conventions did establish rules concerning maritime delimitation in three different zones: the territorial sea, the contiguous zone and the continental shelf (they did not include "internal waters"). In this respect, it should be recalled that in the preparatory works prior to 1958, it was made very clear by participating States that specific rules had to be agreed upon, to avoid leaving a wide margin to international courts and tribunals deciding on maritime delimitation. This was done by means of the express rejection of any decision *ex aequo et bono*, only possible under Article 38, paragraph 2 of the ICJ Statute.[50]

However, it is noteworthy that in relation to the 1958 Geneva Conventions herein examined, even though the provisions for the territorial sea and the continental shelf seem to be similar, they still bear some differences. At least two are worth noting: continental shelf provisions make a distinction between States with adjacent coasts, for which the rule was the "equidistance line" (referred to as the "principle of equidistance"), and States with opposite coasts, for which the rule was the "median line". It follows that the terminology took account not of a difference in methods, since both resorted to the equidistance method, but a difference in geography. The "median line" would be preferred for a line dividing States with opposite coasts, whereas the "equidistance line" would be preferred for a line dividing States with adjacent coasts.[51] In fact, as has been pointed out by the ICJ in the *Black Sea* judgment,[52] both formulas are considered to reflect the same method. The second difference is the reference to historic title as a special circumstance in the territorial sea convention that was not included in the Continental Shelf Convention.

Besides that, Article 6 of the 1958 Convention on the Continental Shelf (CCS) was to a certain extent the reason for the famous disputes concerning the *North Sea Continental Shelf* between, on the one hand, Denmark and the Netherlands, and, on the other, the Federal Republic of Germany. In those cases, the Court rejected the method of equidistance invoked by Denmark and the Netherlands on the basis of two related reasons: Germany had not ratified the CCS, and the rule contained in its Article 6 did not reflect customary international law. Furthermore, in this case the utmost importance of geography in maritime delimitation was acknowledged in view of the concavity of the German coast. Because of that concavity, if equidistance had been applied, Germany would have ended up being squeezed between Denmark and the Netherlands. The concavity of the coast was therefore considered a circumstance justifying the adjustment of the equidistance line in order to achieve an equitable result.[53] In this regard the Court held that Article 6 of the Convention did not have customary character. Rather, it held that it was customary to effect delimitation in accordance with equitable principles, taking into account all relevant circumstances.[54]

In the case of the contiguous zone, Article 24, paragraph 3, of the 1958 Convention on the Territorial Sea and the Contiguous Zone (CTS) provides for the same rule analysed above but without considering any variation by reason of historical title or "special circumstances". The reason for that difference seems to have been the limited powers attributed to coastal States in the contiguous zone.[55] In any case, the 1982 United Nations Convention on the Law of the Sea[56] did not establish any rule directly related to the delimitation of the contiguous zone since, pursuant to that Convention, that zone is absorbed by the concept of the exclusive economic zone, the delimitation of which, as it will be seen later, is enshrined in Article 74, paragraph 1 of UNCLOS.

A discussion on the rules applicable to the contiguous zone was undertaken by the ICJ in another case filed by Nicaragua against Colombia.[57] In the preliminary phase of those proceedings, Nicaragua claimed that, after the Court's ruling of 19 November 2012,[58] several declarations made by Colombia's highest authorities which culminated with the enactment of a Presidential Decree that declares an "Integral Contiguous Zone" (24 miles measured from the baselines),[59] demonstrated that Colombia was in breach of, *inter alia*, its obligation not to violate Nicaragua's maritime zones as delimited in paragraph 251 of the ICJ Judgment of 19 November 2012. Indeed, in its Application, Nicaragua requested the Court to adjudge and declare, also, that Colombia is in breach of its obligation not to violate Nicaragua's rights under customary international law as reflected in Parts V and VI of UNCLOS.[60] In its final Judgment, dated 21 April 2022, the Court found the "integral contiguous zone", established by Colombia by Presidential Decree 1946 of 9 September 2013, as amended by Decree 1119 of 17 June 2014, is not in conformity with customary international law.[61]

In relation to the delimitation of internal waters, the 1958 Geneva Conventions did not tackle the issue, as that maritime space, lying between the baselines and the low water line, falls under the full sovereignty of the coastal State.[62] In any case, it seems possible to apply by analogy the same rule, agreement/equidistance/special circumstances.

The 1958 Geneva Conventions on the Law of the Sea entered into force during the 1960s. Instead of an all-encompassing convention that would – it was thought – have gathered little acceptance, four separate conventions (and an optional protocol) were adopted. Notwithstanding this effort, the number of ratifications and accessions was lower than expected.[63] In particular, South American States[64] and Iceland[65] remained out of it under the belief that the conventions would harm their interests.

With hindsight, the Geneva Conventions ("the Geneva regime") are now considered the epitome of the traditional law of the sea, as it emerged from the codification efforts of the 1930s and the 1950s. That regime recognised only two maritime spaces (beyond the notion of territorial waters): the territorial sea, most of the time a narrow band measuring three nautical miles, and the high seas.

The United Nations Convention on the Law of the Sea

In 1967, Maltese Ambassador to the United Nations Arvid Pardo proposed, in a speech delivered to the General Assembly,[66] that all manganese nodules found in the seabed beyond areas of national jurisdiction were part of what he named "common heritage of mankind".[67] This speech had a significant impact on the law of the sea: first, as a key factor in the adoption, in 1970, of the Declaration of Principles governing the seabed and its subsoil,[68] and second, as the basis upon which Part XI of UNCLOS would be drafted.

In that context, a number of States that had opposed the Geneva Regime, together with most South American States and Iceland, gave their support to the General Assembly to call for a new conference on the law of the sea. Additionally, States that in the past had reacted against unilateral extensions of the territorial sea and other forms of coastal State jurisdiction also favoured the new conference, claiming that centuries of legal development could not be disregarded and that hence the integrity of the Geneva Regime was to be preserved.[69]

The Third United Nations Conference on the Law of the Sea lasted from 1973 to 1982, although the most important period was between 1973 and 1976, when the main tenets of the "package deal" were agreed upon.[70] Understandably, in retrospect, negotiation concerning Part XI (i.e. the regime of "the Area") caused delay until 1982. That is why the main innovation of the Law of the Sea Convention was precisely the concept of common heritage of mankind. The other crucial element resulting from UNCLOS III was the concept of the "exclusive economic zone".[71] Within this context of radical change in the law of the sea, contained in UNCLOS and its deliberation, negotiations concerning the rules on maritime delimitation took place.

As regards delimitation of the territorial sea, UNCLOS substantially reproduced the provisions of the 1958 CTS in its now-customary Article 15,[72] making it the only maritime area for which the equidistance method is expressly mentioned.

The rule discussed amounts to a *juris tantum* presumption in favour of equidistance, only overridden by the presence of special circumstances.[73] A clear distinction between historic title and special circumstances is necessary, in the sense that the former implies the existence of a title while the latter, on the other hand, stands for circumstances of geographical or geological nature. In any case, it has to be recalled that even historic waters can be delimited.

Concerning the continental shelf, the 1969 *North Sea Continental Shelf* judgment, as stated before, had introduced the notion of equitable principles as overriding the equidistance method established in Article 6 of the 1958 CCS. Hence, in Negotiating Group No. 7,[74] participating delegations took positions defending either equidistance or equitable principles, according to their particular interests.[75] This conflict of legal views was the reason why Article 83, paragraph 1 and Article 74, paragraph 1, for that matter, are vague and imprecise. Both provisions are identical mutatis mutandis and establish the agreement/equitable solution rule.

It can therefore be stated that both Article 74, paragraph 1 and Article 83, paragraph 1 set an obligation of result rather than one of means: that the boundary be equitable, and that they both now reflect customary international law.[76] It is, however, also important to mention that this formula being the result of so complex a negotiation was accepted by all, as a compromise, precisely because it could allow for different interpretations.

Notes

1 It should be mentioned, however, that they are often referred to as "methods", for instance, the *tracé parallèle* method. In this work, the word "technique" will be preferred.

2 With respect to early case law, the famous 1910 *Grisbadarna* arbitration stands out as the first maritime delimitation dispute in the twentieth century. In it, the Arbitral Tribunal rejected both the median line and the thalweg methods. Instead, it decided to draw a line perpendicular to the general direction of the coast, alleging that that was the rule of international law in the seventeenth century. This however is not considered to have been a generally accepted rule at the time; see: *Decision of the Permanent Court of Arbitration in the Matter of the Maritime Boundary Dispute between Norway and Sweden, AJIL*, Vol. 4, pp. 226–236. See also *RIAA*, Vol. 11, p. 147. This case was not included in a list of "modern maritime boundary decisions" referred to by James Crawford in an oral pleading before the International Tribunal for the Law of the Sea; see: *ITLOS Pleadings, Delimitation of the maritime boundary in the Bay of Bengal (Bangladesh/Myanmar)*. Bangladesh's first round of oral argument (Counsel: James Crawford), 8 September 2011, p. 20.

3 Whittemore Boggs (1930), *ibid*., pp. 543–544.

4 It has been claimed that while the *tracé parallèle* technique was promoted by lawyers and diplomats, the arcs-of-circles technique was preferred by geographers and hydrographers; see for instance: *Maritime Dispute* (*Peru* v. *Chile*), Rejoinder of the Government of Chile, 11 July 2011, Appendix A, "Historical Development of techniques to measure the outer limit of maritime zones", pp. 286–304.

5 Weil, Prosper (1989), *ibid*., p. 208.

6 *North Sea Continental Shelf, Judgment, I.C.J. Reports 1969*, para. 47.

7 *Continental Shelf* (*Tunisia/Libyan Arab Jamahiriya*), *Judgment, I.C.J. Reports 1982*, para. 70.

8 *North Sea Continental Shelf, Judgment, I.C.J. Reports 1969*, para. 92.

9 *Territorial and Maritime Dispute* (*Nicaragua* v. *Colombia*), *Judgment, I.C.J. Reports 2012*, para. 140.

10 *Continental Shelf* (*Tunisia/Libyan Arab Jamahiriya*), *Judgment, I.C.J. Reports 1982*, para. 73.

11 *Maritime Delimitation in the Black Sea* (*Romania* v. *Ukraine*), *Judgment, I.C.J. Reports 2009*, para. 77.

12 *Dispute concerning delimitation of the maritime boundary between Bangladesh and Myanmar in the Bay of Bengal (Bangladesh/Myanmar), Judgment, ITLOS Reports 2012*, para. 397. But see Nicaragua's maritime boundary original claim in the *Territorial and Maritime Dispute (Nicaragua* v. *Colombia)* case: Application of the Government of Nicaragua, 6 December 2001, para. 8; and Memorial of the Government of Nicaragua, 28 April 2003, pp. 266 and 267; and then how it later shifted its original claim so as to transform it into a continental shelf delimitation: Reply of the Government of Nicaragua, 18 September 2009, p. 12, paras. 25 and 26. In this respect, see also: *I.C.J. Pleadings, Territorial and Maritime Dispute (Nicaragua* v. *Colombia)*. Colombia's first round of oral arguments (Counsel: James Crawford), 26 April 2012 (CR 2012/11), p. 23, para. 19.

13 *Territorial and Maritime Dispute between Nicaragua and Honduras in the Caribbean Sea (Nicaragua* v. *Honduras), Judgment, I.C.J. Reports 2007*, para. 269 *et seq*. This seems to be reflected in the writing by an author: Cazala, Julien (2008), "Retour sur les méthodes de délimitation juridictionnelle d'espaces maritimes mises en œuvre dans quelques affaires récentes", *AFDI*, Vol. 54, p. 412.

14 The expression "lines in water areas" has been taken from Whittemore Boggs, Samuel (1951), "Delimitation of Seaward Areas under National Jurisdiction", *AJIL*, Vol. 45, pp. 240–266, at p. 240, footnote 2. Note that Whittemore Boggs, after being appointed in 1921, became the second geographer for the US Department of State. The first geographer was Colonel Lawrence Martin, appointed in 1921, with the establishment of The Office of Geographer in the State Department, an office created, *inter alia*, to take care of the maps that had been acquired by the Department after the Paris Peace Conference of 1919–1920, see: Alexander, Lewis M. (1958), "Samuel Whittemore Bogs: An appreciation", *Annals of the Association of American Geographers*, Vol. 48, Issue 3, pp. 237–244.

15 In this sense, see for instance: Tanaka, Yoshifumi (2006), *Predictability and Flexibility in the Law of Maritime Delimitation*, Oxford: Hart, p. 19. See, at the end, under "Sources", the list in section II.A. of treaties that involve some kind of lines in water areas, both in Latin America and the Caribbean, and elsewhere.

16 Whittemore Boggs (1951), *ibid*., p. 240.

17 Smith, Herbert A. (1942), *The Law and Custom of the Sea*, London: Stevens & Sons, p. 12.

18 Riesenfeld, Stefan A. (1942), *Protection of Coastal Fisheries under International Law*, Washington, DC: Carnegie Endowment for International Peace, p. ix.

19 *Annuaire de l'Institut de droit international*, Vol. 13, p. 329.

20 ILA (1895), Resolution on "Rules of Jurisdiction in Territorial Waters", *Report of the 17th Conference*; and ILA (1926), "Draft Convention on the Law of Maritime Jurisdiction in Time of Peace", *Report of the 34th Conference*.

21 Tanaka (2006), *ibid*., pp. 21–22.

22 Storni, Segundo (1924), *Mar Territorial: conferencia*. Buenos Aires: International Law Association, 55 pp. See also: Storni, Segundo (1916), *Intereses Argentinos en el mar*, Buenos Aires: Moen, 110 pp.

23 Gidel, Gilbert (1934), *Le droit international public de la mer. Le temps de paix*, tome III, Paris: Duchemin, p. 768.

24 Tanaka (2006), *ibid*., p. 23.

25 Reeves, Jesse S. (1930), "The Codification of the Law of Territorial Waters", *AJIL*, Vol. 24, p. 486. For an account of the conference, from a Latin American perspective, in a book dealing primarily with the 1958 Conference on the Law of the Sea see for instance: García Robles, A. (1959). *La Conferencia de Ginebra y la Anchura del Mar Territorial*. Mexico: Fondo de Cultura Económica, pp. 51–65.

26 Committee of Experts for the Progressive Codification of International Law (1927), *Report to the Council of the League of Nations on the Questions which Appear Ripe*

for International Regulation, pp. 29 and 39. See also Rosenne, Shabtai (1972), *League of Nations Committee of Experts for the Progressive Codification of International Law 1925–1928*, Vol. 2, New York: Ocean, p. 68.

27 Memorandum by M. Schücking, League of Nations C.44M 21–1926; Report of the Sub-Committee in: Rosenne, Shabtai (ed.), *League of Nations Committee of Experts for the Progressive Codification of International Law 1925–1928*, vol. II (New York: Ocean, 1972), p. 68.

28 Committee of Experts for the Progressive Codification of International Law (1927), *Report to the Council of the League of Nations on the questions which appear ripe for International Regulation*. Third Session, p. 42.

29 *North Sea Continental Shelf, Judgment, I.C.J. Reports 1969*, p. 3, para. 48. See: Voelckel, Michel (1979), "Aperçu de quelques problèmes techniques concernant la détermination des frontières maritimes", *AFDI*, Vol. 25, p. 693, footnote 1.

30 In this sense, see: Whittemore Boggs, Samuel (1930), "Delimitation of the territorial sea. The method of delimitation proposed by the Delegation of the United States at The Hague Conference for the Codification of International Law", *AJIL*, Vol. 24, p. 542.

31 Oxman, Bernard H. (2006), "The Territorial Temptation: A Siren Song at Sea", *AJIL*, Vol. 100, pp. 831–832.

32 See, for instance, *I.C.J. Pleadings, Maritime Dispute* (*Peru* v. *Chile*). Peru's first round of oral argument (Counsel: Tullio Treves), 3 December 2012 (CR 2012/27), p. 47.

33 Proclamation No. 2668, Policy of the United States with Respect to Coastal Fisheries in Certain Areas of the High Seas, 28 September 1945. The Proclamation was accompanied by Executive Order No. 9634, Providing for the Establishment of Fishery Conservation Zones, 28 September 1945.

34 An author would even doubt whether it "laid claim" to anything; see: García-Amador, Francisco V. (1974), "The Latin American Contribution to the Development of the Law of the Sea", *AJIL*, Vol. 68, p. 34.

35 Presidential Proclamation No. 2667 Concerning the Policy of the United States with respect to the Natural Resources of the Subsoil and Sea Bed of the Continental Shelf, 28 September 1945, "U.S. Statutes at Large", Vol. 59, p. 884; "Federal Register", Vol. 10, p. 12303; "Department of State Bulletin", Vol. 13, p. 485; in: *UNLS*, *National Legislation and Treaties relating to the Law of the Sea*, ST/LEG/SER.B/1, pp. 38–40. For a contemporary commentary, see for instance: Borchard, Edwin (1946), "Resources of the Continental Shelf", *AJIL*, Vol. 40, pp. 53–70; and Young, Richard (1948), "Recent Developments with Respect to the Continental Shelf", *AJIL*, Vol. 42, pp. 849–857.

36 *I.C.J. Pleadings, Maritime Dispute* (*Peru* v. *Chile*). Peru's first round of oral argument (Counsel: Tullio Treves), 3 December 2012 (CR 2012/27), p. 48.

37 See *infra*, *inter alia*: Mexico; Argentina; Chile; Peru; Costa Rica (Decree-Law No. 803, concerning continental and insular shelf, 2 November 1949, "La Gaceta," Vol. 71, No. 249 (5 November 1949), p. 2046; in: *UNLS*, ST/LEG/SER.B/1, 1951, pp. 9–10); Honduras (Congressional Decree No. 102, amending the Political Constitution, 7 March 1950, "La Gaceta: Diario Oficial de la República de Honduras", Vol. 75, No. 14055 (16 March 1950), p. 2; in: *UNLS*, *ibid*., pp. 11–12); El Salvador (Decree No. 1961 of 25 October 1955 (Maritime Hunting and Fishing Act); in: *UNLS*, ST/LEG/SER.B/6, 1956, pp. 490–492.

38 *North Sea Continental Shelf, Judgment, I.C.J. Reports 1969*, p. 3, para. 47.

39 *Petroleum Development* (*Trucial Coast*) *Ltd. And Sheikh of Abu Dhabi*, August, 1951, *ILR*, Vol. 18, p. 155. See also: Jennings, Robert (1969), "The Limits of Continental Shelf Jurisdiction: Some possible implications of the North Sea Case Judgment", *ICLQ*, Vol. 18, pp. 819–832.

40 United Nations (1956), *Yearbook of the International Law Commission, 1949*, New York. See also: García Robles (1959), *ibid*., pp. 81–91.

41 United Nations, *Yearbook of the International Law Commission, 1953*, Vol. II, New York. Information and observations submitted by the Governments regarding the question of the delimitation of the territorial sea of two adjacent States. See also: *Case concerning delimitation of the maritime boundary in the Gulf of Maine Area*, Vol. II, Memorial of the United States of America, para. 262 *et seq*.
42 Belgium, Burma, Denmark, Dominican Republic, El Salvador, France, Netherlands, Norway, Sweden, UK, US and Yugoslavia.
43 *Continental Shelf (Tunisia/Libyan Arab Jamahiriya), Judgment, I.C.J. Reports 1982*, para. 119. See also Canada's CM, para. 637, citing the 1953 Yearbook, p. 79 and the *Official Records of the United Nations Conference on the Law of the Sea*, Vol. VI, p. 93).
44 *Yearbook of the International Law Commission*, Vol. II, 1956, p. 158.
45 United Nations (1957), *Yearbook of the International Law Commission, 1956*, Vol. 2, New York.
46 *North Sea Continental Shelf, Judgment, I.C.J. Reports 1969*, p. 3, para. 48.
47 *Corfu Channel, Merits, Judgment, I.C.J. Reports 1949*, p. 4; *Fisheries, Judgment, I.C.J. Reports 1951*, p. 116; and *Nottebohm, Second Phase, Judgment, I.C.J. Reports 1955*, p. 4. In the *Nottebohm* case, issues concerning "genuine link" were touched upon. The concept of genuine link was also at stake in: *M/V "SAIGA" (No. 2) (Saint Vincent and the Grenadines v. Guinea), Judgment, ITLOS Reports 1999*.
48 Dean, A.H. (1958). "The Geneva Conference on the Law of the Sea: What was Accomplished", *AJIL*, Vol. 52, pp. 607–628; more recently, see: Treves, Tullio (2008), "The 1958 Geneva Conventions on the Law of the Sea", *United Nations Audiovisual Library of International Law*. For a comment on the second Geneva Conference on the Law of the Sea, see: Dean, A.H. (1960). "The Second Geneva Conference on the Law of the Sea: The Fight for Freedom of the Seas", *AJIL*, Vol. 54, pp. 751–789.
49 Convention on the Territorial Sea and the Contiguous Zone, CTS (Signature: 29 April 1958; entry into force on 10 September 1964), *UNTS*, Vol. 516, p. 206; Convention on the High Seas, CHS (Signature: 29 April 1958; entry into force: 30 September 1962), *UNTS*, Vol. 450, p. 11; Convention on Fishing and Conservation of the Living Resources of the High Seas CFCLR, (Signature: 29 April 1958; entry into force: 20 March 1966), *UNTS*, Vol. 559, p. 285; Convention on the Continental Shelf, CCS (Signature: 29 April 1958; entry into force: 10 June 1964), *UNTS*, Vol. 499, 1964, p. 312; and Optional Protocol of Signature concerning the Compulsory Settlement of Disputes, OPSD (Signature: 29 April 1958; entry into force: 30 September 1962), *UNTS*, Vol. 450, p. 169.
50 *North Sea Continental Shelf, Judgment, I.C.J. Reports 1969*, para. 88. See also: Antunes, Nuno (2003), *Towards the Conceptualization of Maritime Delimitation. Legal and Technical Aspects of a Political Process*, Leiden: Martinus Nijhoff, p. 109. Regarding the delimitation of the territorial sea, see Art. 12 of the 1958 Geneva Convention on the Territorial Sea and Contiguous Zone, which enshrined the rule agreement/equidistance/special circumstances, also found in Article 6 of the 1958 Convention on the Continental Shelf.
51 Caflisch, Lucius (1985), "La délimitation des espaces entre Etats dont les côtes se font face ou sont adjacentes", in: Dupuy, René-Jean and Daniel Vignes (eds.), *Traité du Nouveau Droit de la Mer*, Paris: Bruylant, p. 377, especially footnote 5.
52 See: "No legal consequences flow from the use of the terms 'median line' and 'equidistance line' since the method of delimitation is the same for both"; *Maritime Delimitation in the Black sea (Romania* v. *Ukraine), Judgment, I.C.J. Reports 2009*, p. 61, para. 116.
53 In the oral pleadings of the *Bay of Bengal* case, this situation (the situation of concavity in the *North Sea* case) was referred to as being similar to that of Bangladesh "pinched" between India and Myanmar; see: *ITLOS Pleadings, Delimitation of the maritime*

boundary in the Bay of Bengal (*Bangladesh/Myanmar*). Bangladesh's first round of oral argument (Counsel: Paul Reichler), 8 September 2011, p. 12.

54 *North Sea Continental Shelf, Judgment, I.C.J. Reports 1969*, para. 85. James Crawford compared this case and the *Bay of Bengal* case in the following terms: "Mr. President, members of the Tribunal, this is your first delimitation case; this is your North Sea Continental Shelf case. It is brought under the 1982 Convention, the greatest diplomatic achievement in the field of general international law of our shared professional lives. That is the heritage that you will leave to your successors, and your decision in this case will be a notable part of that heritage"; see: *ITLOS Pleadings, Delimitation of the maritime boundary in the Bay of Bengal* (*Bangladesh/Myanmar*). Bangladesh's first round of oral argument, Counsel: James Crawford, 8 September 2011, p. 35.

55 Caflisch, Lucius (1991), "The Delimitation of Marine Spaces between States with Opposite or Adjacent Coasts", in: Dupuy, René-Jean and Daniel Vignes (eds.), *A Handbook on the New Law of the Sea*, Dordrecht: Martinus Nijhoff, p. 443 (and the French version: *ibid*., pp. 392–394). For an account of the development of the contiguous zone, from the British practice, see: Lowe, Vaughan (1981), "The Development of the Concept of the Contiguous Zone", *BYIL*, Vol. 52, pp. 109–169.

56 United Nations Convention on the Law of the Sea, adopted in Montego Bay, Jamaica, 10 December 1982, see: *UNTS*, Vol. 1833, p. 397; *ILM*, Vol. 21, 1982, p. 1261. For an overview of "UNCLOS at 30", see: Freestone, David (2012), "The Law of the Sea Convention at 30: Successes, Challenges, and New Agendas", *IJMCL*, Vol. 27, pp. 675–682. See also: Statement by H.E. Ban Ki-moon, Secretary-General of the United Nations, 67th Session of the United Nations General Assembly, 10 December 2012; and Statement by H.E. Judge Shunji Yanai, President of the International Tribunal for the Law of the Sea, at the Plenary of the Sixty-seventh session of the United Nations General Assembly on the occasion of the commemoration of the thirtieth anniversary of the opening for signature of the 1982 United Nations Convention on the Law of the Sea, New York, 10 December 2012; available at ITLOS' website.

57 *Alleged Violations of Sovereign Rights and Maritime Spaces in the Caribbean Sea* (*Nicaragua* v. *Colombia*), *Preliminary Objections, Judgment, I.C.J. Reports 2016*, p. 3. In that Judgment, the Court found it has jurisdiction, on the basis of Article XXXI of the Pact of Bogotá. See also: *Alleged Violations of Sovereign Rights and Maritime Spaces in the Caribbean Sea* (*Nicaragua* v. *Colombia*), *Judgment, 21 April 2022*.

58 *Territorial and Maritime Dispute* (*Nicaragua* v. *Colombia*), *Judgment, I.C.J. Reports 2012*.

59 Presidential Decree 1946 of 9 September 2013.

60 Application of Nicaragua of 26 November 2013; available at the ICJ's website. On 1 October 2021, public hearings on the merits in the case concerning Alleged Violations of Sovereign Rights and Maritime Spaces in the Caribbean Sea (Nicaragua v. Colombia) concluded. By the time of submission of this manuscript, the Court was still conducting its deliberation.

61 *Alleged Violations of Sovereign Rights and Maritime Spaces in the Caribbean Sea* (*Nicaragua* v. *Colombia*), *Judgment, 21 April 2022*, paras. 170–187.

62 Examples of such agreements include the 2011 Ecuador/Peru Agreement, the 1999 Bosnia-Herzegovina/Croatia treaty (Art. 4, para. 3), and the 1900 Honduras/Nicaragua agreement that established a partial maritime boundary within the Gulf of Fonseca.

63 As at 7 June 2020, the number of States bound by the Conventions and the Protocol are: for the CTS, 52; for the CHS, 63; for the CFCLR, 39; for the CCS, 58; and for the OPSD, 38. As can be seen, the number of ratifications and accessions corresponding to the CFCLR and the OPSD were especially low.

64 With the exception of Venezuela, that ratified all four Geneva Conventions (CTS, CHS, and CCS, on 15 August 1961; and CFCLR, on 10 July 1963 – yet not the OPDS), and Colombia, that ratified two of them (CCS, on 8 January 1962; and CFCLR, on

3 January 1963) and signed, together with Bolivia and Uruguay, the optional protocol (OPDS); the remaining South American countries did not ratify any of the 1958 Geneva Convention on the Law of the Sea. See also: Statement by Venezuela at 26° Meeting of States Parties to the 1982 UN Convention on the Law of the Sea (26 SPLOS), available at UN Papersmart.

65 As a country whose people are overwhelmingly dependent upon its coastal fisheries, Iceland was not satisfied with only a "recommendation" (adopted by the First United Nations Conference on the Law of the Sea) whereby in order to limit the total catch of a stock of fish in an area of the high seas adjacent to its territorial sea, any other States fishing in that area "should collaborate" with Iceland by establishing agreed measures having regard to the interests of the other States. In the view of Iceland, more than a recommendation was necessary. First it was to be included in a specific article and, second, a more effective procedure was to be called for. Since Iceland did not achieve this, it did not ratify any of the Conventions; see: "Iceland: proposal", A/CONF.19/C.1/L.7. For an appraisal of Iceland's position on whaling, see: "Tomas H. Heidar: Why Iceland will continue to hunt whales", 23 June 2010, available on: www.independent.co.uk/news/world/europe/tomas-h-heidar-why-iceland-will-continue-to-hunt-whales-2008456.html (accessed on 1 March 2022).

66 See: "Examination of the question of the reservation exclusively for peaceful purposes of the sea-bed and the ocean floor, and the subsoil thereof, underlying the high seas beyond the limits of present national jurisdiction, and the use of their resources in the interest of mankind", United Nations (1967), Official Records of the 22nd General Assembly, A/6695; A/C.1/952.

67 See *inter alia*: Tladi, Dire (2014), "The Common Heritage of Mankind and the Proposed Treaty on Biodiversity in Areas Beyond National Jurisdiction: The Choice between Pragmatism and Sustainability", *Yearbook of International Environmental Law*, Vol. 25, Issue 1, pp. 113–132; Lodge, Michael (2012), "The Common Heritage of Mankind", *IJMCL*, Vol. 27, pp. 733–742; Kiss, A. (1985). "The Common Heritage of Mankind: Utopia or Reality?", *International Journal*, Vol 40, pp. 423–441; and Weisseberg, G. (1969), "The Maltese proposal on the sea-bed and ocean floor – Its fate in two cities", *ICLQ*, Vol. 42.

68 General Assembly Resolution No. 2749 (XXV) of 17 December 1970. It was adopted by 108 votes for, none against and 14 abstentions.

69 Stevenson, John R. and Bernard H. Oxman (1974), "The Preparations for the Law of the Sea Conference", *AJIL*, Vol. 68, pp. 1–32, at p. 2.

70 About UNCLOS III, see among others: Stevenson, John R. and Bernard H. Oxman (1975), "The Third United Nations Conference on the Law of the Sea: The 1974 Caracas Session", *AJIL*, Vol. 69, pp. 1–30; Stevenson, John R. and Bernard H. Oxman (1975), "The Third United Nations Conference on the Law of the Sea: The 1975 Geneva Session", *AJIL*, Vol. 69, pp. 763–797; Galindo, Reynaldo (1979), "Latin America's influence and role in the Third Conference on the Law of the Sea", *Ocean Development and international law*, Vol. 7, pp. 65–87; Oxman, Bernard H. (1982), "The Third United Nations Conference on the Law of the Sea: The Tenth Session (1981)", *AJIL*, Vol. 76, pp. 1–23; Amerasinghe, Hamilton S. (1985), "The Third United Nations Conference on the Law of the Sea", in: Nordquist, M. (ed.). *United Nations Convention on the Law of the Sea, 1982 – A Commentary*, Vol. 1, The Hague: Martinus Nijhoff, pp. 1–10; Koh, Tommy (1985), "A Constitution for the Oceans", in: Nordquist, *ibid.*, pp. 11–16; See also generally: De Yturriaga, J.A., "Orígen, desarrollo y resultados de la III Conferencia de las Naciones Unidas sobre el Derecho del Mar", in: *Tendencias y perspectivas actuales del Derecho del Mar. Cuadernos de la Escuela Diplomática, España*, Vol. 32, pp. 13–38.

71 Scovazzi, Tullio (2010), "The Seabed Beyond the Limits of National Jurisdiction: General and Institutional Aspects", in: Molenaar, E. and Alex O. Elferink, *The International*

Legal Regime of Areas Beyond National Jurisdiction. Current and Future Developments, Leiden: Martinus Nijhoff, pp. 44–60. For an account of the origins of the EEZ, see: Hollick, Ann L. (1977), "The Origins of 200-Mile Offshore Zones", *AJIL*, Vol. 71, pp. 494–500.

72 The ICJ referred to the customary character of Article 15 of UNCLOS in its *Qatar* v. *Bahrain* judgment on the merits; see: *Maritime Delimitation and Territorial Questions between Qatar and Bahrain, Merits, Judgment, I.C.J. Reports 2001*, p. 94, para. 176.

73 For an analysis of equidistance as a presumption in international law, see: Sandonato de León, Pablo (2013), *Les présomptions judiciaires en droit international public*, PhD Thesis, Institut de hautes études internationales et du développement, Genève, pp. 388 *et seq*.

74 At its 90th meeting (during UNCLOS III), in 1978, seven groups "of limited size" were established to deal with "hard-core issues". The seventh group (known as "negotiating group 7" or simply NG7) tackled the issue of "Delimitation of maritime boundaries between adjacent and opposite States and settlement of disputes thereon"; see Document: A/CONF.62/62.

75 For a list of States in each position which were organised into "informal groups", see for instance: Caflisch (1985), *ibid.*, p. 418, footnotes 127 and 128. Among delegations who favoured equidistance (the so-called median line group) was the UK, whereas in the second group, favouring equitable principles one could find France. As for States that remained neutral, it has been claimed that it was so because one method favoured them on one coast and the other on the other coast; see for instance, Anderson, David (2008), *Modern Law of the Sea. Selected Essays*, Leiden: Martinus Nijhoff, p. 444. See also the English Channel Arbitration, for how British and French positions were at the core of that litigation, in: *Case Concerning the Delimitation of the Continental Shelf between the United Kingdom of Great Britain and Northern Ireland, and the French Republic, RIAA*, Vol. 18, pp. 3–413.

76 *Maritime Delimitation in the Area between Greenland and Jan Mayen, Judgment, I.C.J. Reports 1993*, p. 59, para. 48, in which the Court referred to the customary character of Articles 74, paragraph 1, and 83, paragraph 1; see also *I.C.J. Reports 2012*, p. 50, para. 139. In *Nicaragua* v. *Colombia* (merits), the Court was asked to assess the customary character of Article 76; see: *I.C.J. Reports 2012*, para. 118. See similarly Anderson, David (2005), "Developments in Maritime Boundary Law and Practice", in: Colson, David A. and Robert W. Smith (eds.), *International Maritime Boundaries*, Vol. V, Leiden: Martinus Nijhoff, pp. 3211–3212.

4 Latin America and the Caribbean and the Law of the Sea

Although not always acknowledged,[1] the contribution of Latin America and the Caribbean to the modern law of the sea has no parallel.[2] That contribution comprises a number of unilateral claims that followed the 1945 Truman Proclamations and, more importantly, of the 200-nautical-mile Declaration made by Ecuador, Peru and Chile in 1952, which were followed by other important Declarations in the region.

Unilateral Claims

Although different in importance and geographical extent, national claims were indeed formulated by Latin American States both before and after the Truman Proclamations. Prior to the 1945 Truman Proclamations, national claims reflected a common practice in the nineteenth and early twentieth centuries whereby States would establish a certain breadth of their territorial sea.

After the 1945 Truman Proclamations, a wave of similar but ultimately quite distinct unilateral claims made by Latin American States followed. Similar because it is evident that they understood the rationale behind the US proclamations, but distinct because some of the Latin American claims were of an additional nature.[3] Mexico and Argentina, as will be seen, being States endowed with natural continental shelves, quickly followed the Truman Proclamation on the Continental Shelf. Chile and Peru, on the other hand, having no physical continental shelves, went way beyond that, perhaps even "far ahead of their time",[4] and put forward the 200-nautical-mile thesis as a kind of compensation.[5]

Mexico

On 29 October 1945, by means of a Declaration made by the president of Mexico, Manuel Avila Camacho, with respect to the continental shelf, Mexico laid claim to the whole of the continental shelf and to "each and all of the natural resources existing there, whether known or unknown". At the same time, it decided to take steps to "supervise, utilise and control the closed fishing zones necessary for the conservation of this source of well-being."[6]

By doing that, Mexico's Declaration did not restrict itself to establishing conservation zones in the high seas contiguous to its coasts, as did the Truman

DOI: 10.4324/9781003290452-6

Proclamation on fisheries limited to US nationals carrying out fishing activities near US coasts, but claimed the right to take unilateral measures to protect living resources in fishing zones irrespective of the nationality of the fishermen.[7] It is worth mentioning that the Declaration did not seek to disregard the rights of free navigation on the high seas.

Argentina

On 11 October 1946, Argentina proclaimed sovereignty over the epicontinental sea and the continental shelf.[8] The Declaration claimed that those spaces were "subject to the sovereign power of the Nation" but also stipulated, in line with its Mexican precedent, that "[f]or purposes of free navigation" the waters situated "in the Argentine Epicontinental Sea and above the Argentine Continental Shelf" remained unaffected by it.[9] In 1966, Law No. 17.094 on the adjacent sea and the continental shelf confirmed that declaration.[10] It should be noted that, contrary to the previous proclamation, this one does include the water column.

Chile

Chile's claim of 23 June 1947, enshrined in the form of a Presidential Declaration,[11] came as a reaction to the threat to South-East Pacific fisheries – and hence to the national interest of Chile and Peru[12] – and to the side effects of the Truman Proclamations.[13] Indeed, during the 1940s, the whaling industry of Chile and Peru had expanded, in part as a result of World War II, during which time European whaling around Antarctica had been suspended.[14] The Declaration hence proclaimed Chile's

> national sovereignty over the seas adjacent to its coasts whatever may be their depths, and within those limits necessary in order to reserve, protect, preserve and exploit the natural resources of whatever nature found on, within and below the said seas, placing within the control of the government especially all fisheries and whaling activities with the object of preventing the exploitation of natural riches of this kind to the detriment of the inhabitants of Chile.

The Declaration added that the protection and control was being declared "over all the seas contained within the perimeter formed by the coast and the mathematical parallel projected into the sea at a distance of *200 nautical miles*" (emphasis added) from the coasts of Chile. This was the first formulation ever made by a State on a 200-nautical-mile zone. It met with strong opposition from the international community.[15]

Peru

Peru's proclamation was adopted by means of a Supreme Decree enacted on 1 August 1947.[16] In addition to the threat to the Peruvian whaling industry, the fishing industry also felt the pressure caused by foreign fishing vessels, which had been driven away from their traditional fishing grounds in the North Pacific as a result of overfishing and of the 1945 Truman Proclamation. This is why Peru's Supreme Decree declared that national sovereignty and jurisdiction were to be "extended to the submerged continental or insular shelf adjacent to the continental or insular shores of national territory", no matter what depth and extension the shelf may have. It also claimed the exercise of national sovereignty and jurisdiction

> over the sea adjoining the shores of national territory whatever its depth and in the extension necessary to reserve, protect, maintain and utilize natural resources and wealth of any kind which may be found in or below those waters.

It finally declared that it would exercise the same control and protection over the seas adjacent to Peru's coast up to a distance of 200 nautical miles, drawing protests similar to Chile's claim.[17]

In this manner, Chile and Peru asserted a general claim to a 200-nautical-mile zone, following a similar approach and purpose, however independently.[18] In general, it is possible to say that the claims made by Chile and Peru were different from the Truman Proclamation on the Continental Shelf, as well as from the Mexican and Argentinean claims, in at least three respects: they were made against international law "as it stood at the time", they were radically innovative in as much as they extended to a distance of 200 nautical miles, and they included a new element: the socio-economic factor.[19]

The 1952 Santiago Declaration on the Maritime Zone

Following the unilateral claims made by Chile and Peru in 1947, these two countries, together with Ecuador, in an expression of regional solidarity decided to cooperate, with the aim of protecting the resources of their adjacent sea from the predatory activities of foreign fleets (intensive foreign whaling and increasing foreign fishing).[20] Chile, Ecuador and Peru thus adopted, on 18 August 1952, the Declaration on the Maritime Zone, better known as the 1952 Santiago Declaration.[21]

The Declaration proclaimed "as a norm" of the three countries' "international maritime policy" that they "possess exclusive sovereignty and jurisdiction over the sea along the coasts of their respective countries to a *minimum* distance of 200 nautical miles" (emphasis added). Hence, the Declaration aimed at announcing to the world that the three States were extending their national jurisdiction seawards, up to at least 200 nautical miles, and, at the same time, excluding vessels from third States from their fishing and whaling grounds.

It is in this manner that the main tenets of the future 200-nautical-mile exclusive economic zone were laid down. It would later be enshrined in the 1982 United Nations Convention on the Law of the Sea.

This was well illustrated, for instance, in a 1979 Letter from the Heads of Delegation of Chile, Colombia, Ecuador and Peru to the president of UNCLOS III, Sri Lanka's Ambassador Hamilton Shirley Amerasinghe. In it, protesting against manifestations of the US Government's policy concerning the instructions given to US vessels and aircraft to defy the maritime jurisdiction asserted by those States, they claimed that

> in the present state of development of the new law of the sea, it is unusual to attempt to deny the validity of the new provisions, whose initial and clearest expression is found in the *Santiago Declaration on the Maritime Zone of 200 miles*, which contains principles that represented a *major and genuinely Latin American contribution* to the discussions of the Third United Nations Conference on the Law of the Sea [emphasis added].[22]

In the same vein, few years later, in a Joint Declaration made by Chile, Colombia, Ecuador and Peru, dated 28 April 1982, also in the framework of UNCLOS III, it was stated that

> The delegations of Chile, Colombia, Ecuador and Peru wish to point out that the universal recognition of the *rights of sovereignty and jurisdiction of the coastal State within the 200-mile limit* provided for in the draft Convention is a fundamental achievement of the countries members of the Permanent Commission of the South Pacific, in accordance with the basic objectives stated in the *Santiago Declaration* of 1952.
>
> Those objectives have been compiled and developed by the Convention on the Law of the Sea, which incorporates into international law principles and institutions which are essential for a more appropriate and fairer exploitation of the resources contained in coastal waters, to the benefit of the over-all development of the peoples concerned, on the basis of the duty and the right to protect those resources and to conserve and guarantee that natural wealth for those peoples [emphasis added].[23]

There is no doubt, in light of the foregoing, that the 1952 Declaration of Santiago, some 30 years earlier, established the basis for what would be known as the exclusive economic zone. This is one of the main contributions of Latin America to the modern law of the sea.[24]

The 1970 Montevideo Declaration on the Law of the Sea

A number of diplomatic conferences were organised in the 1970s to reach a regional accord on the law of the sea, or at least to "coordinate" positions.[25] The context was one of lack of uniformity on matters related to the law of the sea in Latin America[26] caused, to a certain extent, by a diverse range of claims made by coastal States before and after the Santiago Declaration. Such claims included Costa Rica's 1948 proclamation, El Salvador's Constitution of 1950

(200-nautical-mile territorial sea) and Honduras' 1951 Legislative Decree.[27] Similarly, Ecuador, Panama and Brazil claimed 200-nautical-mile territorial seas in 1966, 1967 and 1970, respectively.[28]

Consequently, in May 1970 a conference was held in the capital of Uruguay with the participation of nine Latin American States having claimed 200-nautical-mile zones.[29] The official outcome was a Declaration composed of six basic principles ("Basic Principles of the Law of the Sea"),[30] namely: (1) right of the coastal State over the natural resources of the adjacent sea for economic purposes; (2) right to establish the limits of their maritime sovereignty and jurisdiction according to their geographical and geological characteristics; (3) right to explore and conserve the adjacent marine resources and regulate fishing and hunting activities; (4) right to explore, conserve and exploit the natural resources on the continental shelf; (5) right to explore, conserve and exploit the natural resources of the seabed and its subsoil; and (6) right to enact regulatory measures to achieve the above-mentioned goals without prejudice to the freedom of navigation and overflight of vessels and aircraft of any flag.[31]

Although the conference was considered by one author as unsuccessful,[32] in part because eight of the nine participants formulated declarations that seemed to undermine the impact of the main text,[33] it can yet be said that the Declaration of Montevideo was the expression of a regional contribution to the progressive development of international law from a Latin American perspective. This helped such Latin American countries gain support for their claims from the international community,[34] a position that appears to have been finally included in the 1972 Santo Domingo Declaration.

The 1970 Lima Declaration of Latin American States on the Law of the Sea

Pursuant to the 1970 Montevideo Declaration, another conference took place later that year. This time the venue was Lima, Peru, and it was held between 4 and 8 August 1970. The outcome was a Declaration[35] aimed at coordinating the diplomatic positions of the attending countries, which were not only Latin American but also from other regions,[36] concerning some aspects of the law of the sea. In relation to maritime delimitation, point 2 of the Declaration (following the Montevideo Declaration) referred to the right of every State "to establish the limits of its maritime sovereignty or jurisdiction in accordance with reasonable criteria, having regard to its geographical, geological and biological characteristics, and the need to make rational use of its resources". It did not make any reference whatsoever to a method of maritime delimitation.

From a political perspective, it is worthwhile noting that in his welcoming remarks, Peru's Foreign Minister stated that "the expansion of maritime jurisdictions for economic purposes and the principle of freedom of the seas could be mutually reconciled" and that "each State is to establish its own maritime boundaries based on its own geographic and geological characteristics and its need for national utilisation".[37]

Additionally, the participating States approved six resolutions dealing with some aspects of the law of the sea[38] that were to be discussed at the United Nations General Assembly of September 1970, and also at the United Nations Committee on the Peaceful Uses of the Seabed and the Ocean Floor beyond the Limits of National Jurisdiction.[39]

In sum, the Lima Declaration, while reaffirming the principles of the Montevideo Declaration, included two additional concepts: the right of the coastal State to prevent contamination of the waters and other dangerous and harmful effects that may result from the use, exploration or exploitation of the area adjacent to its coast; and the right of the coastal State to authorise, supervise and participate in all scientific research activities carried out in the maritime zone and to be informed of the findings and the results of this research.

It has been claimed that these rules and principles are "the most detailed formulation of the content of the legal regime ever to be produced by any State, or geographical group, regarding the conduct of scientific research offshore a coastal State";[40] and that clearly reflect some of the main tenets incorporated into Parts XII and XIII of the Law of the Sea Convention.[41]

Both marine scientific research and the protection and preservation of the marine environment were questions dealt with at the Lima Conference and the object of recommendations later reflected in the United Nations Convention on the Law of the Sea.[42]

It is hence possible to say they were also part of the contribution of Latin America to the modern law of the sea.[43]

The 1972 Declaration of Santo Domingo

In the framework of the "Specialised Conference of the Caribbean Countries on Problems of the Sea", held in Santo Domingo on 9 June 1972, of all the attending States, ten Latin American and Caribbean States signed the Declaration of Santo Domingo.[44] This declaration articulated the concept of the "patrimonial sea" the breadth of which was not to exceed a *maximum* of 200 nautical miles, one of the key differences with Santiago's *minimum* 200-nautical-mile distance. But perhaps the most striking difference of the "patrimonial sea" concept was referred to by Venezuelan Ambassador Andrés Aguilar:

> An economic zone, called the patrimonial sea, not more than 200 miles in breadth from the base line of the territorial sea. In that zone, there would be freedom of navigation and overflight but the coastal State would have an exclusive right to all resources.[45]

Thus, the "patrimonial sea" was well received at the international level as an effort put forward by some Latin American and Caribbean States (Colombia, Mexico and Venezuela playing a leading role) to reach a compromise between the two views opposing at the time.[46] As it is known, some States claimed a 200-nautical-mile jurisdiction over all marine resources (the "territorialist" group),[47] whereas others defended the traditional view of a narrow territorial sea and large areas of high seas where they could exercise all freedoms of the seas (major maritime powers). A compromise could be envisaged, especially by some Caribbean costal States modestly endowed with natural resources and whose geography would not allow exceed a maximum distance of 200 nautical miles.[48]

While including certain legal principles relating to maritime areas, such as the territorial sea, continental shelf, international seabed and the high seas, as well as issues such as marine pollution and regional cooperation, the most important legacy of this declaration is the notion of the "patrimonial sea" that "became a major cornerstone in the final and successful construction of the new law of the sea",[49] because it helped shape what would later become the exclusive economic zone.

Despite their varied interests and geographical characteristics, Latin American and Caribbean States, through diplomatic efforts displayed in Santiago, Montevideo, Lima and Santo Domingo, advanced a position, first radical then moderated, so as to persuade the international community of the necessity of change in the law of the sea.[50] After having coordinated their positions, their views were eventually enshrined in the 1982 United Nations Convention on the Law of the Sea.[51]

Finally, one common aspect concerning Latin American and Caribbean declarations is their acknowledgement of a geographic, economic and social relationship between the sea, the land and the people who live on the land. This constitutes the basis of coastal populations' lawful priority regarding the utilisation of the natural resources in the sea adjacent to their coasts and also – more importantly for the purposes of this book – of the need to establish the limits of coastal States' maritime jurisdiction, considering the geographic, geological and biological features of the concerned areas.[52]

Regional International Law in Latin America and the Caribbean?

The notion of regional international law is herein presented so as to examine the existence of regional rules concerning maritime delimitation in Latin America and the Caribbean.

Unlike universal or general international law, regional international law regulates a group of States linked geographically, ideologically or otherwise that may recognise special rules applying only to them, such as EU law and rules on diplomatic asylum in Latin America.[53] As it is known, in the *Asylum* case the ICJ laid down a high standard as regards the notion of "constant and uniform usage" in order to establish a regional custom.[54]

Despite this, the existence of a regional practice of using lines of latitude and longitude as maritime boundaries was argued by Honduras in its maritime delimitation dispute with Nicaragua.[55] Similarly, that there is a regional custom in the South-Eastern Pacific has been advanced in academia.[56] Yet none of these views has prevailed.

In the region, one could refer to the cases of maritime boundaries between Colombia and Ecuador, to one segment of the maritime boundary between

Colombia and Panama in the Pacific Ocean, to the maritime boundary between Ecuador and Peru, and even to the first segment of the maritime boundary between Peru and Chile. Almost all of these run (at least partially) along geographical parallels, but that practice alone is insufficient to infer the existence of a rule of customary international law.

To sum up, there is no indication whatsoever of the existence of regional rules relating to maritime delimitation in Latin America and the Caribbean. In relation to the foregoing, it is significant to recall the position of former ICJ Judge Alejandro Alvarez concerning the specificity of the Latin American legal tradition.[57] Alvarez considered Latin American international law to be a sub-division of what he called American international law. He claimed that American international law had exercised a considerable influence over universal international law and had given it its peculiar character.[58] It seems that Alvarez's thesis also comprised the objective of improving the standing and stature of Latin American States within the international community. In his article published by the *American Journal of International Law* in 1909, Judge Alvarez claimed that "the entry of Latin America into the community of nations is one of the most important facts in the history of civilisation."[59] Yet, it is clear, as stated earlier, that in the law of maritime delimitation neither regional nor sub-regional rules are applicable to Latin America and the Caribbean.

Notes

1 The contribution of Latin America and the Caribbean to the modern law of the sea seems not to be always acknowledged. Some accounts on the history or development of the law of the sea do not mention the Latin American claims made in the 1940s and 1950s; see for instance: Roach, J. Ashley and Robert W. Smith (2012), *Excessive Maritime Claims*, Third Edition, Leiden: Martinus Nijhoff, pp. 845–860 (Appendix XII: Evolution of the Modern Law of the Sea).

2 Writing in 1974, García-Amador considered Latin America's contribution to be restricted to the exploration, exploitation, and conservation of natural resources of the sea; see: García-Amador (1974), *ibid.*, p. 33. Other authors that wrote on the Latin American contribution to the law of the sea include: Vargas Carreño, Edmundo (1973), *América Latina y el Derecho del Mar*, Mexico: Fondo de Cultura Económica, 167 pp.; De Soto, Alvaro (1973), "The Latin American View of the Law of the Sea", *India Quarterly*, Vol. 29, pp. 126–137; Zacklin, Ralph (1974), "Latin America and the Development of the Law of the Sea", in: Zacklin, Ralph (ed.), *The Changing Law of the Sea. Western Hemisphere Perspectives*, Leiden: Sjithoff, pp. 57–78; De la Colina, Rafel (1974), "Evolución del Derecho del Mar en América: Contribución latinoamericana", in: Secretaría de Relaciones Exteriores de Mexico, *México y el régimen del mar*, Mexico: Tlatelolco, pp. 37–80; Galindo, Reynaldo (1976), "Contribución de América Latina a la Conferencia de Caracas", in: Vargas, Jorge A. and Edmundo Vargas Carreño (eds.), *Derecho del mar: una visión latinoamericana*, Mexico: Editorial Jus, pp. 53–77; Vargas, Jorge A. (1981), *Contribuciones de la América Latina al derecho del mar*, Mexico: UNAM, 138 pp.; Dupuy, René-Jean and Daniel Vignes (eds.) (1985), *ibid.*, especially Chapter 2, Division C "Universalism and regionalism of the law of the sea", pp. 42–60; Aguilar, Andrés (1992), "The Latin American contribution to the modern law of the sea", *Netherlands International Law Review*, Vol. 39, pp. 63–88; and Ferrero Costa, Eduardo (2013), "Latin America and the Law of the

Sea", in: Scheiber, Harry and Jin-Hyun Paik (eds.), *Regions, Institutions and Law of the Sea*, Leiden: Martinus Nijhoff, pp. 383–410.

3 "In contrast with [the 1945 Truman claims], a majority of the Latin American claims introduced true innovations in the traditional international law of the sea"; see: García-Amador (1974), *ibid.*, p. 34.

4 *I.C.J. Pleadings, Maritime Dispute* (*Peru* v. *Chile*). Peru's first round of oral argument (Counsel: Sir Michael Wood), 3 December 2012 (CR 2012/27), p. 58, para. 6.

5 For an account of "The Latin American claims", see: *I.C.J. Pleadings, Maritime Dispute* (*Peru* v. *Chile*). Peru's first round of oral argument (Counsel: Tullio Treves), 3 December 2012 (CR 2012/27), pp. 48–49, paras. 18–20. See also: Ulloa, Alberto (1957), *Derecho Internacional Público*, Vol. I, Madrid: Ediciones Iberoamericanas, p. 565.

6 Presidential Declaration with respect to continental shelf, 29 October 1945. English text available at: *UNLS: Laws and Regulations on the Regime of the High Seas,* 1951, Vol. I, (ST/LEG/SER.B/1), pp. 13–14. For a commentary see: García-Amador (1974), *ibid.*, pp. 71–72.

7 García-Amador (1974), *ibid.*, p. 34.

8 Declaration proclaiming sovereignty over the epicontinental sea and the continental shelf, 9 October 1946. English text available at: *AJIL*, Vol. 41, No. 1, Supplement: Official Documents, pp. 11–12. For a commentary, see for instance: García-Amador (1974), pp. 71–72; and also: Pfirter de Armas, Frida (1974), "Argentina and the Law of the Sea", in: Zacklin, Ralph (ed.), *ibid.*, pp. 169–187.

9 The "Epicontinental Sea" refers to the waters above the continental shelf.

10 Pfirter de Armas (1974), *ibid.*, pp. 173–174.

11 Presidential Declaration concerning the continental shelf, 23 June 1947. English text available at: *UNLS*, *ibid.*, Vol. I (ST/LEG/SER.B/1), pp. 6–8. For a commentary, see for instance: Oda (1969), *ibid.*, pp. 434–435.

12 *Maritime Dispute* (*Peru* v. *Chile*), Counter-Memorial of the Government of Chile (CMC), Vol. I, 9 March 2010, para. 2.23, and in general, paras. 2.24–2.26.

13 *Maritime Dispute* (*Peru* v. *Chile*), Memorial of the Government of Peru (PM), Vol. I, 20 March 2009, para. 4.44.

14 *Maritime Dispute* (*Peru* v. *Chile*), PM, para. 4.42; see also: Hollick (1977), *ibid.*, pp. 497–498.

15 E.g. Protest by the United Kingdom Government against the Declaration by the President of Chile of 23rd June 1947, available at *Maritime Dispute* (*Peru* v. *Chile*), CMC, Vol. III, 9 March 2010, Annex 56. In it, His Majesty's Government stated that "in the United Kingdom are gravely disquieted by the implications of the above claims [it refers to the three claims contained in Chile's Presidential Declaration of 1947, namely: national sovereignty over the continental shelf adjacent to its national territory; national sovereignty over the seas adjacent to its coast; and protection and control over all the seas contained within the perimeter formed between the coast and the mathematical parallel projected into the sea at a distance of 200 nautical miles] which go far beyond those put forward in the earlier declarations referred to above of the United States of America and Mexico".

16 Supreme Decree No. 781, concerning submerged continental or insular shelf, 1 August 1947. English text available at: *UNLS, ibid.*, Vol. I (ST/LEG/SER.B/1), pp. 16–19.

17 Note No. 11 (152/8/48) of February 1948, from the Ambassador of the United Kingdom to the Minister of Foreign Affairs of Peru, available at: *Maritime Dispute* (*Peru* v. *Chile*), Memorial of the Government of Peru, Vol. III, 20 March 2009, Annex 61.

18 *Maritime Dispute* (*Peru* v. *Chile*), Memorial of the Government of Peru, para. 4.59. Note that these claims were the object of different interpretations in the dispute between Peru and Chile before the ICJ. In that regard see: Rejoinder of the Government of

Chile, Vol. I, 11 July 2011, para. 8.2; and *I.C.J. Pleadings, Maritime Dispute* (*Peru* v. *Chile*). Peru's first round of oral argument (Counsel: Sir Michael Wood), 3 December 2012 (CR 2012/27), pp. 62–67, paras. 16–35.

19 *Maritime Dispute* (*Peru* v. *Chile*), Memorial of the Government of Peru, paras. 4.24–4.26.

20 In that sense, it has also been claimed that the signatory States were not satisfied with the 1946 International Whaling Convention, which they signed but never ratified, because of its being in favour of larger whaling powers to the detriment, specially, of the whaling industries of Chile and Peru; see: *Maritime Dispute* (*Peru* v. *Chile*), Memorial of the Government of Peru, para. 4.43. Hence, those two countries decided to adopt their own approach to the whaling problem, that is to say, they proceeded to adopt unilateral claims.

21 Declaration on the Maritime Zone, 18 August 1952. English text available at: *UNTS*, Registration Number 14758. Signed originally by Chile, Ecuador, and Peru at the First Conference on the Exploitation and Conservation of Marine Resources of the South Pacific. Colombia joined this Declaration by accession on 16 April 1980. In the framework of that Conference, the Permanent Commission of the South Pacific (known by its acronym in Spanish, CPPS, standing for *Comisión Permanente del Pacífico Sur*), was also created. Its legal character was the object of interpretation by the International Court of Justice in its Judgment of 27 January 2014.

22 Letter dated 20 August 1979 from Heads of Delegations of Chile, Colombia, Ecuador and Peru to the President of UNCLOS III; see: Document A/CONF. 62/85.

23 Joint Declaration of the Representatives of Chile, Colombia, Ecuador and Peru at the Third United Nations Conference on the Law of the Sea, 28 April 1982; see: Letter to the President of the Conference, A/CONF.62/L.143, 29 April 1982. In this sense, see also: Hollick (1977), *ibid.*, pp. 494–500.

24 It should be recalled that the 1952 Declaration of Santiago has been considered by some as a multilateral treaty that – while involving all aspects mentioned before – established at the same time maritime boundaries between Ecuador and Peru and between Chile and Peru; see: *I.C.J. Pleadings, Maritime Dispute* (*Peru* v. *Chile*). Chile's first round of oral argument (Counsel: Pierre-Marie Dupuy), 7 December 2012 (CR 2012/32), pp. 12–28. The question was settled by the International Court of Justice in its judgment of 27 January 2014, which is commented upon elsewhere in this book.

25 The 24th Session of the United Nations General Assembly, in Resolution 2574A (15 December 1969), recommended that a survey be made concerning revision of the regimes of the high seas, the continental shelf, the territorial sea, the contiguous zone, conservation of the living resources of the high seas, and particularly, an internationally accepted definition of the area beyond the limits of national jurisdiction. This, for the United Nations Secretary-General to gather the views of States regarding the convening of a new United Nations Conference on the Law of the Sea. Note that Peru's Ambassador Alfonso Arias Schreiber was appointed as rapporteur of the conference.

26 The lack of uniformity was also acknowledged by García-Amador, Francisco (1974), *ibid.*, pp. 45–47.

27 García-Amador, Francisco (1974), *ibid.*, pp. 36 and 37.

28 *Ibid.*, pp. 38 and 39.

29 The participating States were: Argentina, Brazil, Chile, Ecuador, El Salvador, Nicaragua, Panama, Peru and Uruguay.

30 UN Doc. A/AC.138/34 (8 May 1970); see: Vargas, Jorge F. (2011), *Mexico and the Law of the Sea. Contributions and Compromises*. Leiden: Martinus Nijhoff, pp. 178–179.

31 Acta Final de la Reunión de Montevideo sobre el Derecho del Mar (1970), *RPDI*, XXVIII, pp. 128–146. It includes three resolutions: (1) Basis for the answers to the question put forward by the United Nations Secretary-General on the calling of a

conference on the Law of the Sea; (2) Basis for the answers to the questions put forward by the US and the USSR concerning the calling of a conference on certain aspects of the Law of the Sea; and (3) Coordinating measures.

32 For Vargas, the conference was a "diplomatic and political failure", see: Vargas (2011), *ibid.*, p. 143. The same author claimed this Declaration "lost a unique opportunity" of adopting a more conciliatory position with respect to the 200-nautical-mile zone; *ibid.*, pp. 144–145.

33 All participating States, except from the host, Uruguay.

34 In his speech, Ecuador's delegate stated that the Montevideo meeting worked on the basis of a rich historical continental contribution ("*sobre la base de un rico aporte histórico continental*"); see: *RPDI*, XXXVIII, p. 144. In this context, it is important to mention as another antecedent a Declaration containing "Mexico's Principles on the Legal Regime of the Sea" ("*Principios de México sobre Régimen Jurídico del Mar*") adopted on 3 February 1956 whereby it was established that each State had the right to establish its territorial sea extending until "reasonable limits" taking into account geographical, geological and biological factors; see: *RPDI*, XXXVIII, p. 143.

35 See also, in general, Speech by the Meeting's President, Enrique García Sayán, available at: *RPDI*, XXXVIII, pp. 185–188.

36 Argentina, Brazil, Chile, Colombia, Dominican Republic, Ecuador, El Salvador, Guatemala, Honduras, Mexico, Nicaragua, Panama, Peru and Uruguay voted in favour of the Declaration. Bolivia, Paraguay and Venezuela voted against the Declaration. Other States participated as observers: Costa Rica, Canada, Haiti, Iceland, India, Senegal, South Korea, the United Arab Republic and Yugoslavia.

37 See: Speech by Gen. Edgardo Mercado Jarrín, Minister for Foreign Affairs of Peru, *Exposiciones Oficiales Peruanas* (1972), Ministerio de Relaciones Exteriores, Lima, pp. 11–18; and also: *Final Minute of the Latin American Meeting on the Law of the Sea*, UNGA Doc. A/AC. 138/28 of 14 August 1970.

38 See in particular, Resolution 2, available at: *RPDI*, XXXVIII, pp. 173–174. Also, Resolution 1, for instance, recommended that the participating States give priority to the adoption of a "Declaration of Principles" on the seabed and ocean floor beyond the limits of national jurisdiction, a Declaration that eventually became one of the cornerstones of the notion of "common heritage of mankind". Also, Resolution 5 recommended reaffirming, *inter alia*, that all scientific research carried out within the maritime jurisdiction of the State shall be subject to this State's previous authorisation; that the coastal State has the right to obtain benefits out of the data obtained from the research carried out within its jurisdiction; and that all the samples obtained as a result of research of this kind shall become property of the State under whose jurisdiction is being carried out.

39 United Nations General Assembly Resolution No. 2749 (XXV), 17 December 1970.

40 Vargas (2011), *ibid.*, p. 149.

41 See for instance, UNCLOS Articles 240 and 245 and 246 and 249.

42 See, in particular, Resolution 3, available at: *RPDI*, XXXVIII, pp. 175–177. Other sources known to lay at the basis of the relevant LOSC texts include: the United Nations Conference on the Human Environment held in Stockholm in 1972 (Stockholm Declaration, especially: principles 21 and 22); the *Torrey Canyon* oil spill in 1967, and a number of IMO instruments; see for instance: IMO Secretariat (2012), *Implications of the United Nations Convention on the Law of the Sea for the International Maritime Organization*, LEG/MISC.7, 19 January 2012.

43 For a discussion of all Resolutions part of the Lima Declaration, see generally: Vargas (2011), *ibid.*, pp. 148–150. Concerning the "legitimate priority right" to use "the natural resources of the marine environment" by coastal populations, and the reference to "a geographical, economic and social link between the sea, the land and man who inhabits it" (preamble of Declaration); it can be said it found its inspiration in the 1952

Santiago Declaration which, in turn, took account of Peru's Supreme Decree 781 of 1947, the so-called Bustamante Decree, named after the Peruvian president at the time (and later judge of the ICJ), José Luis Bustamante y Rivero. See: Speech by Minister of Foreign Affairs of Peru to commemorate the 25th anniversary of Supreme Decree 781, in 1972; see Vargas (2011), *ibid.*, p. 146, note 70.

44 States that signed the declaration: Colombia, Costa Rica, Dominican Republic, Guatemala, Haiti, Honduras, Mexico, Nicaragua, Trinidad and Tobago, and Venezuela. States that, while attending, did not sign the declaration: Barbados, El Salvador, Guyana, Jamaica and Panama.

45 UN Doc. A/AC.138/SR.64.

46 Zacklin (1974), *ibid.* p. 71; and Vargas (2011), *ibid.*, p. 151. See specially, note 85.

47 This includes States such as Chile, Costa Rica, El Salvador, Honduras and Peru that had claimed a 200-nautical-mile zone, not necessarily "territorial sea"; but also States such as Brazil, Ecuador and Panama that expressly claimed a 200-nautical-mile territorial sea.

48 García-Amador (1974), *ibid.*, p. 46.

49 Vargas (2011), *ibid.*, p. 151.

50 In this train of thought, it is important to refer also to a Resolution dated 9 February 1973, adopted by the Inter-American Juridical Committee (ILM, 12, 1972, pp. 711–713). The document is significant, among other reasons, due to its being an effort to close the gap between the "territorialists" and the "patrimonialists".

51 The author is not unaware of the impact that meetings held in regions other than Latin America and the Caribbean had on the development of the law of the sea. For instance: Meetings of the Asian-African Legal Consultative Committee (1970–1982), in: Report of the Sub-Committee on the Law of the Sea by the Asian-African Consultative Committee, Colombo, 18–27 January 1971; the African States Regional Seminar on the Law of the Sea, held in Yaoundé, Cameroon (1972), which resulted in a document labelled "Yaoundé Conclusions", comparable to the proposals of the Lima Declaration, in: Conclusions in the General Report of the African States Regional Seminar on the Law of the Sea, held at Yaoundé, 20–30 June 1972. United Nations Legislative Series, ST/LEG/SER.B/16, p. 601; the meeting of the Council of Ministers of the Organisation of African Unity (OAU), which resulted in the OAU Declaration on Issues of the Law of the Sea (1973) also known as the Addis Ababa Declaration, in: UN Doc. A/CONF.62/33; and the Group of 77 meeting on the Law of the Sea issues, Nairobi, Kenya (1974), which failed to produce an agreed document.

52 García-Amador, F.V. (1974), *ibid.*, p. 50. See also, generally, the reference to regional declarations made prior to the Third United Nations Conference, in the *South China Sea Arbitration Award of 12 July 2016*, paras. 512 *et seq.*

53 Shaw, Malcom (2008), *International Law*, 6th edition, Cambridge (etc.): Cambridge University Press, p. 2; and also, generally, SFDI (1976), *Colloque de Bordeaux, Régionalisme et universalisme dans le droit international contemporain*, Paris: Pedone, pp. 257–262.

54 *Colombian-Peruvian asylum case, Judgment, I.C.J. Reports 1950*, pp. 276–277.

55 *Territorial and Maritime Dispute between Nicaragua and Honduras in the Caribbean Sea* (*Nicaragua* v. *Honduras*)*, Judgment, I.C.J. Reports 2007*, para. 246; and *I.C.J. Pleadings, Territorial and Maritime Dispute between Nicaragua and Honduras in the Caribbean Sea* (*Nicaragua* v. *Honduras*). Honduras' first round of oral argument (Counsel: David Colson), 16 March 2007 (CR 2007/10), pp. 31–32, paras. 149, 150, 152–154. Regarding the inequitableness of using parallels or meridians, see: *I.C.J. Pleadings, Territorial and Maritime Dispute between Nicaragua and Honduras in the Caribbean Sea* (*Nicaragua* v. *Honduras*). Nicaragua's first round of oral argument (Agent: Carlos Argüello), 5 March 2007 (CR 2007/1), p. 19, paras. 15 and 16.

56 Llanos Mardones, Ignacio (2000), *El Derecho de la Delimitación Marítima en el Pacífico Sudeste*, Santiago de Chile: RIL, pp. 162–164.

57 For a reference to the long-standing tradition of Latin American international legal thinking see: *Pulp Mills on the River Uruguay* (*Argentina* v. *Uruguay*), *I.C.J. Reports 2010, Separate Opinion of Judge Cançado Trindade*, p. 154, especially footnote 57. Cf. Becker Lorca, Arnulf (2006), "International Law in Latin America or Latin American International Law? Rise, Fall, and Retrieval of a Tradition of Legal Thinking and Political Imagination", *Harvard International Law Journal*, Vol. 47, 1, pp. 283–305.

58 *Colombian-Peruvian asylum case, Judgment, I.C.J. Reports 1950, Dissenting Opinion of Judge Alvarez*, pp. 293–294.

59 Alvarez, Alejandro (1909), "Latin America and International Law", *AJIL*, Vol. 3, p. 269.

5 Law of Maritime Delimitation Through Case Law

The law of maritime delimitation has evolved a great deal since 1945, most prominently in the last four decades. Today, coastal States find themselves more often than not either negotiating or litigating so as to resolve their maritime boundary disputes. Prior to that evolution, States would generally not allocate much importance to negotiating the limits of a narrow belt of waters, measuring often three nautical miles,[1] the economic importance of which was rather limited.

In that context, two main causes explain the increasing frequency of maritime delimitation disputes being settled by agreement or by third-party adjudication. First, the emergence of new maritime areas under State jurisdiction which has brought about a dramatic extension of the potential resources at stake;[2] second, each State's search for legal certainty to conduct its relations with other States, reflected in the need to extend those new maritime spaces as much as possible, and ideally establish a final and permanent boundary line.[3]

The extension of maritime spaces under coastal State jurisdiction has given coastal configuration and the presence of islands the ability to transform a case of maritime delimitation between adjacent States into maritime delimitation between opposite States. A few examples in Latin America and the Caribbean are cases such as Mexico and the US in the Gulf of Mexico; and Belize, Guatemala and Honduras in the Caribbean.[4] Similarly, it can be argued that while Colombia envisaged negotiating maritime boundaries with Venezuela[5] or with Ecuador, and while Venezuela could expect to do so with the Netherlands (on account of Aruba, Bonaire and Curaçao), it seems less likely that, before the emergence of the modern law of the sea, Haiti ever imagined it would negotiate maritime boundaries with the US (on account of Puerto Rico) or that Costa Rica thought it could need to establish maritime boundaries with Ecuador.[6] Those situations are clearly the consequence of the dramatic extension of maritime spaces under coastal State jurisdiction.

As of 2022, over 230 maritime boundaries laid down by agreements, judgments or awards have been produced publicly.[7] Since most maritime boundaries have been established by agreement rather than by a judicial or arbitral body, maritime boundary negotiations constitute a significant means whereby States come up with a negotiated solution.[8] What is more, there are even some cases where third-party adjudication was involved but decisions still had to be "translated" into

DOI: 10.4324/9781003290452-7

agreements because the Parties had expressly requested that the Court establish principles and rules instead of drawing a line.

This was the case, for instance, of the maritime delimitation treaties concluded by Germany and Denmark and by Germany and the Netherlands, after the 1969 *North Sea* judgment;[9] the 1986 treaty between Libya and Malta that followed the 1985 ICJ Judgment;[10] and the 1988 treaty concluded by Libya and Tunisia after the 1982 ICJ Judgment.[11] In the maritime delimitation case between Nicaragua and Honduras before the ICJ, the Court, while drawing most of the line, established the obligation of the Parties to negotiate the first three miles of their maritime boundary. This could be contrasted with the 2012 ICJ Judgment concerning *Nicaragua* v. *Colombia*, where Colombia announced that the judgment of the ICJ "is not applicable without a treaty".[12]

Most maritime boundary agreements in existence were concluded after the First Geneva Conference on the law of the sea (i.e. after 1958).[13] Yet, as will be seen later in this book, a great number of them were concluded during UNCLOS negotiations in the 1970s, and ever since they remain a frequent issue in international relations. Today, in some cases, depending on the existence of special circumstances, maritime boundary negotiations could consist of discussions about the number and choice of base points to be taken into account (contributing points) after having posited a provisional equidistance line.

Where an agreement through negotiation could not be reached or negotiations never took place,[14] recourse to third-party adjudication has been an option. The latter situation can be divided in two: cases in which the Parties to the dispute seized jointly the ICJ, the International Tribunal for the Law of the Sea (ITLOS), or an arbitral tribunal by means of a special agreement (*compromis*); and cases brought before the ICJ, ITLOS or Annex VII Arbitrations by unilateral application.[15]

In fact, it seems that more and more maritime delimitation cases are being submitted by unilateral application, unlike earlier times when the rule was the submission of cases to international adjudication by special agreement. This may amount to the strengthening of the rule of law at the international level, since it gives States possibilities that not so long ago were hardly conceived of: the possibility of bringing a dispute before a judge or arbitrator and settling long-term disputes peacefully.[16]

Cases brought to the Court (or to ITLOS) by unilateral application can, in turn, be sub-divided in two. On the one hand are cases in which the respondent did not consent to litigation and therefore challenged the Court's jurisdiction by entering preliminary objections. Four cases fit this situation:[17] *Aegean Sea Continental Shelf* (*Greece* v. *Turkey*); *Maritime Delimitation and Territorial Questions* (*Qatar* v. *Bahrain*); *Land and Maritime Boundary* (*Cameroon* v. *Nigeria*); and *Territorial and Maritime Dispute* (*Nicaragua* v. *Colombia*).

The other subcategory is that of cases in which the Court (or ITLOS), while seized by means of a unilateral application, did not have to settle an issue of jurisdiction or admissibility. In that sense, in the *Maritime Delimitation on the Area between Greenland and Jan Mayen* (*Denmark* v. *Norway*), Norway did not contest the jurisdiction of the Court; in the *Maritime Delimitation between*

Guinea-Bissau and Senegal, the proceedings were discontinued following the agreement concluded between the Parties on 14 October 1993; in the *Territorial and Maritime Dispute Between Nicaragua and Honduras in the Caribbean Sea* (*Nicaragua* v. *Honduras*), Honduras contested neither the jurisdiction of the Court nor the admissibility of the claim; in the *Maritime Delimitation in the Black Sea* (*Romania* v. *Ukraine*), Ukraine did not challenge the jurisdiction of the Court; in the *Maritime Dispute* (*Peru* v. *Chile*), Chile decided not to object ICJ's jurisdiction; in *Costa Rica* v. *Nicaragua*, the latter did not object the Court's jurisdiction either; and in *the Maritime Delimitation in the Indian Ocean* (*Somalia* v. *Kenya*), the Court found its jurisdiction on the declarations made by the two countries, pursuant to Article 36, paragraph 3 of the Statute.

The dispute settlement system available for maritime delimitation disputes, like all inter-State dispute settlement mechanisms, is founded upon Article 2, paragraph 3 of the Charter of the United Nations, whereby all States are bound to a primary obligation to settle disputes through peaceful means. If the Parties to a given maritime delimitation dispute are also Parties[18] to UNCLOS, Part XV of the said Convention applies.

In that case, Article 279 of the Convention, in accordance with the United Nations Charter, underscores the importance of settling disputes by peaceful means, while Article 283, paragraph 1 of UNCLOS requires that in the case of a dispute arising between States Parties with respect to its interpretation or application, the Parties to the dispute shall proceed to an exchange of views regarding its settlement by negotiation or other peaceful means. Failing negotiations, there are other methods of dispute resolution that involve the participation of a third Party and that can be either non-binding or binding. The former, if resorted to, may be good offices, mediation and conciliation.[19] The latter include compulsory procedures under Section 2 of Part XV, the choice of which is governed by Article 287.[20]

This provision (Article 287)[21] allows a State party, by means of a written declaration, to choose one or more of the means of dispute settlement listed therein: the ITLOS, the ICJ, an Arbitral Tribunal constituted under Annex VII of the Convention[22] or a special arbitral tribunal according to Annex VIII of UNCLOS.[23] If a State party opted not to make any declaration, it is deemed, by operation of Article 287(3), to have accepted arbitration in accordance with Annex VII.

In this context, the number of cases settled by the ICJ, Arbitral Tribunals, and the ITLOS, has increased. Such cases unavoidably create tension between geography, history, politics and law, which, in the absence of an agreement, shall be resolved by reaching an equitable solution.[24] As rightly pointed out by former ICJ President Rosalyn Higgins when referring to disputes about the use of the ocean or the delimitation of maritime zones: "[T]hey can create bitter political relations or be perceived as threatening ways of life that have existed for centuries", adding that "Sometimes a judicial institution can, in providing an impartial pronouncement on the underlying claims, defuse these high tensions".[25]

The 2021 *Somalia* v. *Kenya* judgment rendered by the ICJ was its 16th maritime delimitation decision and, without counting the *Grisbadarna* arbitration,[26] the 31st judicial decision in general concerning maritime delimitation. The full list includes ICJ cases, ITLOS cases, ad hoc tribunals (including two domestic disputes), Annex VII tribunals and a conciliation commission, under Annex V of UNCLOS. It was delivered after the second maritime delimitation decision rendered by the International Tribunal for the Law of the Sea on 23 September 2017 in the *Dispute concerning delimitation of the maritime boundary between Ghana and Côte d'Ivoire in the Atlantic Ocean* (*Ghana/Côte d'Ivoire*) and the 2018 ICJ ruling on *Costa Rica* v. *Nicaragua*. With the creation of a standing special chamber to deal with maritime delimitation disputes in 2007,[27] and given the number of States having chosen ITLOS in accordance with Article 287,[28] it seems possible to state that ITLOS' jurisdiction to adjudicate maritime boundary disputes poses no risk of fragmentation.

In fact, in both its 2012 *Bangladesh/Myanmar* and its 2017 *Ghana/Côte d'Ivoire* judgments, the Law of the Sea Tribunal confirmed, to a great extent, the established jurisprudence (i.e. mostly ICJ-made jurisprudence) concerning the law of maritime delimitation. In so doing, it demonstrated that the risk of fragmentation of international law, due in part to several courts and tribunals adjudicating upon the same body of law, ended up being unfounded. Far from undermining the unity of international law, "decisions by different courts and tribunals on the same law may be a source of richness and not of contradiction", stated Judge Treves in his Declaration.[29]

The Emergence of the Three-Stage Methodology

When States undertake the task of settling a maritime delimitation dispute, be it by negotiation or by third-party adjudication, they have to look at international law, and more particularly, at the law of the sea, in order to identify the rules that are applicable and relevant.

First, as a general rule, maritime delimitation has to be effected by agreement in accordance with international law; in other words, no delimitation can be established unilaterally. Second, the need for delimitation entails that States are under an obligation to enter into negotiations so as to reach an agreement.[30] Third, maritime delimitation must not lead to encroachment by one party on the other.[31] Finally, maritime delimitation must lead to an equitable solution.[32]

Before dealing specifically with the way in which the three-stage methodology concerning maritime boundary delimitation has emerged, it is useful to touch upon an essential element in the law of maritime delimitation, namely, its normative density.

As has been stated before, Article 74, paragraph 1 and Article 83, paragraph 1 of UNCLOS establish a formula that is difficult to implement. In fact, the vagueness of the equitable solution is explained by the efforts put forward during UNCLOS III so as to accommodate two prevailing and antagonist views, namely, equidistance vis-à-vis equitable principles. In that scenario, it has been case law (i.e. the interpretation of said rules carried out by judges and arbitrators over the course of decades) that has allowed the evolution of the law of maritime delimitation.[33] Hence, departing from the traditional "method" of creation of international custom (i.e. the assessment of State practice and the consideration of the *opinio juris*), in this field of international law the rule has been to declare through international adjudication what was to be considered a customary rule. This is the reason why it is possible to qualify the law of maritime delimitation as "judge-made" law or praetorian law,[34] which according to some has even led to a kind of "praetorian subjectivism".[35] However, it has been also claimed that thanks to that case law "the elements of subjectivity and uncertainty in the determination of maritime boundaries and in the choice of methods employed to that end" have been reduced.[36]

The so-called *longue marche du droit de la délimitation maritime*, as described by Prosper Weil,[37] goes back to the conclusions reached by the International Court of Justice in the first maritime delimitation case with which it dealt.

In the *North Sea Continental Shelf* cases, which have been commented upon above, the Court concluded that there was no mandatory method, and that coastal configuration could render an equidistance line inequitable. In that sense, it held that "delimitation must be the object of agreement between the States concerned, and that such agreement must be arrived at in accordance with equitable principles."[38]

This was confirmed in the 1982 *Tunisia/Libya* judgment, where the Court stated that the application of the equitable principles must be equitable, adding that it is "the result which is predominant; the principles are subordinate to the goal".[39]

In that context, the 1985 *Libya/Malta* judgment put forward the idea of separate stages,[40] which was confirmed by the 1993 *Jan Mayen* judgment and other subsequent cases.[41] More recently, in the 2017 *Ghana* v. *Côte d'Ivoire* ruling, the *Costa Rica* v. *Nicaragua* 2018 judgment and the 2021 *Somalia* v. *Kenya* judgment, the Law of the Sea Tribunal and the ICJ, in turn, referred to the established methodology in three stages.[42]

It then follows that in order for the Court to establish that the chosen method is equitable,[43] it has applied the test of proportionality,[44] so as to verify ex post the equitableness of its envisaged decision.[45] In this respect, it is also worth recalling one paragraph of the *Barbados/Trinidad and Tobago* arbitral award:

> [t]he real role of proportionality is one in which the presence of different lengths of coastlines needs to be taken into account so as to prevent an end result that might be "disproportionate" and hence inequitable. In this context, proportionality becomes the last stage of the test of the equity of a delimitation. It serves to check the line of delimitation that might have been arrived at in consideration of various other factors, so as to ensure that the end result is equitable and thus in accordance with the applicable law under UNCLOS.[46]

To sum up, it can be stated that the general rule is that delimitation must be achieved through agreement between the Parties concerned, in accordance with international law. In its absence, and once recourse to third-party settlement has been agreed or established, equitable principles shall prevail.[47] This is to be done by application of the equidistance method unless such method results in an inequitable situation,[48] that is to say, if there are special/relevant circumstances.[49] In that case the provisional equidistance line would have to be shifted or adjusted,[50] or another method would have to be employed.

Having reviewed the most relevant cases of maritime delimitation where the court or tribunal proceeded by stages, it can be said that although in some cases, such as *Jan Mayen*, *Qatar* v. *Bahrain* and *Barbados/Trinidad and Tobago*, the court or tribunal preferred to proceed in two stages, the prevailing jurisprudence points to a common understanding that the process is rather divided in three stages. In fact, the above-described case law suggests that the Court, the ITLOS, and arbitral tribunals have actually consolidated this three-stage methodology, labelled – not without some controversy[51] – as the "standard method" (equidistance/relevant circumstances),[52] the "established jurisprudence", "the established methodology" and even a real "*acquis judiciaire*".

In light of the foregoing, it is possible to claim that, unlike the late 1960s, the current state of the law of maritime delimitation provides for a set of rules and case law that has come to be called a "three-stage methodology". In fact, the ICJ, the ITLOS and several arbitral tribunals have played a decisive role in clarifying those rules through an increasingly important number of judgments and arbitral awards.

Notes

1 It is well known that in the middle of the twentieth century, State jurisdiction would seldom extend more than three nautical miles offshore, see: Prescott, Victor and Clive Schofield (2005), *The Maritime Political Boundaries of the World*, Leiden: Martinus Nijhoff, p. 215.

2 This goes hand in hand with the development of technology to recover hydrocarbons and other non-living resources of the seabed and subsoil; see: Charney, J. (1993), "Introduction", in: Charney, J. and L. Alexander (eds.), *International Maritime Boundaries*, Vol. I, Dordrecht: Martinus Nijhoff, p. xxiii. In fact, now living resources include marine genetic resources; see, for instance: Vidas, Davor (ed.) (2010), *Law, Technology and Science for Oceans in Globalisation*, Leiden: Martinus Nijhoff; and Hamon, G., Arico, S. and C. Monagle, C. (2009), "Marine Genetic Resources: A Review of Scientific and Commercial Interest", *Marine Policy*, Vol. 33, pp. 183–194.

3 Lucchini, Laurent (2006), "La délimitation des frontières maritimes dans la jurisprudence internationale: vue d'ensemble", in: Lagoni, Rainer and Daniel Vignes (eds.), *Maritime Delimitation*, Leiden: Martinus Nijhoff, p. 2.

4 See generally: Remiro Brotóns, Antonio (1993), *ibid.*, p. 124.

5 They indeed made efforts to reach an agreement in the 1970s, see *infra* section on "Unresolved maritime boundaries".

6 Remiro Brotóns, Antonio (1993), *ibid.*, p. 124.

7 International Maritime Boundaries, by International Mapping. See also: Prescott and Schofield (2018), as well as Østhagen, Andreas, Lines at Sea: *Why do States resolve their Maritime Boundary Disputes*, PhD dissertation submitted at the University of British Columbia (2010). In Africa only, of around 90 potential maritime boundaries, only 29 have been duly established; see: Wood, Marissa, *ibid.*

8 For appraisals on maritime boundary negotiations, see *inter alia*: Anderson, David (2008), *ibid.*, pp. 417–435; Feldman, Mark B. and David Colson (1981), "The Maritime Boundaries of the United States", *AJIL*, Vol. 75, pp. 729–763; Guillaume, Gilbert

(1983), "Les accords de délimitation maritime passés par la France", *Colloque de Rouen: Perspectives du droit de la mer à l'issue de la 3e conférence des nations unies*, Paris: Pedone, pp. 276 *et seq*.

9 *North Sea Continental Shelf, Judgment, I.C.J. Reports 1969*, p. 3.

10 *Continental Shelf* (*Libyan Arab Jamahiriya/Malta*), *Judgment, I.C.J. Reports 1985*, p. 13.

11 *Continental Shelf* (*Tunisia/Libyan Arab Jamahiriya*), *Judgment, I.C.J. Reports 1982*, p. 18. See generally: Scovazzi, Tullio, (2004/2005), *ibid*., pp. 429–438.

12 "Declaración del Presidente Juan Manuel Santos sobre la estrategia integral de Colombia sobre el Fallo de la Corte Internacional de Justicia", contained in Nicaragua's Application (to the ICJ) of 26 November 2013.

13 Johnston, D. M. (1988), *The Theory and History of Ocean Boundary*-Making, Kingston: McGill Queen's University Press, p. 213. Following an analysis of State practice in maritime delimitation, one of the leading studies claimed in 1993 that "no normative principle of international law ha[d] developed that would mandate the specific location of any maritime boundary line"; see: Charney, Jonathan I. (1993), "Introduction", in: Charney, Jonathan I. and Lewis M. Alexander (eds.), *ibid*., p. xlii.

14 For instance, in the *Guyana/Suriname* Arbitration, Guyana claimed it instituted proceedings because of Suriname's "repeated refusal" to a maritime boundary agreement; see: Memorial of the Republic of Guyana, Vol. I, 22 February 2005, para. 1.4. In the *Maritime Dispute* (*Peru* v. *Chile*), currently pending before the ICJ, Peru stated it made several attempts to negotiate but it was never accepted by Chile; see: PM, paras. 16–20. More recently (although this is not properly a case of maritime delimitation), in its Notification and Statement of Claim, the Philippines held that exchange of views with China dated back "at least to 1995", yet that after more than 17 years "no settlements have been reached" on any of the disputed matters; see: Notification and Statement of Claim of the Republic of the Philippines, 22 January 2013, paras. 25–26.

15 Note that in the *Dispute concerning delimitation of the maritime boundary between Bangladesh and Myanmar in the Bay of Bengal* (*Bangladesh/Myanmar*), the Government of the People's Republic of Bangladesh first instituted proceedings against the Union of Myanmar (and the Republic of India, for that matter), on 8 October 2009, pursuant to Annex VII of the United Nations Convention on the Law of the Sea. However, following Myanmar's proposal to Bangladesh that the matter be submitted to the International Tribunal for the Law of the Sea and the two countries' Declarations accepting ITLOS' jurisdiction, dated 4 November and 12 December 2009, respectively, this case is finally considered to have been submitted to ITLOS by special agreement. See also: *Dispute concerning Delimitation of the Maritime Boundary between Mauritius and Maldives in the Indian Ocean* (*Mauritius/Maldives*), which was brought before ITLOS by Special Agreement dated 24 September 2019.

16 Horna, Angel V. (2013), "Procedural Aspects Concerning Jurisdiction and Admissibility in Cases of Maritime Delimitation Before the ICJ", in: Boschiero, N. et al. (eds), *International Courts and the Development of International Law. Essays in Honour of Tullio Treves*, The Hague: Asser, p. 178.

17 Note that the author is aware about other (law of the sea) cases before standing international courts or tribunals in which such issues were discussed upon. However, they were not maritime delimitation cases. At ITLOS for instance, one could refer to: *M/V "SAIGA"* (*No. 2*) (*Saint Vincent and the Grenadines* v. *Guinea*), *Judgment, ITLOS Reports 1999*, pp. 30–48, where the jurisdiction of the Tribunal was briefly discussed upon followed by a lengthier discussion on the admissibility of the claims put forward by the Applicant. For an appraisal of the first case of the ITLOS, see, e.g., De la Fayette, L. (2000), "The M/V 'Saiga' (No. 2) Case (St. Vincent and the Grenadines v. Guinea), Judgment", *ICLQ*, Vol. 49, pp. 467–476.

18 Even though a Party to a maritime delimitation case would normally be a State, the term "Party" or "State Party" should not be confined to States only, because it also

includes international organisations which are parties to the Convention, pursuant to Article 1, paragraph 2(2) of the Convention. In that sense, see for instance *Case concerning the Conservation and Sustainable Exploitation of Swordfish Stocks in the South-Eastern Pacific Ocean* (*Chile/European Union*)*, ITLOS Reports*.

19 Article 284 and Annex V of UNCLOS consider conciliation as a means of dispute settlement. In this regard, it is important to highlight the Timor Sea Conciliation: *PCA Case No. 2016–10 In the Matter of the Maritime Boundary Between Timor-Leste and Australia before A Conciliation Commission constituted under Annex V to the 1982 United Nations Convention on the Law of the Sea between the Democratic Republic of Timor-Leste and the Commonwealth of Australia, 9 May 2018*.

20 See, in this regard, *Maritime Delimitation in the Indian Ocean* (*Somalia v. Kenya*)*, Preliminary Objections, Judgment, I.C.J. Reports 2017*, p. 3, para. 125 *et seq*.

21 This is contained in Section II: Compulsory Procedures Entailing Binding Decisions of Part XV of UNCLOS, and is also referred to as the Montreux formula because it was in that Swiss city, near Geneva, that the respective agreement was concluded. See: Nordquist, M.; Rosenne, S. and L. Sohn (1989), *United Nations Convention on the Law of the Sea 1982. A Commentary*, vol. V, Dordrecht: Martinus Nijhoff, p. 8; and Rosenne, S. (1986), "UNCLOS III – The Montreux (Riphagen) Compromise", in: Bos, A. and H. Siblesz (eds.), *Realism in Law-Making: Essays on International Law in Honour of Willem Riphagen*, Dordrecht: Martinus Nijhoff, p. 169. For an up-to date list of the official texts of declarations and statements, which contain the choice of procedure under Article 287 of the Law of the Sea Convention and optional exceptions to applicability of Part XV, Section 2, under Article 298 of the Convention, see DOALOS' website and for instance: Song, Yann-huei (2013), "Survey of Declarations or Statements Made by the Parties to the Law of the Sea Convention: 30 Years after Adoption", *IJMCL*, Vol. 28, pp. 5–59.

22 A dispute may be submitted to Annex VII arbitration, in accordance with Part XV of UNCLOS, when parties are unable to settle it by negotiation, conciliation or other peaceful means. Indeed, pursuant to Article 287 there is a choice of compulsory dispute settlement procedures, namely, ITLOS, ICJ, Annex VII arbitral tribunal, or Annex VIII special arbitral tribunal for specific categories of disputes. For those States that did not make a written declaration selecting their choice of procedure, Annex VII arbitration is the default option.

23 As for the special arbitral tribunal constituted under Annex VIII of UNCLOS, they are only applicable to disputes covering fisheries, protection and preservation of the marine environment, marine scientific research or navigation, including pollution from vessels and dumping.

24 The expression "tension between geography and law" has been borrowed from Nuno Antunes. However, the terms "history" and "politics" have been added because, in this author's opinion, they also play a great role within the present topic, see: Antunes, Nuno (2003), *ibid*., p. 109. Also see in this regard: Weil, Prosper (1989), *The Law of Maritime Delimitation – Reflections*, Cambridge: Cambridge Grotius, p. 281.

25 Statement of Judge Rosalyn Higgins, President of the International Court of Justice, on the occasion of the tenth anniversary of the International Tribunal for the Law of the Sea, available online at the ICJ's website.

26 *Decision of the Permanent Court of Arbitration in the Matter of the Maritime Boundary Dispute between Norway and Sweden, AJIL*, Vol. 4, 1910, pp. 226–236. See also *RIAA*, Vol. 11, p. 147. In this case, the Arbitral Tribunal delimited the territorial sea purportedly applying the law of the seventeenth century (drawing a line perpendicular to the general direction of the coast). This is why it is not included in the full list of judicial decisions.

27 ITLOS Press Release 108, 16 March 2007, available online at ITLOS' website. See also the section on "Competence of the Tribunal in maritime delimitation cases", in: *Yearbook of the International Tribunal for the Law of the Sea*, Vol. 10, Leiden: Martinus Nijhoff, 2006, pp. 51–52.

28 As of 2022, 54 States have made declarations in accordance with Article 287 of UNCLOS; see: "Declarations of States Parties relating to settlement of disputes in accordance with Article 287 (choice of procedure)", available online at ITLOS' website (consulted on 22 March 2022).

29 *Delimitation of the Maritime Boundary in the Bay of Bengal* (*Bangladesh/Myanmar*), *ITLOS Reports 2012, Declaration of Judge Treves*, pp. 1–2.

30 Whilst there is an obligation to negotiate, there is no obligation to actually reach an agreement; see *Railway Traffic between Lithuania and Poland, Advisory Opinion, 1931, P.C.I.J., Series A/B, No. 40*, p. 116; and *I.C.J. Reports 1969*, p. 3, para. 85. More recently, see *Obligation to Negotiate Access to the Pacific Ocean* (*Bolivia* v. *Chile*), *Judgment, I.C.J. Reports 2018*, p. 507.

31 *Continental Shelf* (*Libyan Arab Jamahiriya/Malta*), *Judgment, I.C.J. Reports 1985*, p. 30, para. 46.

32 Articles 74, paragraph 1, and 83, paragraph 1, of UNCLOS establish that delimitation must lead to an "equitable solution". See also: *Territorial and Maritime Dispute* (*Nicaragua v. Colombia*), *I.C.J. Reports 2012*, paras. 190–193; *Maritime Delimitation in the Black Sea* (*Romania v. Ukraine*), *Judgment, I.C.J. Reports 2009*, pp. 101–103, paras. 120–122; and p. 129, para. 211.

33 See for instance: Churchill, Robin and Vaughan Lowe (1999), *The Law of the Sea*, Manchester: Manchester University Press, p. 181; Evans, Malcolm (2015), "Maritime Boundary Delimitation", in: Rothwell, Donald, Elferink, Alex, Scott, Karen, and Tim Stephens (eds), *The Oxford Handbook of the Law of the Sea*, Oxford: Oxford University Press, pp. 254–279.

34 Prosper Weil refers to the normative power of the international judge and to the so-called *droit prétorien*; see: Weil, Prosper (1988), *Perspectives du droit de la délimitation maritime*, Paris: Pedone, p. 168.

35 *Continental Shelf* (*Libyan Arab Jamahiriya/Malta*), *Judgment, I.C.J. Reports 1985, Separate Opinion of Judges Ruda, Bedjaoui and Jiménez de Aréchaga.*

36 *Delimitation of the Maritime Boundary in the Bay of Bengal* (*Bangladesh/Myanmar*), *ITLOS Reports 2012*, para. 226.

37 *I.C.J. Pleadings, Maritime Delimitation and Territorial Questions between Qatar and Bahrain, Merits*. Bahrain's second round of oral arguments (Counsel: Prosper Weil), 29 June 2000 (CR 2000/25), p. 25, para. 21.

38 *North Sea Continental Shelf, Judgment, I.C.J. Reports 1969*, para. 85. See also: Evans, Malcom (2006), "Maritime Boundary Delimitation: Where Do We Go From Here?", in: Freestone et al. (eds). *The Law of the Sea: Progress and Prospects*, Oxford: Oxford University Press, p. 138.

39 *Continental Shelf* (*Tunisia/Libyan Arab Jamahiriya*), *Judgment, I.C.J. Reports 1982*, para. 70.

40 "In applying the equitable principles thus elicited, within the limits defined above, and in the light of the relevant circumstances, the Court intends to proceed *by stages*; thus, it will first make a provisional delimitation by using a criterion and a method both of which are clearly destined to play an important role in producing the final result; it will then examine this provisional solution in the light of the requirements derived from other criteria, which may call for a correction of this initial result", *Continental Shelf* (*Tunisia/Libyan Arab Jamahiriya*), *Judgment, I.C.J. Reports 1982*, para. 60.

41 *Maritime Delimitation in the Area between Greenland and Jan Mayen, Judgment, I.C.J. Reports 1993*, p. 38, para. 51; *Maritime Delimitation and Territorial Questions between Qatar and Bahrain, Merits, Judgment, I.C.J. Reports 2001*, para. 230; *Barbados/Trinidad and Tobago, Award of 11 April 2006, RIAA*, Vol. 27, para. 242. Note that this approach was followed in the Guyana/Suriname Arbitration; see: *Guyana/Suriname Arbitration, Award of 17 September 2007 ILM*, Vol. 47, para. 342; *Maritime Delimitation in the Black Sea* (*Romania* v. *Ukraine*), *Judgment, I.C.J. Reports 2009*, para. 155. See also: *Delimitation of the Maritime Boundary in the Bay of Bengal*

(*Bangladesh/Myanmar*), *ITLOS Reports 2012*, paras. 233 and 275; *Maritime Delimitation in the Black Sea* (*Romania* v. *Ukraine*), *Judgment, I.C.J. Reports 2009*, para. 190; *Territorial and Maritime Dispute* (*Nicaragua* v. *Colombia*), para. 191; *Maritime Dispute* (*Peru* v. *Chile*), *Judgment of 27 January 2014*, para. 180.

42 *ITLOS Reports 2017*, paras. 372 *et seq*.; *Costa Rica* v. *Nicaragua*, paras. 135 *et seq*., and 168 and 176, for both the Pacific Ocean and the Caribbean Sea; and *Maritime Delimitation in the Indian Ocean* (*Somalia* v. *Kenya*), *Judgment, I.C.J. Reports 2021*, para. 131.

43 Jennings, Robert (1986), "Equity and Equitable Principles," *Annuaire suisse de droit international*, Vol. 42, pp. 27–38.

44 Tanaka (2001), *ibid*., pp. 433–463.

45 *North Sea Continental Shelf, Judgment, I.C.J. Reports 1969*, para. 101; *Continental Shelf* (*Tunisia/Libyan Arab Jamahiriya*), *Judgment, I.C.J. Reports 1982*, p. 43, para. 37; *Case Concerning the Delimitation of the Continental Shelf between the United Kingdom of Great Britain and Northern Ireland, and the French Republic*, *RIAA*, Vol. 18, p. 57, para. 99; and the *Continental Shelf* (*Libyan Arab Jamahiriya/Malta*), *Judgment, I.C.J. Reports 1985*, pp. 48–49, para. 66.

46 *Barbados/Trinidad and Tobago, Award of 11 April 2006, RIAA*, Vol. 27, para. 240.

47 In *Tunisia/Libya*, the ICJ highlighted the importance of equity in international law: "Equity as a legal concept is a direct emanation of the idea of justice. The Court whose task is by definition to administer justice is bound to apply it. In the course of the history of legal systems the term "equity" has been used to define various legal concepts . . .; the legal concept of equity is a general principle directly applicable as law," *Continental Shelf* (*Tunisia/Libyan Arab Jamahiriya*), *Judgment, I.C.J. Reports 1982*, p. 60, para. 71.

48 For a distinction between this and Judge Sorensen's interpretation of *justitia distributive*, *North Sea Continental Shelf, Judgment, I.C.J. Reports 1969*, p. 255; see also: Hossain, K. (1980), "Equitable Solutions in the International Law of the Sea: Some Problems", in: Hossain, K. (ed.), *Legal Aspects of the New International Economic Order*, London: Frances Pinter, p. 205.

49 One may recall here the reasoning of the International Court of Justice in the *North Sea* cases, when, departing from a mechanical application of the method of the equidistance which would have reduced the continental shelf of the Federal Republic of Germany, it applied the concept of proportionality, see: *I.C.J. Reports 1969*, p. 50, para. 91.

50 In the *Cameroon* v. *Nigeria* case, the ICJ held that the general rule regarding the delimitation of the continental shelf (and for that matter of the EEZ), in the absence of agreement, consisted in drawing an equidistance line (provisionally), the adjustment of which could be effected in case of special circumstances in order to achieve an equitable result; see *Land and Maritime Boundary Dispute between Cameroon and Nigeria* (*Cameroon* v. *Nigeria: Equatorial Guinea intervening*), *Judgment, I.C.J. Reports 2002*, p. 303, para. 288.

51 See the critical appraisal made by Judge Abraham concerning the *Nicaragua* v. *Colombia* 2012 Judgment; see: *Separate Opinion of Judge Abraham, I.C.J. Reports 2012*, paras. 21–34.

52 *Territorial and Maritime Dispute* (*Nicaragua* v. *Colombia*), *Judgment, I.C.J. Reports 2012*, para. 199.

6 Trends in Maritime Boundary Delimitation

There are certain trends in maritime boundary-making, relating mainly to adjudication, although they may also apply to the negotiation of maritime boundaries[1] and beyond.

First, there is a consistent approach: the three-stage methodology. As an initial step, courts and tribunals draw a provisional equidistance line, followed by a consideration of whether it produces an equitable solution unless relevant circumstances call for the adjustment of the provisional equidistance line. Adjustments, as applicable, are made at the end, in case of a significant disproportion.

Second, there is the establishment of single maritime boundaries, also called "all-purpose boundaries", which are lines for all maritime zones and hence regulate several activities including fisheries, pollution controls, oil and gas operations, and overflight.[2] In this sense, the ICJ has stated that "the concept of a single maritime boundary does not stem from multilateral treaty law but from State practice".[3]

Third, there is the unification of customary and conventional law. This reflects the unity of the law based on different sources, which has allowed States that are not Parties to UNCLOS to still invoke the application of the law of maritime delimitation contained therein, on the basis of its customary nature.[4]

Fourth, there is the harmonisation of different zones, which implies a certain assimilation of the legal principles and rules relating to maritime delimitation of the territorial sea, the EEZ and the continental shelf. However, in some cases differences between regimes applicable in several zones are still valid and necessary, like in the case between Belgium and the Netherlands. In it, two different treaties were concluded with different methods of delimitation.[5]

Fifth, there is the growing interest in the continental shelf beyond 200 nautical miles, or the outer limit of the "extended continental shelf".[6] If after the case of *Libya/Malta* the geological importance of the continental shelf was neglected on the basis of the legal continental shelf concept, beyond 200 nautical miles geophysical and geomorphologic dimensions have retained their utmost relevance to determine the possible entitlement of a specific coastal State to an extended shelf. This has to be done in accordance with Article 76 of UNCLOS and the Rules of Procedure of the Commission on the Limits of the Continental Shelf.

However, that is to be clearly distinguished from continental shelf delimitation under Article 83 of UNCLOS.[7] Reference can be made, in this respect, to the

DOI: 10.4324/9781003290452-8

precisions made in recent cases concerning delimitation of the continental shelf under UNCLOS Article 83 and the delineation of its outer limits under UNCLOS Article 76.[8] The bottom line is that the issuance of recommendations by the United Nations Commission on the Limits of the Continental Shelf (CLCS) is not a prerequisite for maritime delimitation of the extended continental shelf or even for a court or tribunal to entertain an Application.[9]

Related to the foregoing is the issue whether continental shelf claims beyond 200 nautical miles trump continental shelf claims within 200 nautical miles. In that regard, it should be recalled that there is only one continental shelf, irrespective of its length. This was clearly articulated by the Annex VII Arbitral Tribunal that settled the maritime boundary dispute between Barbados and Trinidad and Tobago. It pointed out, in that regard, that "in any event, there is in law only a single 'continental shelf' rather than an inner continental shelf and a separate extended or outer continental shelf".[10]

On the other hand, the making of interim or provisional arrangements of a practical nature seems to be a further trend. This has been enabled by Article 74, paragraph 3 and Article 83, paragraph 3 of the Law of the Sea Convention. Such arrangements have proven successful and include the joint development of mineral resources (e.g. 1993 Colombia/Jamaica); special areas for fisheries (e.g. 2001 Honduras/UK (Cayman Islands); provisional arrangements (e.g. 1977 Cuba/US, 2002 Algeria/Tunisia);[11] bilateral cooperation as (e.g. 2003 EEZ Cooperation Treaty Barbados/Guyana); and coordinated patrols in non-delimited waters.[12]

Whether the successful recourse to conciliation proceedings under UNCLOS to settle the maritime dispute between Australia and Timor-Leste becomes a trend remains to be seen. However, it signals an important avenue to explore for outstanding maritime delimitation disputes.

Similarly, in recent decades there has been increasing concern over the effects of climate change on the oceans. In this regard, the current work of the International Law Commission relating to Sea Level Rise (in particular, aspects pertaining to the law of the sea) will certainly have an influence on the future of maritime boundary delimitation.[13]

Although not a novel issue, the recourse to technical experts and highly specialised legal skills is another growing trend. Hydrographers and cartographers specialising in geodesics and computing[14] are also vital in negotiations concerning maritime boundaries and in litigation. What is more, it seems that different methods of maritime delimitation may require different technical considerations.[15] This is why, ideally, when negotiating maritime boundaries, in addition to putting up a negotiating team, such teams should also be equipped with negotiation strategy and tactics, as well as treaty-drafting skills.

Finally, I should also refer, within the framework of energy projects,[16] to the importance of the industry in the field of maritime delimitation. There are vast supplies of oil and natural gas with the potential to boost economic growth and the much-needed post-pandemic recovery. Indeed, according to the International Energy Agency, there could be "around 270 billion barrels of recoverable oil alone in deep water worldwide".[17]

Indeed, with a long history of energy projects relating to deep-water technologies (i.e. what lies beneath the world's oceans, including in Latin America and the Caribbean) some international companies, like Shell, have been exploring and extracting oil and gas from beneath deep waters for decades. They are hence attracted to the region – for instance to the US (Gulf of Mexico) and Brazil – in search for their resources, in this case, oil and natural gas.[18]

Notes

1 Anderson, David (2008), *ibid.*, pp. 403–416.
2 Concerning oil and gas, it is noteworthy to mention recent maritime boundary developments in the Eastern Mediterranean, where access to oil and gas is at stake, such as the maritime delimitation treaty between Egypt and Greece, signed on 6 August 2020. In this regard, bear in mind, however, that Turkey has rejected that agreement, suggesting that it is "null and void".
3 *Maritime Delimitation and Territorial Questions between Qatar and Bahrain, Merits, Judgment, I.C.J. Reports 2001*, para. 173.
4 Some examples include: *Nicaragua* v. *Colombia*, in connection to the outer continental shelf; see: *Territorial and Maritime Dispute (Nicaragua* v. *Colombia), Judgment, I.C.J. Reports 2012*, para. 137; and *Maritime Dispute (Peru v. Chile), Judgment of the I.C.J. of 27 January 2014*.
5 Anderson, David (2008), *ibid.*, p. 409. See: Treaty between the Kingdom of the Netherlands and the Kingdom of Belgium on the Delimitation of the Territorial Sea (Signature: 18 December 1996; entry into force: 1 January 1999). Text of the treaty available at DOALOS' website. This agreement was based on the principle of equidistance; see also: Treaty between the Kingdom of the Netherlands and the Kingdom of Belgium on the Delimitation of the Continental Shelf (Signature: 18 December 1996; entry into force: 1 January 1999). Text of the treaty available at DOALOS' website. It should be noted that the same approach was also employed in the agreements signed between Belgium and France in 1990.
6 See generally: Nelson, Dolliver (2002), "The Continental Shelf: Interplay of Law and Science", in: Ando, N. et al. (eds.), *Liber Amicorum Judge Shigeru Oda*, The Hague: Kluwer Law International, pp. 1235–1253; and Ocean Policy Research Foundation (Ship and Ocean Foundation) (2007), *The Establishment of the Outer Limits of the Continental Shelf beyond 200 Nautical Miles – Its international circumstances, and its scientific and technical aspects*, Tokyo, 223 pp. See also: Cook, Peter and Chris Carleton (2000), *Continental Shelf Limits: The Scientific and Legal Interface*, Oxford: Oxford University Press, 363 pp.
7 In March 2012, while reaffirming this difference, the International Tribunal for the Law of the Sea became the first standing court to establish a maritime boundary beyond 200 nautical miles (*Delimitation of the Maritime Boundary in the Bay of Bengal (Bangladesh/Myanmar), ITLOS Reports 2012*, paras. 394 *et seq.*). In the 2012 *Nicaragua* v. *Colombia* judgment, however, the Court was not in a position to delimit the continental shelf boundary between the Parties, as requested by Nicaragua, because it [Nicaragua] had not established that it possessed a continental margin extending far enough to overlap with Colombia's 200-nautical-mile entitlement to the continental shelf (*Territorial and Maritime Dispute (Nicaragua* v. *Colombia), Judgment, I.C.J. Reports 2012*, paras. 129–131). Later, on 16 September 2013, Nicaragua filed a new Application before the ICJ instituting proceedings against Colombia, whereby it requested the Court to adjudge and declare "the precise course of the maritime boundary between Nicaragua and Colombia in the areas of the continental shelf which appertain to each of them beyond the boundaries determined by the Court in its judgment of 19 November 2012".

Nicaragua claimed that, having submitted its final information to the Commission on the Limits of the Continental Shelf of 24 June 2013, it was possible to demonstrate that its continental margin extended more than 200 nautical miles from the baselines from which the breadth of the territorial sea of Nicaragua had been measured (*Question of the Delimitation of the Continental Shelf between Nicaragua and Colombia beyond 200 nautical miles from the Nicaraguan Coast* (*Nicaragua* v. *Colombia*), available at the ICJ's website).

8 See: *Dispute concerning delimitation of the maritime boundary between Bangladesh and Myanmar in the Bay of Bengal* (*Bangladesh/Myanmar*), *Judgment, ITLOS Reports 2012*, para. 376. More recently, it is known that Bangladesh has provided to the United Nations CLCS scientific and technical data in support of its entitlement to continental shelf beyond 200 nautical miles, but taking into account the boundaries with Myanmar and India.

9 See, in this regard, *Question of the Delimitation of the Continental Shelf between Nicaragua and Colombia beyond 200 nautical miles from the Nicaraguan Coast* (*Nicaragua v. Colombia*), para. 114.

10 *Barbados/Trinidad and Tobago, Award of 11 April 2006, RIAA*, Vol. 27, para. 213.

11 In the case of the provisional arrangement between Algeria and Tunisia, it was superseded by the 2011 Convention Regarding Delimitation of the Maritime Boundaries between the People's Democratic Republic of Algeria and the Tunisian Republic; see: Lathrop, Coalter (2020), *International Maritime Boundaries*, Vol 8, Brill, pp. 1–20. For an account of the obligation not to jeopardise or hamper the reaching of a final agreement, under Article 83, para. 3, of UNCLOS, see: Separate Opinion of Judge Paik, in the *Dispute concerning delimitation of the maritime boundary between Ghana and Côte d'Ivoire in the Atlantic Ocean* (*Ghana/Côte d'Ivoire*).

12 Coordinated patrols between Malaysia and Indonesia; see: Report of the UN Secretary-General on Oceans and Law of the Sea 2004 (UN Doc. A/59/62, para. 27).

13 UN Doc. A/76/10, and UN Doc. A/73/10, pp. 326–334. See also, *inter alia*, Hioureas, Christina and Alejandra Torres Camprubí (2020), "Legal and Political Considerations on the Disappearance of States due to Sea Level Rise", in: Heidar, Tomas (Ed.), *New Knowledge and Changing Circumstances in the Law of the Sea*, Brill–Nijhoff, pp. 407–426.

14 See generally: IHB (2006), *A Manual on Technical Aspects of the United Nations Convention on the Law of the Sea – 1982. Prepared by the IHO, IAG, IOC Advisory Board on Law of the Sea* (*ABLOS*), Special Publication No. 51, 4th Edition, Monaco; Antunes, Nuno (2003), *ibid.*; and *International Boundaries Research Unit Maritime Briefings*, Vol. 3.

15 Antunes, Nuno (2005), "Some Thoughts on the Technical Input in Maritime Delimitation", in: Colson, D.A. and R.W. Smith (eds.), *International Maritime Boundaries*, Vol. V, p. 3382.

16 Note that oil and gas are never explicitly mentioned in UNCLOS; see Treves, Tullio, "The International Tribunal for the Law of the Sea and the Oil and Gas Industry", in: Second International Oil and Gas Conference, London, 20–21 September 2007.

17 See, for instance: www.shell.com/energy-and-innovation/deep-water.html (recovered on 22 March 2022).

18 This refers to the US (Gulf of Mexico) and Brazil. See also: "Deepwater set to dominate exploration in 2022", available in www.oedigital.com/subsea/deepwater (recovered on 22 March 2022).

Part II

Impact of State Practice and Case Law

The practice of States[1] is one of the necessary elements for the formation of a rule of customary international law.[2] Irrespective of whether one takes a restrictive or broad definition,[3] State practice is any act or statement made by a State from which its views about customary law can be inferred.[4] It includes physical acts and claims,[5] declarations,[6] national legislation, national judgments, omissions and treaties.[7] The weight attributed to treaties as authority for customary law depends on the scope to be given to the definition of State practice and, more importantly, on the fact that, even if regarded as general practice, in order to give rise to customary law, that practice will still need to be accepted as law (*opinion juris*).[8]

For present purposes two kinds of State practice will be taken into account: treaties (maritime delimitation agreements, with the potential of generating customary international law)[9] and unilateral claims (acts of States, such as the Truman Proclamations and a number of Latin American claims[10] that declared certain rights and jurisdiction over the resources of the sea and its subsoil). That said, despite the importance of maritime boundary negotiation, it could be claimed that in the field of maritime delimitation law, State practice has not received enough attention from legal scholarship,[11] hence the relevance of this subject matter.

Almost 80 years of State practice in the form of maritime delimitation agreements in Latin America and the Caribbean are now to be dealt with. It is not envisaged, however, to analyse every aspect of that practice, as this would go well beyond the scope of this book. Rather, the aim is to identify key developments during those years; the most relevant actors, including their "approaches" to maritime delimitation and a brief description of the delimitation treaties they concluded; and finally to identify potential patterns.

In the time frame spanning 1942–2021, a number of key developments can be pointed out. The first agreement ever signed on continental shelf delimitation was concluded in 1942 between the UK and Venezuela. Unilateral claims were then advanced by some Latin American States in 1947 following the 1945 relevant Truman Proclamation. Those Latin American unilateral claims then translated into the tripartite 1952 Declaration of Santiago.

Similarly, Latin American and Caribbean States took part in the Geneva Conferences on the Law of the Sea (1958 and 1960), and years later, Latin American and Caribbean States convened several regional law of the sea conferences so as

DOI: 10.4324/9781003290452-9

to build more leverage within the international community regarding the need for change in the field. Shortly after, they participated in UNCLOS III, which against all odds enshrined a 200-nautical-mile exclusive economic zone and the concept of common heritage of mankind.

Particular attention is merited by the multilateral framework set by the Caribbean coastal States at Mexico's initiative, known as the "Conference on Maritime Delimitation in the Caribbean".[12] It was created in 2002 with the mandate of facilitating, mainly through technical assistance, the voluntary undertaking of maritime delimitation negotiation between Caribbean coastal States. The first plenary session took place in Mexico City in May 2002, while the first meeting held outside Mexico was the 2006 fourth plenary session, in Santo Domingo. It may be claimed that the Conference on Maritime Delimitation in the Caribbean constitutes an interesting feature of Mexico's approach to the law of maritime delimitation.[13] Even though it is not necessarily the best solution for multi-oceanic States (such as France or the US), it seems to be an optimal alternative for States bordering a regional sea. In this regard, it establishes a model that could be followed in other regions.

In addition to the foregoing, 43 bilateral agreements on maritime delimitation were concluded and a number of maritime boundary disputes adjudicated by international judicial and arbitral bodies. Similarly, some provisional arrangements were established and there are multiple ongoing negotiations on maritime boundaries.

In light of the above, it is plain that States progressed from a situation of almost complete absence of clear rules available to the negotiators who divided the Gulf of Paria in 1942, to a well-established body of law dealing with maritime delimitation that, by 2021, could boast the existence of a "standard method" to delimit the exclusive economic zone and the continental shelf.[14]

Specific approaches to maritime delimitation appear to be typical of certain areas of the world.[15] The following pages will deal with key actors and the way in which they have approached the issue of maritime delimitation in Latin America and the Caribbean.

The US

With the largest number of maritime boundaries, established or to be established,[16] the US has several maritime delimitation agreements and "maritime boundary situations" in Latin America and the Caribbean.[17] A brief account of them will follow, so as to be able to discern the US approach to maritime boundary delimitation.

The US and Mexico have so far concluded three maritime delimitation agreements[18] and a provisional arrangement,[19] concerning their overlapping entitlements in the Gulf of Mexico and the Pacific Ocean. In all their treaties they employed a simplified equidistance line. Similarly, in the Straits of Florida, connecting the Gulf of Mexico and the Atlantic Ocean, every two years since 1977 the US and Cuba have renewed a provisional arrangement concerning their maritime delimitation.

With respect to Puerto Rico and the US Virgin Islands, the US has concluded an agreement with Venezuela in the Caribbean Sea,[20] applying a modified equidistance; and two agreements with the UK in the Atlantic Ocean,[21] employing, this time, a simplified equidistance.

However, for the 1970 Rio Grande and Colorado River Agreement with Mexico, all of the maritime boundary agreements concluded by the US followed the 200-nautical-mile fishery conservation zone established in 1976.

Regarding the preparatory phase, before the beginning of each negotiation the US of course had to determine its maritime boundary position. This needed to take into account the political, security and economic interests of all US agencies concerned, a task that was coordinated by the Department of State.

Hence, all these agreements reflect a similar format, with a technical part and a legal part. The technical part consists of indicating geographic coordinates and the geodetical datum (computational basis for determining those coordinates).[22] The legal part sets out the legal effect of the boundary (hereinafter referred to as "LEB clause") and contains a "law of the sea disclaimer" (hereinafter referred to as "LOS disclaimer").[23]

As for the LEB clause, it stipulates that the boundary is an all-purpose maritime boundary or general maritime boundary, in the sense that it includes all maritime spaces without the need to make an explicit reference to them.[24] Its language indicates:

> They shall permanently represent the maritime boundaries between the two Contracting States; on the north side of these boundaries Mexico shall not, and on the south side of them the United States shall not, for any purpose claim or exercise sovereignty, sovereign rights or jurisdiction over the waters, air space, or seabed and subsoil.[25]

As for the LOS disclaimer, it appears to be aimed at avoiding any prejudice on the position of the contracting Parties, mainly that of the US, in relation to the development of the law of the sea. One instance is the need to avoid any kind of acceptance of the existence of a privileged method of maritime delimitation, considering the US position whereby maritime boundaries are to be established by agreement in accordance with equitable principles. In other words, they are based on the Parties' mutual interest and apply any method that expresses that interest in every given situation.[26]

Colombia

The geography of Colombia, like that of Venezuela, allows for a significant maritime projection into the Caribbean Sea. Because of that position it has negotiated and concluded no less than eight maritime delimitation agreements, although one has not been ratified and at least one has been left without object by the ICJ's judgment on the *Nicaragua* v. *Colombia* case.[27]

Colombia first delimited its maritime boundary with Ecuador in 1975, with Panama in 1976 and with the Dominican Republic and Haiti in 1978. It then concluded two maritime delimitation treaties with Costa Rica, one (which has not been ratified) in 1977 concerning their overlapping zones in the Caribbean Sea, and the other in 1984 regarding maritime zones in the Pacific Ocean. Similarly, it signed another treaty with Honduras in 1986 and with Jamaica in 1993. Concerning its maritime delimitation with Nicaragua, it was decided upon by the ICJ in 2012, as will be seen later in this book. On the other hand, Colombia has yet to delimit its maritime spaces with Venezuela in Lake Maracaibo.

Venezuela

Without Venezuela's economic interest in the underwater resources of Lake Maracaibo, Latin America would probably have had to wait several more years before constituting the object of an agreement delimiting marine areas. It is therefore due to having concluded the famous 1942 Gulf of Paria Treaty with the UK, and to its prominent geographical position in the north of South America – with a dominant projection towards the Caribbean Sea, a feature shared with neighbouring Colombia – that Venezuela is considered one of the States whose practice has contributed a great deal to the conclusion of other similar agreements in the region, and hence to the development of the law of the sea.[28]

As mentioned earlier, Venezuela concluded the 1942 agreement with the UK, concerning present-day Trinidad and Tobago. Then, between 1978 and 1980, it managed to persuade three other metropolitan powers to agree to a rather controversial triad of maritime boundary agreements: the US (Puerto Rico and the US Virgin Islands), the Netherlands (Saba and Sint Eustatius), and France (Martinique and Guadeloupe), which gave either full or almost full weight to Aves Island, a miniscule rock. It concluded the 1979 maritime delimitation agreement with the Dominican Republic using a modified equidistance line, and the 1990 treaty with Trinidad and Tobago (then already independent) a boundary formed by simplified and modified equidistance lines. These agreements were important developments in the practice of maritime delimitation and have had quite an impact, especially in the complex situation of the Caribbean Sea, not to mention the ongoing dispute between Venezuela and Guyana, as well as the pending issues that still oppose Venezuela to Colombia.

Argentina

Following Mexico's 1945 proclamation, Argentina made a similar claim in 1946 concerning its "epicontinental" sea. It has concluded two maritime delimitation agreements – the only two possible, in fact – with Uruguay in 1973, with a modified equidistance line, and the other with Chile in 1984, which is the case of the concurrent use of different methods in the form of a "composite line". Yet, despite its limited number of bilateral maritime delimitation treaties, Argentina's contribution to practice in the region remains important. On the one side, the 1973 Río de la Plata Treaty not only established a boundary at the mouth of the river but also seaward following a modified equidistance. At the same time, it defined a starting point of the seaward boundary from the midpoint of the straight baseline that closes the estuary of the Río de la Plata that has come to be regarded as an important precedent of historic waters.

On the other hand, the 1984 Treaty with Chile, negotiated under the auspices of the Holy See's mediation after Argentina's initial rejection of the Beagle Channel Award, established a maritime boundary starting from the terminus of the delimitation effected in that Award, and from there along a line drawn by employing a combination of methods including loxodromes, meridians and a geographical parallel.[29]

France

France is a world maritime power that, despite possessing a territorial area a little over half a million square kilometres, possesses the second largest exclusive economic zone in the world, only exceeded by that of the US. It has concluded eight maritime delimitation agreements in the region and is yet to agree on two maritime boundaries: with Antigua and Barbuda and with Saint Kitts and Nevis.

By the time it started conducting maritime boundary negotiations concerning its possessions in Latin America and the Caribbean, France had already settled, through arbitration, an important delimitation dispute with the UK relating to the English Channel.[30] Perhaps that was even the reason why France went on to negotiate maritime delimitation agreements concerning its numerous possessions around the world.

Be it as it may, its first maritime delimitation agreement in the region was concluded in 1980 with Venezuela (Aves Island) concerning its overseas departments of Martinique and Guadeloupe. A single line (the 62nd meridian) was used to effect a double-sector delimitation.

It then proceeded to conclude two more agreements in the region, first with Brazil concerning French Guyana, with a line running along the perpendicular to the general direction of the coast; and then with Saint Lucia regarding Martinique, using a simplified equidistance line. In a second wave of delimitation treaties, France concluded agreements with Dominica in 1987, a composite delimitation that ended up with a "railway track–shaped" maritime boundary; with the UK in 1996, where the boundaries had segments of simplified and modified equidistance; with Barbados in 2009, one of the few cases of strict equidistance; and with Suriname and with Antigua and Barbuda, both in 2017.

All of the maritime delimitation treaties concluded by France, in the region, between 1980 and 1981 (with Venezuela, Brazil and Saint Lucia) – unlike any one by the US, which include the so-called LOS disclaimer – stated in their preamble that they would proceed to delineate its maritime spaces "taking into consideration" the work being carried out by the Third United Nations Conference on the

Law of the Sea. Evidently, that language was not used after the adoption of UNCLOS in 1982. Whereas in the 1987 treaty with Dominica reference was made to "the rules and principles of relevant international law as they are expressed in the United Nations Convention on the Law of the Sea", in the 1996 treaties with the UK, still non-Party to UNCLOS, no mention at all was made to the Montego Bay Convention.

Except for the agreement concerning French Guyana, in which France seemed to have been particularly concerned with Brazil's 200-nautical-mile claimed territorial sea, in both the treaty with Venezuela and with Saint Lucia a clause was introduced stating, with slightly different wordings, that the limit being defined shall be the maritime boundary between the zones over which the Parties "exercise or will exercise", in accordance with international law, sovereign rights or jurisdiction. The wording "exercise or will exercise" was resorted to because those States had not yet created an economic or fisheries zone,[31] in order to avoid the need to sign another treaty at an ulterior time. By the same token, in the case of the 1987 agreement with Dominica, since that island-State had already established its economic zone, the clause referred to the maritime boundary between the areas in which the parties "exercise, in accordance with international law, their sovereignty or sovereign rights".

In the 1996 treaties with the UK there appears to be a different approach. Together with the absence of any express reference to the 1982 Law of the Sea Convention, no dispute settlement procedure was established, and the contracting States decided to add an article establishing "open-ended" boundaries (tripoints).[32]

Since France, like the US, still has some outstanding maritime boundaries not only in the region[33] but also in Europe and in the Pacific,[34] it would seem important for it to ensure that every negotiation is coherent with the positions that it defends elsewhere. However, it appears that part of France's approach to maritime delimitation is to not discuss such issues in a multilateral framework, for example that provided by the Caribbean Conference on Maritime Delimitation, for those issues constitute a sensitive aspect of sovereignty, not to mention the economic interests at stake.

The UK

Once the foremost global power known as the British Empire, the UK has still a number of overseas possessions in the Caribbean. It is with respect to one of those territories that, already in 1942, the UK inaugurated the maritime boundary delimitation practice beyond the territorial sea, the Gulf of Paria Treaty. At a time when the law of maritime delimitation was yet to be developed, the Parties came up with a boundary now considered a composite delimitation.[35]

Only 50 years later would the UK take part again in maritime delimitation agreements concerning the region. It returned to the scene in 1993, with the two agreements concluded with the US that were already commented upon (relating to Puerto Rico and the Virgin Islands). It then went on to negotiate and close similar deals with France in 1996, another with the Dominican Republic later that year,[36] with Honduras in 2001, and recently with Antigua and Barbuda (27 July 2021). Whereas with the Dominican Republic the method employed was the coastal length comparison, with Honduras the Parties chose a composite delimitation. Also, in its delimitation with Antigua and Barbuda, the line of delimitation is based on equidistance, which is considered an equitable solution.

Although regarding a different region, it is worth noting that following both, the 2019 Advisory Opinion of the ICJ on the *Legal Consequences of the Separation of the Chagos Archipelago from Mauritius in 1965*,[37] and the 2021 Judgment of ITLOS in the case *Mauritius* v. *Maldives*,[38] there is a difference of views regarding whether the UK is a member of the Indian Ocean Tuna Commission (IOTC) as a coastal State or under a different legal basis.

In summary, it can be said that because of the number of maritime boundary situations that they face, the US and France have exercised considerable influence in the negotiation of maritime delimitation agreements in the region. It can be added, especially in relation with the Caribbean Sea, that the presence of those world maritime powers (including the UK), together with the Netherlands, has had a particular impact on maritime delimitation negotiations. This has been and is the case because those maritime powers, often much more experienced in boundary-making than their counterparts, are also able to offer trade-offs unrelated to the law of maritime delimitation ("legal policies").[39] As regards Latin American and Caribbean States, Venezuela and Colombia have been the leaders in the Caribbean Sea because of their dominant projection over that semi-enclosed sea, one on the Eastern Caribbean and the other on the Western half, and the number of maritime boundary situations that they face. Similarly, claims made by South American coastal States on the Pacific – in particular, Chile and Peru – pioneered the 200-nautical-mile zone and therefore brought about the extension of maritime zones that, as has been seen, is at the origins of the sharp increase in maritime delimitation agreements. Another observation is that States do not make use of only one but rather several methods of maritime delimitation, depending on the circumstances of coastal configuration and on geography in general.

Notes

1 As it is known, State Practice plays a significant role in the formation of every field of law, and is particularly important in public international law and usually related to the question of the "sources of international law"; see, e.g., Boisson de Chazournes, Laurence (2004), "Qu'est-ce que la pratique en droit international?", in: SFDI, *Colloque de Genève – La pratique et le droit international*, Paris: Pedone, pp. 13–14; and also: Kohen, Marcelo (2004), "La pratique et la théorie des sources du droit international", in: SFDI, *Colloque de Genève – La pratique et le droit international, ibis.*, p. 111.

2 Draft conclusions on identification of customary international law (document A/73/10); see also United Nations General Assembly resolution 73/203 of 20 December 2018.

3 Note the different views on the kinds of acts considered State practice put forward by Anthony D'Amato (restrictive definition) and Michael Akehurst (broader definition). See: D'Amato, Anthony (1971), *The Concept of Custom in International Law*, p. 88 and Akehurst, Michael (1977), "Custom as a Source of International Law", *BYIL*, Vol. 47, pp. 1–3.

4 Akehurst (1977), *ibid.*, p. 53; Shaw, Malcom (2008), *International Law*, 6th ed., Cambridge: Cambridge University Press, p. 84.
5 This was discussed in *Dissenting Opinion of J. E. Read, Anglo-Norwegian Fisheries* case, *I.C.J. Reports 1951*, pp. 75–81.
6 This could also take the form of pleadings before international courts; see: Akehurst (1977), *ibid.*, p. 2.
7 About a restrictive view whereby claims were not to be given the status of State practice, Akehurst said: "One of the ways in which a treaty can help to create customary law is by asserting claims against non-parties; it is inconsistent to regard such a treaty as evidence of customary law while denying that status to claims made unilaterally by one State against another", Akehurst (1977), *ibid.*, p. 3.
8 In the *North Sea* cases, the Court dismissed an argument by Denmark and the Netherlands that various bilateral treaties for the delimitation of the continental shelf were to be regarded as evidence that the rule set in Article 6 of the CS Convention had become a rule of customary law. The Court held that the treaties showed nothing of the sort because they were not accompanied by *opinio juris*; see: *North Sea Continental Shelf cases*, *I.C.J. Reports 1969*, para. 85. More recent instances of third-party adjudication confirm that State practice, at least in maritime boundary delimitation, is not such an important source of guide, as opposed to case law; see: *Maritime Delimitation in the Black Sea* (*Romania* v. *Ukraine*), *Judgment, I.C.J. Reports 2009*, para. 174; and *Guyana/Suriname Arbitration, Award of 17 September 2007 ILM*, Vol. 47, para. 334.
9 For instance: "La pratique des Etats qui se forma entre 1942 [Gulf of Paria Treaty] et 1958 fut cependant suffisante pour justifier l'inclusion de règles concernant ces droits dans une des Conventions de Genève"; Treves, Tullio (1990), "Codification du droit international et pratique des états dans le droit de la mer", *Recueil des Cours de l'Académie de droit international de La Haye*, Vol. 223, p. 35. Furthermore, maritime delimitation treaties, according to their object, could be classified as "traités-contrats", as opposed to "traités-lois"; see: De Visscher, Charles (1955), "Coutume et traité en droit international public", *RGDIP*, Vol. 20, p. 360.
10 The ICJ called them "State proclamations"; see: *North Sea Continental Shelf cases*, *I.C.J. Reports 1969*, para. 47.
11 An author stated that this was due to the "paucity of information"; see: Tanaka (2006), *ibid.*, p. 130.
12 See: OAS Resolution AG/RES. 1902 (XXXII-O/02, Cooperation in the prevention and settlement of maritime boundary disputes among member States in the Caribbean Region, Adopted at the fourth plenary session, 4 June 2002.
13 The first maritime delimitation agreement resulting out of this conference was the Honduras/Mexico 2005 agreement.
14 *Territorial and Maritime Dispute* (*Nicaragua* v. *Colombia*), *Judgment, I.C.J. Reports 2012*, para. 199; or more recently, *Somalia* v. *Kenya, Judgment, I.C.J. Reports 2021*, paras. 128–131.
15 In this respect one could think of the "pragmatism, flexibility and compromise" that appears to be part of the Southeast Asian approach to maritime delimitation; see: Davenport, Tara (2012), "Southeast Asian approaches to maritime delimitation", *Asian ASIL Working Paper*, 2012/7, p. 41; see also: Janis, Mark W. (1975), "The Roles of Regional Law of the Sea", *San Diego Law Review*, Vol. 12, pp. 553–568. Similarly, it seems possible to state that Caribbean coastal States, with the multilateral framework they created in 2002, also have a particular approach. That is the case of the Caribbean Conference on Maritime Delimitation, *supra*. About a "regional approach" in the implementation of the Convention, see also the recommendations of the United Nations Open-ended Informal Consultative Process established by the General Assembly in its resolution 54/33 in order to facilitate review by the Assembly of development in ocean affairs (see A/57/80, paras. 42–47, especially para. 45).

16 See: Feldman and Colson (1981), *ibid.*, pp. 729–730. For a complete list of US maritime boundaries, see: Roach and Smith (2012), *ibid.*, pp. 900–902. Unresolved US maritime boundaries include: US/Bahamas, US/UK (Bermuda), US/Cuba – Eastern Gap, US/Mexico – Eastern Gap, US (Puerto Rico)/Dominican Republic, US (Virgin Islands)/The Netherlands (Saba), US/The Netherlands/Venezuela – Tripoint, US/Dominican Republic/Venezuela – Tripoint, US/Bahamas/Cuba – Tripoint, US/Mexico/Cuba – Tripoint, US (Navassa)/Cuba, US (Navassa)/Haiti (Navassa), US (Navassa)/Jamaica.

17 See: Feldman and Colson (1981), *ibid.*, p. 734.

18 US/Mexico, 1970, see *supra*; US/Mexico, 1978, see *supra*; and US/Mexico, 2000, see *supra*. Only in the 2000 agreement did the Parties include a dispute settlement provision (see Article 8). Note that there is an unsolved maritime boundary between the US and Mexico in the Eastern Gap of the Gulf of Mexico where the continental shelves of those two countries, beyond 200 nautical miles, overlap; see: Roach and Smith (2012), *ibid.*, p. 902.

19 US/Mexico, 1976 (Exchange of Notes and Agreement).

20 US/Venezuela, 1978. This is a controversial agreement because it awarded full weight to Aves Island. It seems to be the first maritime delimitation agreement concluded by the US in Latin America and the Caribbean where the Parties included a dispute settlement provision (Article 5). But there are no dispute settlement provisions in the US/UK 1993 agreements.

21 US (Puerto Rico and US Virgin Islands)/UK (British Virgin Islands), 1993; and US (US Virgin Islands)/UK (Anguilla), 1993.

22 Normally the North American Datum 1983 ("NAD 83"), except in the 1970 agreement. Before 1983, it was the 1927 North American Datum, Clarke 1866 ellipsoid; see also: Annex: Table of Maritime Delimitation Agreements concluded in Latin America and the Caribbean.

23 Feldman and Colson (1981), *ibid.*, p. 742. Note that the wording of the LEB clause is very similar to that used in the 1942 Gulf of Paria treaty.

24 In this sense see: "the boundary established is a general maritime boundary, designed to serve for continental shelf, fisheries, and any other purpose recognised by international law"; Feldman and Colson (1981), *ibid.*, p. 742. A French author described them as "lignes uniques nord-américaines"; see: Beer-Gabel, Josette, "Variations sur la notion de frontière maritime", in: INDEMER (1992), *Droit de la mer. Etudes dédiées au Doyen Claude-Albert Colliard*, Paris: Pedone, p. 18.

25 Article V.C, 1970 US/Mexico treaty.

26 Feldman and Colson (1981), *ibid.*, pp. 742–743. For additional information relating to LEB clauses and LOS disclaimers, consider that: in the 1970 US/Mexico agreement, the LEB clause can be found in Article III.C, and the LOS disclaimer Article III.D. It should be noted that this is the only treaty where the LEB clause includes a reference to air space. In the 1978 US/Mexico agreement, the LEB clause is in Article II, and the LOS disclaimer in Article III, second paragraph. In the 1977 US/Cuba modus vivendi, the LEB clause is in Article III, and the LOS disclaimer in Article IV. While in the1978 US/Venezuela treaty the LEB clause and the LOS disclaimer are merged in Article 4, in the 1993 US/UK treaties, the LEB clause is found in "Articles" 3 and the LOS disclaimer in "Articles" 4. Finally, in the 2000 US/Mexico treaty dealing with the outer continental shelf, the LEB clause is in Article 3, and the LOS disclaimer in Article 7. Of course this more modern treaty includes a number of other issues concerning "transboundary reservoirs".

27 *Declaration of Judge ad hoc Cot, I.C.J. Reports 2012*, paras. 10 *et seq.*; and *Declaration of Judge Xue, I.C.J. Reports 2012*, para. 15; and *supra* note 554. Reference should also be made to Colombia's delimitation strategy in the Western Caribbean, as established in September 2013, see: "Declaración del Presidente Juan Manuel Santos sobre

la estrategia integral de Colombia sobre el Fallo de la Corte Internacional de Justicia", contained in Nicaragua's Application (to the ICJ) of 26 November 2013. See also to Decree 1436, of 13 June 1984 establishing "outrageous baselines", in: Remiro Brotóns (1993), *ibid.*, p. 120.

28 See for instance: Morales Paul, Isidro (1974), "Venezuela: the Country in the Caribbean", in: Zacklin, Ralph (ed.), *ibid.*, pp. 125–131.

29 *Dispute between Argentina and Chile concerning the Beagle Channel. 18 February 1977, RIAA*, Vol. 21, pp. 53–264. See also, the Glossary.

30 *Delimitation of the Continental Shelf between the United Kingdom of Great Britain and Northern Ireland, and the French Republic, RIAA*, Vol. 28, pp. 3–413. In this arbitration, the position of the UK was based upon Article 6 of the 1958 CCS (i.e. equidistance), whereas France claimed that that convention was obsolete because of the evolution of customary international law and that equitable principles should prevail. The Tribunal handed down its Award and held that both Article 6 of the CCS and customary international law had the same object, that is to say, the delimitation of the maritime boundary with equitable principles. This, of course, was more in line with France's interests and with all the equitable principles of the informal group at UNCLOS III; see in this regard: Anderson, David (2006), *ibid.*, pp. 444–445. In connection to that, former ICJ President Guillaume wrote: "[i]l n'existe pas, semble-t-il, un dilemme équidistance/équité, mais un objectif, la recherche d'une solution équitable, qui doit être atteint en faisant application de la règle juridique selon laquelle l'équidistance doit être corrigée en fonction des circonstances spéciales"; and then he added: "L'un des grands mérites de la sentence arbitrale franco-britannique de 1977 à cet égard est d'avoir mis fin à ce qui était pris à tort pour une dualité des règles . . . là où il y a en fait unité", see: Guillaume, Gilbert (1983), *ibid.*, p. 280.

31 Guillaume, Gilbert (1983), *ibid.*, p. 279.

32 For an account of tripoints, see: Lathrop, Coalter (2005), "Tripoint Issues in Maritime Boundary Delimitation", in: Colson, David A. and Robert W. Smith (eds.), *ibid.*, pp. 3305–3375.

33 With Antigua and Barbuda; Saint Kitts and Nevis; the Netherlands (Sint Maarten) and Suriname.

34 Unresolved French maritime boundaries in regions other than Latin America and the Caribbean include: with the UK both in the English Channel and concerning the Channel Islands; with Italy – since the only existent delimitation is that of the territorial sea in the Mouths of Bonifacio, between Corsica and Sardinia – there are several open questions of delimitation, including the Tuscan Archipelago; with Spain: negotiations are pending both in the Mediterranean and in the Bay of Biscay; with Vanuatu, concerning New Caledonia; and with Madagascar, in relation to all maritime spaces west of that country since it does not recognise France's sovereignty over the so-called Scattered Islands (*les îles Éparses*) lying in the Mozambique Channel.

35 UK (Trinidad and Tobago)/Venezuela, 1942.

36 UK (Turks and Caicos Islands)/Dominican Republic, 1996.

37 *Legal Consequences of the Separation of the Chagos Archipelago from Mauritius in 1965, Advisory Opinion, I.C.J. Reports 2019.*

38 *Dispute concerning Delimitation of the Maritime Boundary between Mauritius and Maldives in the Indian Ocean (Mauritius/Maldives), Preliminary Objections, Judgment, ITLOS Reports 2021.*

39 Yet it should be added that the possibility to offer "trade-offs" is not restricted to asymmetric negotiations. In that regard, it seems that in negotiations between France and Italy concerning Corsica, France could be offering Italy trade-offs non-related to maritime delimitation. About "political considerations" in maritime delimitation agreements, see: *Barbados/Trinidad and Tobago, Award of 11 April 2006, RIAA*, Vol. 27, para. 346.

7 Maritime Boundaries in Latin America and the Caribbean

This chapter analyses State practice in the form of maritime delimitation agreements concerning Latin America and the Caribbean and concluded between 1942 and 2021. In each case, it also covers a brief account of its rationale and a description of the maritime boundary established.[1]

Before entering into the subject matter, I will briefly discuss some of the patterns identified while examining the practice of States in Latin America and the Caribbean. To that aim, I have divided the time frame sub-analysis into three periods: the pre-codification age (1942–1958), the Geneva Conventions age (1958–1982) and the UNCLOS age (1982–present).

As for the pre-codification period (1942–1958), only the 1942 Gulf of Paria Treaty was concluded. This seems to be explained by the advent of the 1958 Geneva Conference on the Law of the Sea, establishing the first conventional framework for maritime delimitation, as well as by events that took place in the late 1940s and early 1950s involving Chile, Peru and later Ecuador.

Regarding the period corresponding to the Geneva Conventions (1958–1982), when 17 treaties were concluded, it is important to highlight the landmark judgment of the ICJ on the *North Sea Continental Shelf* cases,[2] which was the first time that the 1958 CCS was interpreted and led to a certain degree of confusion, due to the reference to equitable principles as opposed to the equidistance method enshrined in Article 6 of the 1958 Convention.

Against that background, in 1970 Mexico and the US concluded a double frontage delimitation agreement (Gulf of Mexico and the Pacific Ocean) and made recourse to a simplified equidistance line. The other two agreements appear to have been brought about, partly, by Uruguay's willingness not to have the method of the geographical parallel applied to it. Uruguay hence concluded a treaty with Brazil in 1972, establishing a perpendicular to the general direction of the coast as their maritime boundary, and another treaty with Argentina in 1973 that made use of an equidistance line, drawn from the midpoint of the baseline closing the mouth of Río de la Plata.

Later, in the framework of the Third United Nations Conference on the Law of the Sea, a parallel process took place. This process, led mainly (but not exclusively) by sub-regional leaders including Colombia and Venezuela and an extra regional power such as France, was (I claim) directly related to the dynamics of

DOI: 10.4324/9781003290452-10

the conference (Negotiating Group No. 7)[3] and to the development of case law, especially in the case of France.[4] This is what I would call "the Golden Age" in maritime boundary-making in the region, when 16 maritime delimitation agreements were concluded between 1973 and 1982, without counting the 1973 Argentina/Uruguay agreement. That number includes the 1977 Colombia/Costa Rica treaty, which was signed but not ratified, and the 1977 Cuba/US modus vivendi, which is renewed every two years.

Thus, during UNCLOS III Colombia entered into negotiations with a number of neighbouring countries and concluded no fewer than five maritime delimitation agreements with Ecuador, Panama, Costa Rica (albeit non-ratified), the Dominican Republic and Haiti. It seems this was also done so as to counter any claims made by Nicaragua to disputed islands in the Western Caribbean. As for the methods used by Colombia, they range from simplified (Dominican Republic) to modified equidistance (Haiti), and from the geographical parallel (Ecuador) to a combination of methods in a pragmatic way (Panama), which has been referred to in this book as "composite delimitation".

Venezuela, in turn, considering Colombia's approach in the area, concluded four maritime delimitation agreements that related to that country's island territory. While three of them (with the US, the Netherlands and France) were aimed at giving full weight to Aves Island (which it achieved in two out of three), the other one, with the Dominican Republic, which was made after that country had signed a similar agreement with Colombia, dealt with Los Monjes Archipelago. Concerning the methods of maritime delimitation employed by Venezuela, it made use of a modified equidistance in two cases (US and Dominican Republic), a combination of methods in one case (the Netherlands) and a meridian in the other (France).

Last but not least, France took the lead among metropolitan States and concluded three maritime delimitation agreements, one already mentioned with Venezuela, another with Brazil regarding French Guyana, and another with Saint Lucia concerning Martinique. Whereas with Brazil the Parties agreed to a modified equidistance, with Saint Lucia a simplified equidistance was established.

As for the rest, the 1976 Cuba/Mexico agreement utilised a combination of simplified and modified equidistance, as was the case in the 1977 Cuba/Haiti agreement, whereas the 1977 Cuba/US modus vivendi established a simplified equidistance. Similarly, while the 1978 Mexico/US treaty delimited those two States' maritime areas in accordance with a simplified equidistance, the 1980 Costa Rica/Panama agreement established a line perpendicular to the general direction of the coast.

After the adoption of the Law of the Sea Convention (e.g. the UNCLOS period, 1982–present), Latin American and Caribbean States concluded 23 delimitation agreements and one provisional arrangement (although one of them, the 1985 Costa Rica/Ecuador, has yet to be ratified).[5]

Again, Colombia was one of the States quite keen to delimit its maritime boundaries, and took the lead by concluding in that period its agreements with Costa Rica in 1984, with Ecuador in 1985, with Honduras in 1986 and with Jamaica in

1993. It made use of equidistance with Costa Rica, of simplified equidistance with Ecuador and Jamaica, and of parallels and meridians with Honduras.

Particular attention should be given to the 1984 Argentina/Chile maritime boundary delimitation. It came about after a long negotiation that included a mediation by the Holy See and that eventually allowed the Parties to draw a line from the *terminus* of the maritime boundary that had been established in the 1977 Beagle Channel Award,[6] an arbitral decision initially rejected by Argentina. Regarding the methods, they were a combination of loxodromic lines, meridians and a parallel (composite delimitation).

In 1987, Dominica and France, in respect of Guadeloupe and Marie-Galante and Martinique, concluded a maritime delimitation agreement the preamble of which claimed it was based "on the rules and principles of international law as they are expressed" in UNCLOS. This agreement has been labelled as a case study in the region due to the complexity of the geographical situation. Indeed, the island of Dominica lies in between two French dependencies, which has resulted in a maritime boundary with a "railway-track shape". This is why, concerning the methods used, this agreement seems to constitute a pragmatic solution.

Venezuela and Trinidad and Tobago decided in 1990 to subsume their previous agreements, the 1942 Gulf of Paria and another one signed in 1989, into one overarching treaty that delimited the maritime areas that had not previously been delimited with segments of simplified and modified equidistance. The UK, in turn, concluded two treaties with the US on the same day, so as to delimit their maritime spaces in the Atlantic Ocean with a simplified equidistance. Understandably, the Anglo-American treaties took due care not to make any reference to the already-adopted Montego Bay Convention.

Cuba and Jamaica, in turn, signed their maritime delimitation agreement in February 1994. The agreement, like the 1987 Dominica/France one, took into account the relevant provisions of the 1982 Law of the Sea Convention and seems to be one of the rare maritime delimitation agreements that established a strict equidistance as the method.

Apart from the 2000 Mexico/US treaty whereby those two countries, to further their maritime relations, delimited their outer continental shelf with a simplified equidistance line, in the period under analysis the UK seems to have taken a more active role in delimiting the maritime areas of its overseas territories in the Caribbean. It hence concluded four delimitation agreements and fostered an agreement between its own dependencies (Anguilla and the UK Virgin Islands).[7] Two delimitation agreements were established with France in 1996, one between Guadeloupe and Montserrat, and another between Saint Martin and Saint Barthélemy, and Anguilla. Both treaties applied a simplified equidistance method. Also in 1996, the UK concluded a treaty with the Dominican Republic concerning the Turks and Caicos Islands, the delimitation of which was said to have been effected in accordance with the "disparity of coasts" method. Some years later, in 2001, the UK also reached an agreement with Honduras regarding the Cayman Islands. This treaty established a combination of methods, including simplified equidistance and modified/adjusted, as well as a parallel of latitude, that is to say a composite delimitation or simply pragmatic line.

Besides the 2001 treaty with the UK, Honduras concluded two more maritime delimitation agreements, one with Mexico in 2005 that consisted of a simplified equidistance line, and one with Cuba in 2012, which also established a simplified equidistance line. There was also, of course, the 2007 *Nicaragua* v. *Honduras* ICJ judgment that effected an adjusted maritime delimitation in the Caribbean Sea between those two countries using the bisector method.

Other agreements in recent decades are the 2003 Barbados/Guyana provisional arrangement; the 2009 Barbados/France maritime delimitation in respect of Guadeloupe and Martinique, which gave full effect to French Désirade Island and seems to have established another rare strict equidistance line; the 2010 Grenada/Trinidad and Tobago treaty that established only two points with coordinates; the 2011 Ecuador/Peru agreement; and the Bahamas/Cuba agreement that came along after 15 years of negotiations and which appears to be another case of strict equidistance.

More recently, Costa Rica and Ecuador signed their deal in 2014 and France reached agreement with the Netherlands in 2016, relating to Saint Martin/Sint Maarten, and with Suriname and Antigua and Barbuda in 2017.

Having made this preliminary account of State practice in Latin America and the Caribbean concerning maritime boundary delimitation, along three different periods, it follows that between 1942 and 1958 no patterns can be identified since only one treaty was concluded and there was no clear law applicable to the delimitation of maritime boundaries. As for the second period, between 1958 and 1982, not only did States already have few sources of international law available when aiming at delimiting their maritime boundaries, but most of them made use of a kind of equidistance method, and if a pattern is to be found, it is probably the number of claims made by Latin American and Caribbean coastal States that would pave the way for future changes on the law of the sea.

In addition to that, between 1973 and 1982 there was a rush for maritime boundaries, which made it the most prolific decade in terms of the number of maritime delimitation treaties concluded in the region. Hence, during those nine years alone, 17 maritime delimitation agreements were concluded, mainly in the Caribbean Sea. To a certain extent, I argue, those agreements aimed at validating in advance a law of the sea institution that had not yet seen the light, that is to say, the exclusive economic zone. The maritime boundary rush phase was also conspicuous because of Venezuela's (eventually unsuccessful) initiative to have Aves recognised as not being a rock (which is also an island), under international law.[8]

From 1982 onwards, maritime delimitation agreements that include cooperation activities such as navigation safety, search and rescue, hydrographic surveys, scientific research, environmental preservation and protection,[9] as well as exploration for and exploitation of the non-living natural resources and management of the use of living natural resources,[10] are increasingly frequent. They are also characterised by a stronger influence of dictums of international courts and tribunals adjudicating maritime boundary disputes, especially after the *Qatar* v. *Bahrain* judgment on the merits.[11]

It can therefore be said that between 1942 and 2021, a direct relationship developed between the practice of Latin American and Caribbean States concerning maritime boundary delimitation and the law applicable to it. This law, whose codified first version emerged in the late 1950s, developed during UNCLOS III, was enshrined (however uninstructively) in the 1982 Convention, and has ever since been progressively clarified by maritime boundary case law. This progressive clarification of the law has also benefited from the practice of States, among which the practice of Latin American and Caribbean States, first unilateral and then in the form of maritime delimitation agreements, has carried a great weight.

The Pre-codification Age (1942–1958)

From the first period under analysis (1942–1958), the 1942 Gulf of Paria Treaty will be examined. The fact that only one treaty was concluded in this period may be explained by events that took place in the late 1940s and early 1950s involving Chile, Peru and later Ecuador, and by the advent of the 1958 Geneva Conference on the Law of the Sea, establishing the first conventional framework for maritime delimitation. In this initial period, one should also recall the landmark judgment of the ICJ on the *North Sea Continental Shelf*,[12] which, as mentioned before, was the first time that the 1958 CCS was interpreted.

UK (Trinidad and Tobago)/Venezuela – 1942

The treaty between the UK (concerning the territory of present-day Trinidad and Tobago) and Venezuela relating to the submarine areas of the Gulf of Paria, commonly referred to as the "Gulf of Paria Treaty", is mostly considered as the "first bilateral agreement ever signed by any two states regarding the delimitation of the seabed beyond the territorial sea".[13] Although the term "continental shelf" was not included in the Treaty, the use of "submarine areas" clearly referred to the inner continental shelf. In that sense, the agreement has also been considered as the "first international accord reached concerning the division of the continental shelf".[14] For instance, in a book co-authored by Robin Churchill and Vaughan Lowe, while considering it a maritime delimitation agreement, they stated that

> Early delimitations of the continental shelf evidenced the application of no clear principles. The agreed delimitation in the Gulf of Paria in 1942, for example, was said to have secured an "equitable division" between the United Kingdom and Venezuela.[15]

Back in 1923, Venezuela was the first country to conduct effective underwater drilling in Lake Maracaibo. This triggered Britain's interest in approaching Venezuela in relation to the eastern end of its coastline, both before (1936) and during World War II. It was only in the latter period, probably because of the added strategic need for oil and (most importantly) Britain's decision to accept Venezuela's request to link this treaty to the devolution of the island of Patos, that Venezuela agreed to British terms.[16]

Although the treaty did not put forward any method of delimitation per se,[17] the agreement reached by the Parties established in a pragmatic way three segments or lines joining four points (A, B, X, and Y) defined in Article 3,[18] namely, line A–B, line B–Y and line X–Y. The first segment (A–B) may give the impression of an equidistance line but was drawn taking into account two islands: the Island of *Patos* and *Soldado* Rock, and hence has nothing to do with that method. The second (B–Y), located in Serpent's Mouth, followed Venezuela's three-nautical-mile territorial sea. The third line (X–Y), in Columbus Channel, ran along a fixed parallel.

Furthermore, Article 2 established that the Parties will "not assert any claim to sovereignty or control over those parts of the submarine areas of the Gulf of Paria" which lie beyond the lines as described in Article 3, and that they will, in turn, recognise the rights of sovereignty or control of the other Party beyond those lines. Hence, the agreement put forward a "formula", consisting in fact of an abstention, that has been replicated several times in subsequent agreements in the region and elsewhere (the so-called LEB clauses, discussed later in this book).

In the absence (at the time) of any relevant Convention concerning the delimitation of maritime boundaries, general international law governing the delimitation of maritime spaces comprised the works of the 1930 Hague Codification Conference. Other than that, the UK had claimed three nautical miles of territorial waters in 1878, while Venezuela had done the same in 1939.[19]

The Geneva Conventions Period (1958–1982)

In the second period under analysis, which has been called "the Geneva Conventions period" (1958–1982), 17 treaties were concluded, starting with the 1970 Mexico/US agreement, the 1972 Brazil/Uruguay treaty and the 1973 Argentina/Uruguay agreement. At a time when the 1958 Geneva Conventions had already entered into force and the ICJ had handed down its judgment in the *North Sea* cases, Mexico and the US concluded a double frontage delimitation agreement (Gulf of Mexico and the Pacific Ocean) and made recourse to a simplified equidistance line. The other two agreements appear to have been brought about, partly, by Uruguay's unwillingness to have the method of the geographical parallel applied to it. Uruguay thus concluded a treaty with Brazil in 1972 establishing a perpendicular to the general direction of the coast as their maritime boundary, and another treaty with Argentina in 1973 which made use of an equidistance line, drawn from the midpoint of the baseline closing the mouth of Río de la Plata.

Mexico/US – 1970

The agreed maritime boundaries between Mexico and the US are a good example of a several-step maritime boundary negotiation.[20] With the antecedents of the 1848 Treaty[21] concluded at the end of the US-Mexican War, in 1970 the two countries signed the treaty to resolve pending boundary differences and maintain the Rio Grande (*Rio Bravo*) and Colorado Rivers as the international boundary, which established the territorial sea maritime boundary in the Gulf of Mexico and in the Pacific Ocean.[22] It is thought to have been the first case of double-frontage delimitation in the region.

Its main purpose was to settle sovereignty issues over tracts and islands in and near the Rio Grande and the Colorado Rivers, two geographical features of the highest importance for both countries since they form part of the US/Mexico border, which is always a delicate issue.[23] In fact, the instability of the meandering courses of those rivers was a source of friction between the two countries.[24] Hence it is in this manner that the two countries established the first section of their maritime boundaries.

In the Gulf of Mexico, the parties employed an approach that was innovative at the time. The boundary started "at the centre of the mouth of the Rio Grande, wherever it may be located" (a "floating" initial boundary point). From there it ran in a straight line to the point formed by the coordinates 25°57′22.18″N and 97°8′19.76″W (approximately 2000 feet seaward). The treaty then established a simplified line "drawn in accordance with the principle of equidistance".[25]

With respect to the maritime boundary in the Pacific Ocean, the boundary of the territorial sea started from the land boundary terminus ("the western point of the mainland boundary"). It then ran along a simplified equidistance line, "a line the delineation of which represents a practical simplification through a series of straight lines, of the line drawn in accordance with the principle of equidistance".[26]

Brazil/Uruguay – 1972

This was the first maritime delimitation agreement ever signed by either Brazil or Uruguay.[27] A somewhat simple geographical setting, constituted by States with adjacent coasts running in a northeast-southwest direction, allowed for a quite straightforward culmination of negotiations.

While recognising that the land boundary had been established in 1851,[28] the agreement comprised the Joint Declaration on Maritime Jurisdictional Boundaries signed by the Parties on 10 May 1969 and the Joint Declaration issued by the presidents of Brazil and Uruguay on 11 May 1970, which recognised that the lateral limit of their maritime jurisdictions was bounded by an equidistant line as direct antecedents.

It has been claimed that one of the main concerns of Uruguay in seeking to conclude this treaty enshrining the equidistance method was its intention to discard any possibility of applying the geographical parallel in its maritime delimitation with Argentina. The precedent constituted by the criteria applicable in the case of islands that had been included in the 1952 Santiago Declaration appears to have triggered the attention of Uruguay.[29]

The treaty defined their all-purpose maritime boundary at sea through a line running nearly perpendicular to the general line of the coast.[30] However, as stated by Canada in its Counter-Memorial in the *Gulf of Maine* case, "[t]he objective . . .

was to produce a simplified equidistance line".[31] More specifically, pursuant to that treaty, the lateral sea boundary between these two adjacent States

> shall be defined as the loxodrome which runs from the point defined above [that is, the position of the River Chué bar constituted by the intersection of the line running from the existing Chué lighthouse, more or less perpendicular to the general line of the coast, and the azimuth of the lateral sea boundary with the Atlantic Ocean], at an azimuth of one hundred and twenty-eight [128] sexagesimal degrees (from true north), to the outer limit of the territorial sea of both countries.

The line obtained by the application of this method is very close to that obtained with the equidistance method.[32] In so doing, it created a "grey area" where part of the maritime area on the Brazilian side of the maritime boundary is beyond Brazil's 200 nautical miles but within Uruguay's 200-nautical-mile reach.

Argentina/Uruguay – 1973

Argentina and Uruguay concluded a treaty concerning the Río de la Plata and the Corresponding Maritime Boundary (*Tratado del Río de la Plata y su Frente Marítimo*) in November 1973.[33] The Treaty was aimed, among other matters, at establishing the maritime boundary between those two adjacent countries at the mouth of the Río de la Plata and seawards.

Having signed a Joint Declaration on the Outer Limit of the Río de la Plata in 1961[34] whereby Argentina and Uruguay laid claim over the waters of the mouth of that river based, to a certain extent, on historic rights and in accordance with Article 13 of the Geneva Convention on the Territorial Sea, the 1973 Río de la Plata Treaty was the next step. This was worked on in particular after Uruguay signed a delimitation treaty with Brazil the year before.

It should be noted here that the 1961 Declaration, while somehow based on historic rights,[35] took into account Article 13 of the Territorial Sea Convention which relates to rivers that flow directly into the sea and not to those that flow into an estuary or bay.[36] In this sense, it can be stated that the River de la Plata Estuary (a non–salt water area) is a case of the mouth of a river rather than the case of a historic bay.

In its Article 70, the treaty provides that the lateral maritime boundary and the continental shelf boundary between the two countries "are defined by an equidistant line, determined by the adjacent coasts methods", starting (without specifying any coordinates) from the midpoint (also called point 23) of the straight 118-nautical-mile baseline connecting *Punta del Este* (Uruguay) and *Punta Rasa del Cabo San Antonio* (Argentina),[37] a line that had been established pursuant to the 1961 Joint Declaration.

As is evident, the treaty established no more than a general criterion to effect the delimitation in their overlapping maritime spaces, without touching in a detailed manner upon the course of the maritime boundary. This is rather striking for an otherwise thorough international agreement.

Accordingly, the maritime boundary beyond point 23 is composed of six segments. The first sector joins point 23 to point A, drawn from the midpoint of the Río de la Plata closing line, and influenced both by Argentinean's *Punta Médanos* and the Uruguayan *Isla de Lobos*.[38] The following four segments (A–B, B–C, C–D and D–E) appear to be segments of a parabolic curve. Finally, segment E–F reaches a point which is equidistance from *Punta Médanos* and *Isla de Lobos*.[39]

Colombia/Ecuador – 1975

Colombia and Ecuador concluded their first maritime delimitation agreement concerning the Southeast Pacific region in 1975.[40] It involved Ecuador, one of the signatory countries of the 1952 Declaration of Santiago; and Colombia, a country that, due to its geography, seems to be more oriented to the Caribbean Sea than to the Pacific Ocean, and that acceded to the Declaration in 1979.[41] The term "marine and submarine areas" stems from the 1970 modus operandi between Colombia and Venezuela and was applied to areas off the northwest of the Gulf of Venezuela in order to avoid controversial geographical references.[42] The 1975 maritime delimitation agreement, as will be seen below, was complemented by a Joint Declaration made by the Ministers of Foreign Affairs in 2012 concerning the endpoint of the land boundary.

Sharing a land boundary of 586 kilometres, these two South American countries have generally enjoyed an amicable relationship.[43] After having established their land boundary by means of a Treaty in 1916,[44] Colombia and Ecuador deemed it necessary to establish their maritime boundary,[45] taking into account the developments that had occurred in the region (e.g. the 1952 Declaration of Santiago) and elsewhere, including the adoption of the 1958 Geneva Conventions on the Law of the Sea and especially the development of the then-ongoing UNCLOS III.

In its Article 1, the treaty designated the line of the geographical parallel "traversing the point at which the international land frontier between Ecuador and Colombia reaches the sea" as the maritime boundary covering its respective marine and submarine areas. This is a situation where the method of the geographical parallel was explicitly chosen by the Parties as their maritime boundary, in light of the general configuration of the coast.

It is noteworthy that in Article 2, the parties established beyond 12 nautical miles a special zone 10 nautical miles wide on either side of the parallel. The establishment of this area was aimed at ensuring that the accidental presence of fishermen of either country would not be considered a violation of the maritime boundary. Similarly, in Article 4 of the agreement, the parties recognised for each other the right to establish the baselines from which the width of their territorial seas was to be measured.[46]

Even though the parallel of latitude was already established in 1975 as the method applicable to draw the boundary line at sea, the exact point at which the land boundary reached the sea had not been identified. Only in 2012 was that point identified by means of the above-mentioned Joint Declaration, where the coordinates of 1°28′10.49″N and 78°52′07.27″W (WGS84) were established as the *terminus* of the land boundary at the mouth of the river Mataje.[47] Similarly, the terminal point of the maritime boundary for Colombia was positioned on the 200-nautical-mile limit as measured from Isla Malpelo, while Ecuador's boundary terminated on the 200-nautical-mile limit measured from Punta Pasado and Punta Galera located on its northern mainland coast.

Cuba/Mexico – 1976

In 1976, the Governments of Cuba and Mexico exchanged Notes constituting an agreement on the delimitation of their maritime areas[48] in the Yucatan Channel, on the basis of the "principle" of equidistance. The boundary line extends for 352 nautical miles until it reaches a tripoint with Honduras.

Due to its strategic and geopolitical importance as a link between the Gulf of Mexico and the Caribbean Sea, not to mention its high relevance as the shortest route between US ports in the Gulf and the Panama Canal, the Yucatan Channel seems to have been more of a unifier than a divider between Mexico and Cuba. Hence, both Governments have normally kept friendly relations trying to ensure safety for navigation and freedom of the sea in the area. These factors, together with Mexico's urgency to settle its maritime delimitation with Cuba before the entry into force of its EEZ law, triggered the Parties to negotiate and conclude this treaty.

The maritime boundary, formed by 12 segments, divides the maritime zones projected from Cap Catoche in Mexico's Yucatan Peninsula and Cozumel Island, and from Cap San Antonio in Cuba. As mentioned earlier, it is a rather long maritime boundary, stretching more than 350 nautical miles from the Caribbean Sea and ending in the Gulf of Mexico. The agreement was reached by applying the equidistance method disregarding Cuba's baselines but taking into account and giving full effect to the islands and rocks belonging to both States.[49] It hence starts, towards the northwest, at point 1, 24°56′28.83″N and 86°56′16.69″W (Gulf of Mexico) and ends, towards the southeast, at point 13, 19°32′25.80″N and 84°38′30.66″W (Caribbean Sea).[50]

Colombia/Panama – 1976

Colombia and Panama border the Pacific Ocean and the Caribbean Sea. Against the backdrop of Colombia's policy aimed at completing its maritime map,[51] the two coastal States decided in 1976 to establish a "double frontage delimitation" covering both such areas.[52]

It has been claimed that, with the 2012 judgment by the International Court of Justice on *Nicaragua* v. *Colombia*, this treaty, together with the 1977 Colombia/Costa Rica maritime delimitation agreement, was left without object or even "virtually invalidated".[53]

While in the framework of UNCLOS III participants would advance their views on certain principles and rules of international law relating to maritime delimitation, in their home country they would put these principles and rules into practice.

In this case, the Parties would agree on the "principle" of equidistance (Article 1), while Colombia would recognise expressly the status of historic bay to the Gulf of Panama (Article 3).

In the Caribbean Sea the Parties drew a line joining 13 points (A to M). Its starting point (point A) is at Cape Tiburón, 8°41′07.3″N and 77°21′50.9″W. Next, within an adjacency relationship, it follows an equidistant line, with minor deviations (between points F and H, in favour of Colombia), until it reaches point H (12°30′00″N and 78°00′00″W), that is, 40% of the maritime boundary.

From that point until point M, where the boundary is between opposite coasts because it concerns the islands and cays of the San Andrés Archipelago, the line departs from equidistance and follows a stepped-shape combination of latitudes (three) and longitudes (two) conventionally agreed upon,[54] which gives full effect to the Colombian islands. It is presumed that this part of the boundary was envisaged to be in conformity with the meridian that Colombia claimed at the time as the maritime boundary with Nicaragua. Finally, the maritime boundary in its last part, from point M onwards, follows a straight line on azimuth 225° (45°SW) until it reaches a point where delimitation with a third party (Costa Rica) is possible.[55]

In the Pacific Ocean, the Parties chose two different methods. For the first part, from the point at which the international land boundary meets the sea (7°12′39.3″N and 77°53′20.9″W), the maritime boundary follows, except for minor deviations, a median or equidistance line that joins six points (A–M). A second part of the boundary, from point M, located at 5°00′00″N and 79°52′00″W, the delimitation of the maritime boundary follows the line of the 5th parallel until the delimitation must be made with a third country.

In this agreement with Colombia, and in its 1980 agreement with Costa Rica (in both cases, in Article III), Panama managed to get express recognition from the respective counterparts that the Gulf of Panama has the status of historic bay.[56]

Cuba/Haiti – 1977

The maritime delimitation treaty between Cuba and Haiti,[57] which followed the two countries' 200-nautical-mile proclamations at the beginning of 1977, established their maritime boundary along the Windward Passage. While Haiti had closed the Gulf of Gonâve (hence the boundary line was built taking that into account), the maritime frontier did not consider Navassa Island as basepoint (lying approximately 30 nautical miles from Haiti's western end), which was disputed between Haiti and the US.

Unlike the Yucatan Channel between Cuba and Mexico, the Windward Passage seems to have been, at least at the time of the negotiation, more of a separating than a uniting factor.[58] Yet this did not prevent those two Caribbean States from reaching an agreement.

Concerning the method of delimitation, attention should be drawn to the language used in the treaty: the delimitation is said to have been accomplished "on the basis of the principle of equidistance or equity, as the case requires." This meant that, among the 50-segment maritime boundary, created by the joining of

51 points, one can find parts applying strict equidistance, simplified equidistance or radically modified equidistance.[59]

Colombia/Dominican Republic – 1978

The agreement on the delimitation of "marine and submarine areas" and maritime cooperation between Colombia and the Dominican Republic,[60] reached in 1978, used as "a general norm" the "principle of the median line" or rather, it should be clarified, the equidistance method.[61] While seeking mainly to delimit the maritime spaces of the two countries involved, the agreement also established a zone of scientific research and "common" fishing exploitation. Similarly, it is an example of an agreement dealing with maritime areas not (yet) formally declared under the jurisdiction of at least one of the coastal States Party to it.[62]

In the framework of UNCLOS III, this agreement was concluded taking into account the so-called (informal) Single Negotiating Text[63] and hence reflected the views that the Parties would also advance in the conference.[64] This delimitation involved a strategy undertaken by Colombia, and later also by Venezuela, so as to defend their position vis-à-vis a potential delimitation between them off the Gulf of Venezuela.

Having established the median line as the method, the maritime boundary runs along two segments, in the form of simplified equidistance. First, from the point at 15°02′00″N and 73°27′30″W, to another point at 15°00′40″N and 71°40′30″W. Second, from that point towards a third point at 15°18′00″N and 69°29′30″W, until delimitation with a third State is required, in this case, the area in dispute between Colombia and Venezuela.[65] It is, however, important to note that this third point is situated far from the scope of the present delimitation and is therefore used as a reference only. It is hence another case of an "open-ended" maritime boundary.

Furthermore, the treaty, as mentioned before, established what at the time was an innovative zone of joint scientific research and fishing exploitation located within four straight lines drawn between four points, the coordinates of which are specified in Article III of the treaty.[66]

Colombia/Haiti – 1978

In 1978, Colombia and Haiti concluded an agreement on maritime boundary delimitation,[67] whereby they established the method of the median line.[68] They decided to draw a 65-nautical-mile line continuing the boundary line that had been agreed between Colombia and the Dominican Republic shortly before, in January 1978.

These two countries decided to fix the limits of their respective jurisdictions in an area that gained the utmost importance with the opening of the Panama Canal. This was ultimately the last of the group of five maritime delimitation treaties successfully negotiated by Colombia between 1975 and 1978.[69]

With the intention of establishing a median line (i.e. the equidistance method),[70] the boundary was therefore constituted by a straight line joining the point at

14°44′10″N and 74°30′50″W to the point at 15°02′00″N and 73°27′30″W, which is the point where the Colombia/Dominican Republic maritime boundary starts. However, it does not recognise Morant Cays (Jamaica) as base point.

US (Puerto Rico and Virgin Islands)/Venezuela – 1978

The 1978 treaty between the US and Venezuela[71] established "an equitable maritime boundary" (note the willingness to avoid any reference to the equidistance method) "in accordance with international law", although in actual fact equidistance was applied. It included a part of the boundary delimiting the Venezuelan island of Aves and the US island of Saint Croix. The agreement was reached when Venezuela and the Netherlands had come to terms concerning their own delimitation in the so-called Dutch Antilles. Following that, it was with Venezuela, and not with the Netherlands, that the US had to negotiate.[72] One of the main characteristics in this regard was that, in both agreements (with the Netherlands and with the US), Aves Island was given full effect.[73]

One of the main features concerning the method is that here equity was equated with equidistance,[74] due to the absence of special circumstances and the fact that delimitation involved opposite islands. The maritime boundary therefore runs along a first segment, between Aves Island and the US Virgin Islands where equidistance is employed, and then a second segment where base points belonging to a third State (Curaçao and Bonaire [the Netherlands]) were taken into account, and hence it can be said that instead it corresponds to a case of modified equidistance.[75]

The maritime boundary is determined by a number of geodetic lines connecting 22 points listed in Article 2. An interesting aspect is the way in which the agreement refers to its western end. Because of technical uncertainties, the precise western point of the US-Venezuela boundary could not be fixed, and hence the agreement opted to establish a point (with latitude and longitude clearly expressed) beyond which under no circumstance should the boundary extend. In that way, it allowed the results of a US/Dominican Republic maritime delimitation agreement to determine that point.[76]

The Netherlands/Venezuela – 1978

The 1978 maritime delimitation treaty between the Netherlands and Venezuela[77] constitutes "one of the most interesting and complex case studies"[78] of a maritime delimitation that was concluded, as it took into account a number of circumstances different to those used in maritime delimitation law. It established their maritime boundaries in two areas of the Caribbean Sea: a major, U-shaped boundary between mainland Venezuela and Aruba, Bonaire and Curaçao; and a minor, quite short boundary between Venezuela's Aves Island and the two Dutch Lesser Antilles of Saba and Sint Eustatius (Statia). The boundaries concerned their territorial waters, continental shelves, exclusive economic zones "and all other maritime or submarine areas that have been or may be established by the Parties in accordance with international law".

The treaty emerged in the context of a three-century-long relationship between advanced free-trading economies belonging to the Netherlands Antilles and a former Spanish colony. In this framework, Venezuela's main driver to conclude the treaty, in the major areas, was to maintain and ensure free and unimpeded access between the high seas, the Gulf of Venezuela and Lake Maracaibo, the latter rich in crude oil reserves, taking into account the strategic position of Los Monjes Archipelago, a federal dependency of Venezuela located to the northwest of that Gulf. The Netherlands, in turn, was concerned about the economic development of oil resources, pollution-free tourism, renewable marine resources and port facilities.[79] In the minor area, Venezuela again managed to gain full weight recognition for once-disputed Aves Island.[80]

According to the treaty, the maritime boundary is composed of four sectors. Sectors A, B and C – which coincidentally reflect the initials of Aruba, Bonaire and Curaçao – established a three-segment boundary: one between the west of Aruba and Venezuelan territory; another one between the Leeward Islands of the Netherlands Antilles (Aruba, Bonaire and Curaçao) and the north coast of Venezuela; and a last one between Bonaire and Venezuelan territory.[81]

It then seems that these three segments were anchored to two corners, with reference to fixed points on land, formed by pairs of meridians and parallels. Hence, on the west, a point was formed at 70°25′W and 12°21′N (point 3); and on the east, a point was formed at 11°40′N and 67°59′W (point 11). From those points, sector B was first drawn between the three Major Antilles and mainland Venezuela, joining the above-mentioned points 3 and 11, through a number of other points which could represent a simplified equidistance in the sense that, in compensating the line, it grants two small triangles to the Antilles and two larger ones to Venezuela.

With regards to sectors A and C, they were inclined in northeasterly and northwesterly directions, respectively. Sector A, from point 2 (12°49′00″N and 70°25′00″W) to point 1, and sector C, from point 12 (12°27′00″N and 67°59′23″W), to point 13. These two segments depart a great deal from the equidistance line.

Sector D, that is the fourth sector, between the Island of Aves and Saba and Sint Eustatius, was a plain two-segment equidistance line that used maritime features belonging to third States as basepoints (Saint Croix, belonging to the US, and Saint Christopher, belonging at the time to the UK). The boundary, thus, ran along three points: 14, 15 and 16.[82]

Mexico/US – 1978

As antecedents, it is to be recalled that in 1976, in an Exchange of Notes,[83] Mexico and the US provisionally recognised maritime boundaries between them in the Pacific Ocean and the Gulf of Mexico out to 200 nautical miles. The fact that Mexico established its 200-nautical-mile zone shortly before the US seems to have triggered this provisional arrangement. The Parties decided to conclude this agreement, on a provisional basis, due to their belief that further technical studies were needed so as to have more scientific grounds justifying a permanent boundary.

In 1978, Mexico and the US signed a treaty[84] that gave a definitive character to the 1976 Exchange of Notes that had established a provisional arrangement between them in their overlapping maritime zones (i.e. exclusive economic zones and continental shelves) in the Gulf of Mexico and the Pacific Ocean. Indeed, having found no need whatsoever for further technical work relating to the precise location of base points, two years after signing the 1976 Exchange of Notes the two Governments decided to sign a maritime boundary agreement enshrining those same provisions.

This is generally the case with simplified equidistance lines, since in both areas covered by the treaty (the Gulf of Mexico and the Pacific Ocean) some points were omitted. In the Gulf of Mexico, the line was simplified by deleting three points, whereas in the Pacific the line was simplified by deleting 12 turning points.[85]

In the Western Gulf of Mexico, the maritime boundary extends, in general, from the endpoint of the 12-nautical-mile territorial sea limit established in 1970 to a point 200 nautical miles from each coast (in a situation of adjacency). It does so, however, by joining four points (GM.W-1, GM.W-2, GM.W-3 and GM.W-4), the coordinates of which are clearly identified in the treaty. Beyond that point, in the Eastern Gulf of Mexico a gap of approximately 129 nautical miles would follow with no maritime boundary until (in a situation of opposite coasts) it reaches an area of overlapping entitlements projected from the coast of Louisiana and the coast of some Mexican islands north of Yucatan.[86] It then follows three points (GM.E-1, GM.E-2 and GM.E-3), the coordinates of which are also identified in the treaty. In the Pacific Ocean, in turn, the boundary runs in a southwesterly direction joining similarly four points (OP-1, OP-2, OP-3 and OP-4).[87]

Dominican Republic/Venezuela – 1979

As was the case in the 1978 Colombia/Dominican Republic agreement, the treaty between the Dominican Republic and Venezuela, concluded in March 1979,[88] reflects the currently pending potential delimitation between Colombia and Venezuela. Moreover, the agreement is composed of two segments separated by a maritime gap of about 40 nautical miles which should hopefully be at some point delimited by an agreement with the Netherlands (on behalf of Aruba, Bonaire and Curaçao) and the Dominican Republic. Note also that this is the case of delimitation between islands since it relates to the Dominican Republic and Venezuelan Monjes Archipelago.

The importance of maritime traffic to and from Venezuela, expressly included in the treaty's preamble, is one of the clear drivers of this treaty. However, one cannot avoid seeing in it, as well as in the aforementioned treaty (Colombia/Dominican Republic), a close relation to the outstanding delimitation matters between Colombia and Venezuela.

The method used is that of equidistance. Article 2 of the treaty determined the maritime boundary between them by geodesic lines that join a number of points with their respective coordinates. Those lines were, in turn, divided into two sectors: sector A (points 1 to 6) and sector B (starting from point 7 to point 8).

Concerning sector A, the maritime boundary starts at the point of 15°24′48″N and 69°34′38″W (point 1) and ends at the point of 14°57′52″N and 71°24′19″W (point 6). Beyond point 6, between Alto Velo (DR) and Los Monjes Archipelago, the line remains an "open-ended" line following azimuth 270°68′ to another point where delimitation with a third State must be affected.

Sector B, is drawn from point 7 at 15°14′28″N and 68°51′44″W towards a point at 15°12′51″N and 68°28′56″W.[89]

Costa Rica/Panama – 1980

The 1980 maritime delimitation treaty between Costa Rica and Panama,[90] similar to other maritime delimitation treaties concerning such geographical features, constitutes the case of a double-frontage delimitation, one in the Caribbean Sea and the other in the Pacific Ocean. While the method indicated in the treaty is that of equidistance, the method employed most frequently is the perpendicular to the general direction of the coast.[91]

This treaty completed Panama's maritime boundaries, including a maritime area in the Pacific that is crossed by heavy traffic routes from and to the West Coast of the US. From Costa Rica's perspective on the Pacific Ocean, it paved the way to delimiting its maritime spaces with Ecuador.

The maritime boundary in the Caribbean runs along a one-segment line between the *terminus* of the land boundary (mouth of the Sixaola River, at 9°34′16″N and 82°34′00″W) and the tri-junction where it meets the last point of both the Colombia/Panama and the Colombia/Costa Rica boundaries ("where the boundaries of Costa Rica, Colombia, and Panama intersect"). In other words, it is not a median line "every point of which is equidistant from the nearest points on the baselines from which the breadth of the territorial sea of each States is measured in accordance with public international law", as provided for in the treaty, but rather a line perpendicular to the general direction of the coast.

In the case of the maritime boundary between Costa Rica and Panama towards the Pacific Ocean, it can also be said that it runs along a line more akin to a perpendicular to the general direction of the coast than to a median line since, again, it draws a straight line from the southernmost point of the land boundary (*Punta Burica*) joining it to a point at 5°00′00″N and 84°19′00″W.

Note that in this agreement with Costa Rica, as in its 1976 agreement with Colombia (in both cases under Article III), Panama managed to achieve an explicit recognition from its counterpart that the Gulf of Panama is a historic bay.[92]

France (Martinique and Guadeloupe)/Venezuela – 1980

This is the first treaty[93] concluded by France, a major maritime power, concerning delimitation in the Caribbean Sea.[94] It follows a French approach to the negotiation of maritime boundary agreements in the vicinity of its departments and overseas territories (Guadeloupe and Martinique) with States that play the role of a regional leader, to produce an imitation effect ("effet d'entraînement") on the other States of the region.[95] In this case, delimitation was in fact effected between island territories, since it concerned not only those French overseas departments (two at the same time) but also the controversial Venezuelan Aves Island.

Having already signed agreements relating Aves Island with the US and the Netherlands, Venezuela is thought to have taken the initiative in negotiating this treaty already in 1978, as a means to confirm the strategic value of Aves' central location in the Caribbean Sea. From the French viewpoint, it was mainly the interest of fishermen carrying out activities in waters that would no longer be considered as high seas that triggered its will to negotiate and sign this agreement.[96]

The delimitation concerned the maritime spaces located between the west coasts of Guadeloupe and Martinique and the east coast of Aves Island, bearing in mind that the two French departments are separated by Dominica. In other words, the boundary that concerns "the zones over which the . . . Parties exercise or will exercise" sovereign rights or jurisdiction in accordance with international law is composed of two segments, one in the north corresponding to Guadeloupe and one in the south corresponding to Martinique. In between lie the maritime spaces of Dominica.

After having considered other methods during negotiations (including granting Aves only half effect),[97] interestingly enough the Parties came to agree upon a line running along the meridian 62°48′50″ as the maritime boundary for both segments in a seeming attempt at unitising, for the sake of simplicity, the course of the maritime boundary.[98]

Brazil/France (French Guyana) – 1981

The agreement relating to the maritime delimitation between Brazil and French Guyana, the largest overseas department of France, was concluded in Paris on 30 January 1981.[99] As stated elsewhere in this work, this treaty was the result of French policy to achieve a formal recognition of France's presence in those regions.[100]

In this case, modified equidistance between the Parties did not take fully into account the French island of Le Grand Connétable, although this was later compensated in the second half of the boundary.

The line was hence drawn from the midpoint of the closing line of the bay of Oyapock, a binational bay shared by Brazil and France. The midpoint was situated at 4°30.5′N and 51°38.2′W. From that point the boundary line is determined by the true azimuth loxodromic curve 41°30′.[101]

In this case, it seems that strict equidistance would have been inequitable for France because of the orientation of Cape Orange in the bay of Oyapock. This orientation does not reflect the general direction of the coast of the adjacent States and is thought to become more marked year after year.[102] Hence, had that general direction been taken into consideration the result would have been an equidistance line significantly deviated towards the northwest, and therefore inequitable for France.[103]

France (Martinique)/Saint Lucia – 1981

In 1981, France (regarding Martinique) and Saint Lucia, lying only about 30 kilometres from each other, agreed their maritime delimitation.[104] It is hence a case of two island territories with opposite coasts.

The Parties, whilst taking into account the work of UNCLOS III, established the application of the equidistance method, "judged to be in the present case in accordance with equity".[105] The line drawn aimed to join, in a west-east direction, 18 points, the coordinates of which were established in Article 2. The first point westwards (L1), which is the intersection of 14°04′50″N and 62°48′50″W – and at the same time connects with the 62nd meridian established in the 1980 Agreement between France and Venezuela – should go through 17 segments until finally connecting with the last point (L18), identified as 14°06′51″N and 59°59′59″W.[106] The coordinates mentioned in the text of this agreement are expressed according to the geodetic system adopted by the *Institut géographique national français* for Martinique in 1953.[107]

The UNCLOS Age (1982–Present)

The period between the adoption of the Law of the Sea Convention in 1982 and the present day is called the UNCLOS period. Latin American and Caribbean States have been quite prolific during this time. Twenty-five agreements were concluded, although one of them has yet to be ratified (1985 Costa Rica/Ecuador).[108]

Again, Colombia was one of the States quite proactive in delimitation matters and took the lead by concluding in that period its agreements with Costa Rica in 1984, with Ecuador in 1985, with Honduras in 1986 and with Jamaica in 1993. It made use of equidistance with Costa Rica, of simplified equidistance with Ecuador and Jamaica, and of parallels and meridians with Honduras.

The 1984 Argentina/Chile maritime boundary delimitation deserves particular attention. It came about after a long negotiation that included mediation led by the Holy See, and that eventually allowed the Parties to draw a line from the *terminus* of the maritime boundary that had been established in the 1977 Beagle Channel Award,[109] an arbitral decision initially rejected by Argentina. Concerning delimitation methods, a combination of loxodromic lines, meridians and a parallel (composite delimitation) were employed.

In 1987, Dominica and France, in respect of Guadeloupe and Marie-Galante and Martinique, concluded a maritime delimitation agreement, the preamble of which claimed it was based "on the rules and principles of international law as they are expressed" in UNCLOS. This agreement has been labelled as a case study in the region due to the complexity of the geographical situation. Indeed, the island of Dominica lies in between two French dependencies, which results in a maritime boundary with a "railway-track shape". This is why, concerning the methods used, this agreement seems to constitute a pragmatic solution (composite delimitation).

Venezuela and Trinidad and Tobago decided in 1990 to subsume their previous agreements, the 1942 Gulf of Paria and another one signed in 1989, into one overarching treaty that delimited the maritime areas that had not previously been delimited with segments of simplified and modified equidistance. The UK, in turn, concluded two treaties with the US on the same day so as to delimit their maritime spaces in the Atlantic Ocean with simplified equidistance. Understandably enough, the Anglo-American treaties took due care not to make any reference to the already-adopted Montego Bay Convention.

Finally, Cuba and Jamaica concluded their maritime delimitation agreement in February 1994. The agreement, like 1987 Dominica/France, took into account the relevant provisions of the 1982 Law of the Sea Convention and seems to be one of the rare maritime delimitation agreements that employed the method of strict equidistance.

Argentina/Chile – 1984

On 29 November 1984, Argentina and Chile concluded a treaty[110] that established the maritime boundary between them over an area where the Atlantic and the Pacific meet and what the treaty calls the sea of the "Southern Region" (*Mar de la Zona Austral*), situated to the south of the island of *Tierra del Fuego*. Without mentioning it, the treaty alludes to the 1977 Beagle Channel Award[111] in as much as the starting point of the maritime boundary is the last point of the delimitation effected in the said award.

Following the tense situation created between these two South American States after the rejection of the award by the Government of Argentina in January 1978, the Holy See's mediation allowed the Parties to carry out negotiations and finally sign the 1984 Treaty of Peace and Friendship. As pointed out before, Article 7 of the treaty, dealing with the maritime delimitation, begins by accepting the boundary established by the 1977 Award. However, it is thought that the compromise was reached because Chile accepted, to a certain extent, Argentina's bi-oceanic principle which had been dismissed years before in the Beagle award.[112]

The agreement established the course of the maritime boundary following five segments formed by joining loxodromes along points A to F. The first segment, that connects points A and B, has an extension of 12 nautical miles and is drawn towards the southeast. Point A, being the last point established by the Beagle Channel Award, is connected to point B, the coordinates of which are 55°11′0″S and 66°4′7″W. Point B is joined to point C (55°22′9″S and 65°43′6″W), following again a southeasterly direction along a 16.5-nautical-mile line that seems to be equidistant from *Isla Nueva* and *Isla Grande de Tierra del Fuego*. These two first segments give Chile a limited projection towards the Atlantic Ocean.

From then onwards, the remaining three segments of the maritime boundary follow a step-like shape. Hence, the segment connecting C and D (60 nautical miles) runs towards the south along a meridian; the line between points D and E (51 nautical miles) runs towards the west following the geographical parallel; and finally, the line between points E and F (119 nautical miles) continues towards the south along another meridian, the so-called Cape Horn meridian.[113]

It should also be added that in August 2021, the Governments of Chile and Argentina had an exchange of views regarding their outer continental shelves.[114]

Colombia/Costa Rica – 1984 (Pacific Ocean)

According to the terms of its own preamble, this maritime delimitation treaty between Colombia and Costa Rica[115] extends their cooperation in maritime affairs and delimits their marine and submarine areas in the Pacific Ocean. It should be recalled that in 1977 the Parties had already signed another treaty concerning their delimitation in the Caribbean Sea, but it has not been ratified by Costa Rica.[116]

The treaty delimited the marine and submarine areas of both States in the Pacific Ocean with a straight line drawn from a point located at 5°00′00″N and 84°19′00″W of Greenwich (i.e. the end of the maritime boundary between Costa Rica and Panama) southward towards another point located at 3°32′00″N and 84°19′00″W of Greenwich. From this point, the maritime boundary continues along the boundary of the 200-mile maritime zone of the Island of Coco to a point at 3°03′00″N and 84°46′00″W of Greenwich.[117] In this sense, this is the case of a combination of simplified and modified equidistance.

Colombia/Honduras – 1986

Unlike earlier treaties signed by Colombia, this agreement concluded in August 1986[118] did not make any reference to the "developing law of the sea" or to any declarative principles. The Law of the Sea Convention had already been adopted and hence there was probably no need to make such proclamations in the treaty's preamble.

This agreement was, to a certain extent, affected by the 2007 *Nicaragua* v. *Honduras* ICJ judgment,[119] which prompted Honduras' Application for Permission to Intervene in the case concerning the *Territorial and Maritime Dispute* (*Nicaragua* v. *Colombia*).[120]

After settling different views concerning sovereignty and jurisdiction over the Serranilla cays, Colombia and Honduras succeeded in negotiating a maritime delimitation treaty whereby Colombian sovereignty over the cays was recognised by Honduras. This would be strongly protested by Nicaragua,[121] which would later bring claims against both Colombia and Honduras before the International Court of Justice.

Colombia and Honduras established that their maritime boundary in the Caribbean Sea is constituted by joining six points, the coordinates of which are expressly established in the treaty. The first line, joining points 1 and 2, starts at the 82°W meridian and runs along parallel 14°59′08″N (which for the sake of simplicity was known as "the 15th parallel" in the *Nicaragua* v. *Honduras* pleadings)[122] up to the meridian 79°56′00″W, where the maritime boundary turns north until reaching the 12-nautical-mile territorial sea of the Serranilla cays. From there, it continues along the border of a 12-mile arc of circle until reaches parallel 16°04′15″N. It then continues eastwards until it reaches the limits of a third State.[123]

Dominica/France (Guadeloupe and Marie-Galante and Martinique) – 1987

The 1987 agreement on Maritime Delimitation between Dominica and France[124] is the first maritime boundary to be established in the East Caribbean, by negotiation, after the adoption of the United Nations Convention on the Law of the Sea. Due to the geographical fact that Dominica lies in between the French dependencies of Guadeloupe and Marie-Galante and Martinique, the maritime boundary took a "railway-track" shape. In any case, its negotiation is considered a case study in the region.[125] This agreement also falls in the category of agreements fostered by France and its policy to close the maritime areas of its overseas possessions worldwide.

The application of the equidistance method seems to have been discarded in view of the cut-off effect that it would have caused to Dominica's EEZ.[126]

The lines of delimitation between Dominica and Guadeloupe, Saintes and Marie-Galante Islands on the north, and Dominica and Martinique Islands on the south, follow a series of loxodromes joining a number of points, the coordinates of which are established in Article 1 of the treaty.

Hence, in the north, the maritime boundary between Guadeloupe and Dominica starts at a point 1, touching the meridian that had been constituted as the maritime boundary between France and Venezuela (Aves Island). The coordinates of point 1 are 15°03′54″N and 62°48′50″W, and the line follows through eight points until it reaches point 8 at 16°30′03″N and 57°56′54″W.

From that point 8, the line follows an arc of geodetic circle centred at 15°29′30″N and 61°14′52″W with a radius of 200 nautical miles connecting it to point 9 at 16°03′51″N and 57°52′30″W.

Finally, in the south, the maritime boundary starts at point 9 and, following five segments, reaches point 14 at 14°29′19″N and 62°48′50″W until it connects again with the meridian dividing France and Aves Island.[127]

Trinidad and Tobago/Venezuela – 1990

Trinidad and Tobago and Venezuela concluded an agreement on the delimitation of marine and submarine areas in 1990.[128] With the conclusion of this treaty, in accordance with its Article 11, the two previous treaties that engaged the Parties in this matter ceased to have effect. Those treaties were the 1942 Gulf of Paria Treaty, between the UK, on account of Trinidad and Tobago and Venezuela, and the 1989 Treaty between Trinidad and Tobago and Venezuela.

Since the 1942 Gulf of Paria Treaty had not delimited all the maritime areas between these two countries, it was necessary to finalise the task by including all maritime spaces in a new one while keeping the 1942 line. The countries hence started approaching each other on this subject as early as 1975. In the framework of their maritime relations, the Parties also established fishery agreements in the 1970s and 1980s.

The treaty referred to the maritime boundary with respect to the territorial seas, the continental shelves, the exclusive economic zones "and to any other marine and submarine areas which have been or might be established" by the Parties "in accordance with international law", in the Caribbean, the Gulf of Paria, the Serpent's Mouth and the Atlantic Ocean. It appears to be based upon equitable principles,[129] but it cannot be stated that it followed any single method.

The boundary, therefore, is constituted by joining 21 geographical coordinates, extending for about 440 nautical miles. In joining those points, one can identify five different segments concerning methods of maritime delimitation.

As for the first segment, in the open Caribbean sector, the maritime boundary starts at 11°10′30″N and 61°43′46″W (point 1) and runs south through the latter meridian until it reaches point 2.[130] The second segment goes from point 2 to point 8, south of Dragon's Mouth in a part of the Gulf of Paria that was not included in the 1942 Treaty. It follows, from point 2 until point 6, the equidistance method taking account of the islands; and from point 6 to point 8, a meridian and a parallel. The following segment (points 8–9 and 9–10) refers to the Gulf of Paria itself, and is almost as it was delimited in 1942, except for the line joining points 9 and 10 which slightly rectifies the 1942 Treaty. The fourth segment runs along the Columbus Channel and the southeastern sector and is based on equidistance until it reaches point 19 (it was established up to this point in 1989). Finally, in the last segment (added in 1990), the maritime boundary follows a northeastern direction, presumably to allow Venezuela access to the Atlantic (*salida al Atlántico*).[131]

UK (British Virgin Islands)/US (Puerto Rico and US Virgin Islands) – 1993

In 1993 the UK and the US signed two maritime delimitation agreements concerning their Caribbean possessions,[132] one having a total length of 288 nautical miles and the other only 1.34 nautical miles. In their preambles, the agreements made explicit reference to equidistance, and in their (similarly worded) Articles 1 to their being in accordance with international law. They were concluded with as reference the signature, on 27 March 1979, of a reciprocal fisheries agreement applying to the waters between the US Caribbean territories and the British Virgin Islands, whereby the two Governments expressed their shared approach based on the use of an equidistant line in order to divide their respective fisheries jurisdiction.[133]

The method used is equidistance, which both sides then decided to simplify by discarding some 75 turning points that had minimal effect on the line.[134] The maritime boundary ends up being composed by the joining of 50 points whose coordinates are indicated in the Annex to the Treaty.

Starting in the north, the first part of the equidistant line (some 134 nautical miles) is constructed from Puerto Rico's coast. From point 6 (at 19°37′29″N and 65°20′57″W) of the maritime boundary to the southern terminus, at the tripoint with Anguilla, the line is constructed taking into account base points situated in the US Virgin Islands and in the British Virgin Islands.[135]

UK (Anguilla)/US (US Virgin Islands) – 1993

In this agreement, concluded on the same day as the UK (BVI) and US (Puerto Rico, USVI) treaty,[136] the UK and the US established a one-segment maritime boundary, surely one of the shortest in the world, dividing the waters between the island of Anguilla and the US Virgin Islands.

Presumably following the equidistance method, as announced in the preamble, the treaty established a one-segment boundary, about 1.34 nautical miles long, which joined by a geodetic line the two following coordinates: (a) 17°57′51″N and 63°53′53″W; and (b) 17°56′37″N and 63°53′20″W. That was how this simple two-point maritime boundary maritime boundary was drawn between two small island territories.

Colombia/Jamaica – 1993

Colombia and Jamaica signed a treaty in 1993,[137] in order to establish their maritime boundary – between San Andrés Archipelago and the Colombian mainland coast on the one hand, and Jamaica on the other – as well as a joint regime area between San Andrés Archipelago and Jamaica's marine areas.

The background to the agreement was a number of renewable fishing agreements concluded in the 1980s allowing Jamaican flag vessels to undertake fishing activities (according to certain quotas) within the 12-nautical-mile area of Bajo Nuevo and Serranilla Cays.

The maritime boundary line runs along four segments, from east to west, from point 1 (14°29′37″N and 78°38′00″W) to point 4 (14°44′10″N and 74°30′50″W), and from there eastwards in the direction of a fifth point (15°02′00″N and 73°27′30″W), where the delimitation between Colombia and Haiti intersects the dividing line to be decided by Jamaica and Haiti.

The maritime boundary was then constituted by a slightly modified median line, taking as base point the island of Providencia in the Archipelago, Jamaica and the westernmost point of the maritime boundary between Colombia and Haiti. However, the area of Serranilla and Bajo Nuevo was left undelimited and hence brought about the establishment of a Joint Regime Area.[138]

The Joint Regime Area,[139] excluding the 12-nautical-mile zone drawn around the Colombian Cays of Serranilla and Bajo Nuevo, provided for a regime of joint administration, control, exploration and exploitation of living and non-living resources. Jamaica thus recognised Colombia's sovereignty over those rocks, as well as the possibility of projecting a territorial sea. Similarly, both States recognised each other's right to explore and exploit the living and non-living resources of that zone.[140]

Cuba/Jamaica – 1994

The 1994 agreement between Cuba and Jamaica[141] on the delimitation of their maritime boundary was the second agreement to be signed by Jamaica concerning maritime limits. The two States signed this agreement, concerning their EEZs and continental shelves, in the year on which the Law of the Sea Convention came into force.

The Parties stated, in Article 1, that "the equidistance method is the equitable solution" for the establishment of the delimitation line between their EEZ and continental shelves. The boundary, hence, runs in an east-west direction and uses geodesic lines to join 106 points, the coordinates of which are established in Article 2 of the agreement. Judging by the number of turning points, it appears possible to assert that this is a case of strict equidistance.

The agreement also established that from point 106 (19°15′47″N and 78°22′09″W), the delimitation line would proceed in a westerly direction up to a point to be determined by subsequent agreement, presumably with the UK (Cayman Islands).[142]

France (Guadeloupe)/UK (Montserrat) – 1996

This first Anglo-French maritime boundary treaty concerning their Caribbean possessions[143] stated, in its Article 1, that the delimitation between France's overseas department of Guadeloupe and the UK's territory of Montserrat shall be based upon the "principle" of equidistance.

Pursuant to its preamble, the Parties drew a line in accordance with the method of equidistance. The maritime boundary is hence constructed by joining five points with geodesic lines, along a distance of about 74 nautical miles, in a southwest to northeast direction. The boundary starts at point 1 (15°50′31″N and 62°48′50″W), that is, the last point, towards the north, of the maritime boundary between France and Venezuela, and ends at point 5 (16°39′28″N and 61°51′04″W), beyond which the Parties agreed to apply the same equidistance method to join that last point to the tripoint between their maritime areas and that of Antigua and Barbuda.

France (Saint Martin and Saint Barthélemy)/UK (Anguilla) – 1996

The second Anglo-French maritime delimitation treaty,[144] concluded the same day as the previous one, is also based on the "principle" of equidistance and reflects the continuation of the French policy aimed at establishing the maritime boundaries of all of its possessions worldwide.

The boundary line running for a distance of about 83 nautical miles is based on equidistance and follows geodesic lines joining, again from southwest to northeast, eight points whose coordinates are indicated in Article 2. It starts, therefore, at point 1 (17°57′35″N and 63°36′57″W) and ends at point 8 (18°18′29″N and 62°13′59″W).

Like the previous agreement, this treaty provided for a rule concerning the delimitation of points before point 1 and beyond point 8. It established that the line before point 1 (until it reaches the tripoint between the jurisdiction of the Parties and the jurisdiction of the Kingdom of the Netherlands), as well as the line beyond point 8 (until it reaches the tripoint between the jurisdiction of the Parties and that of

Antigua and Barbuda), will be drawn by applying the same method used for establishing all points between 1 and 8 (i.e. the equidistance methodology).

Dominican Republic/UK (Turks and Caicos Islands) – 1996

Just like the other two treaties concluded by the Dominican Republic (with Colombia in 1978 and with Venezuela in 1979), in this agreement concluded in 1996 with the UK[145] the equidistance method seems to have been resorted to.[146] It is to be noted, however, that this agreement has not yet come into force. On the other hand, the archipelagic baseline claim made by the Dominican Republic (Law No. 66–07 of 22 May 2007) does not appear to be consistent with the Law of the Sea Convention and therefore some countries, including the US, have not accepted it.[147]

The text of the agreement does not mention any method and confines itself to declaring that delimitation was being effectuated "in accordance with the principles of international law". Thus, the maritime boundary extends 283 nautical miles along geodesic lines, joining five points, the coordinates of which are indicated in an attachment to the treaty. It starts, towards the west, at point 1 (20°32′43″N and 72°08′50″W) and ends, towards the Atlantic Ocean, at point 5 (22°24′47″N and 67°40′04″W). The line thus established was the object of a seven-nautical-mile adjustment to the north, which appears to reflect the disparity of the respective coastlines.[148]

Mexico/US – 2000

In 2000, Mexico and the US went further in their maritime relations and decided to delimit their overlapping "outer" continental shelves in the Western Gulf of Mexico.[149] One of the drivers for the conclusion of this agreement was the possibility of finding petroleum or natural gas reservoirs across the continental shelf boundary. This includes transboundary hydrocarbons in the deepest portions of the Gulf of Mexico.[150] Even though this agreement represented significant progress for having delimited the "Western Gap", the delimitation of the "Eastern Gap", situated between Mexico, Cuba and the US remains outstanding.

In effecting the delimitation of their continental shelf beyond 200 nautical miles, Mexico and the US determined 16 points, following a simplified equidistance method, whose coordinates are established in Article 1. The line thus established starts at a point 1 (25°42′14.1″N and 91°05′25.0″W) and from there follows in a westerly direction through a number of geodesic lines until it finally reaches point 16 (25°29′49.3″N and 93°26′42.5″W).

Honduras/UK (Cayman Islands) – 2001

The UK, in respect of the Cayman Islands, and Honduras concluded a maritime delimitation agreement in December 2001,[151] following the adoption by Honduras of a system of straight baselines around part of its Caribbean coast in 2000.[152]

The treaty considered the traditional interests of the Cayman Islands in fisheries in areas appertaining to Honduras and "relevant circumstances" of a historical character concerning oil concessions granted by Honduras in the Caribbean Sea.

The boundary was formed by geodesic lines joining three points (A, B and C). It starts, up in the north, along a first segment, from point A (19°27′57″N and 83°35′50″W) following a northwest-southeast direction until point B (17°35′03″N and 82°21′00″W). In this first segment the maritime boundary seems to have been drawn in accordance with the equidistance method between the Swan Islands (*Islas de El Cisne*) and the Cayman Islands.

From there the boundary continues along the 17th parallel of latitude until it reaches 80°49′59″W (point C). Beyond point C, the treaty does not identify any limit although the Parties agreed that, at the appropriate time, the maritime boundary would continue in an easterly direction until it meets the tripoint between the limits of the maritime areas of the two Parties and a third State, Jamaica.

The agreement established also that Honduras would respect Cayman fisheries' rights in Honduran exclusive economic zone in the banks of Rosario and Misteriosa.[153]

Honduras/Mexico – 2005

In April 2005, Mexico and Honduras concluded an agreement delimiting their exclusive economic zones and continental shelves[154] in the Amatique Bay. This agreement is the first to be adopted as a result of the efforts put forward in the framework of the Conference on Maritime Delimitation in the Caribbean. It is therefore the fruit of a multilateral setting established at Mexico's initiative in order to facilitate the negotiation and conclusion of maritime boundary agreements concerning the waters of the Caribbean Sea.

It consists of an equidistance line connecting, in the north, the tripoint of 200 miles from Mexico, Honduras and Cuba; and in the south, the tripoint measured from the coasts of Mexico, Honduras and Belize. The maritime boundary runs therefore along six points (from point HM1 until point XIX).

The equitable character of this agreement has been questioned because the maritime spaces of Belize and Guatemala, which do not seem to have been consulted during negotiations, ended up being enclaved.[155]

Barbados/France (Guadeloupe and Martinique) – 2009

The agreement between France (Guadeloupe and Martinique) and Barbados established the maritime boundary between the overlapping entitlements of the parties.[156] It took three negotiating rounds held in Bridgetown and Paris between May 2006 and November 2007.[157]

Apart from the Parties' desire to "develop relations of good neighbourliness and friendship" between them, the treaty seems to be particularly important for Barbados as a sign of successful cooperation in the region, especially after the

Arbitral Award that settled its maritime boundary, towards the south, with Trinidad and Tobago.

The agreement stated that the line of delimitation was to be based on equidistance "which [wa]s considered an equitable solution in this case" and was constituted by the line joining the points mentioned in Article 2 in geodetic arcs, in a southwest-northeast direction, towards the Atlantic Ocean. The line, hence determined, starts at point 1 (14°06′56.8″N and 59°59′45.6″W)[158] and ends at point 7 (16°01′09.9″N and 57°33′06.7″W), taking into account La Désirade, a French island close to Guadeloupe, which is given full effect, for both the EEZ and the extended continental shelf.

In an interesting and innovative approach, the Parties added two more points defined by their geographical coordinates (points 8 and 9) if the continental shelves of the Parties were to overlap beyond 200 nautical miles.[159]

Grenada/Trinidad and Tobago – 2010

In 2010 Grenada signed a maritime delimitation agreement with Trinidad and Tobago,[160] which is Grenada's first maritime delimitation treaty. After having reached an agreement with Venezuela in 1990, and having settled its maritime boundary with Barbados by arbitration in 2006, Trinidad and Tobago restarted negotiations with Grenada in 2009 so as to establish their maritime boundary and thus (hopefully) close all of its maritime borders.[161]

In its preamble, the agreement makes express reference to Articles 74(1) and 83(1) of the United Nations Convention on the Law of the Sea. It then proceeds to establish a single maritime boundary delimiting the exclusive economic zones and continental shelves of the Parties. The treaty does not mention any method of delimitation, although it can be said that it used the equidistance methodology.

The majority of the line is hence established by joining two points: point TTG1 (11°23′31″N and 61°43′56″W) and point TTG2 (11°59′03″N and 60°54′38″W). The line runs along 60 nautical miles. From then on it continues in a northeast direction in the form of an open-ended maritime boundary along a geodesic azimuth of 58°28′36″ until it reaches the jurisdiction of a third State, in this case Saint Vincent and the Grenadines.

Ecuador/Peru – 2011

Ecuador and Peru concluded their maritime delimitation agreement in 2011 by means of an Exchange of Notes of Identical Content.[162] Prior to that, both countries accepted that the second sentence of point IV of the 1952 Declaration of Santiago applied between them, while not constituting a maritime delimitation agreement in and of itself.[163] Indeed, that provision was considered to have set out a principle applicable between Ecuador and Peru because of the presence of islands near Peru's general maritime zone. Yet, it was still necessary to conclude a proper agreement, and consequently in 2011 Ecuador and Peru reached a comprehensive, all-purpose delimitation agreement which considered the principle established in point IV of the Santiago Declaration.

The implications of this agreement between Ecuador and Peru, which was negotiated and concluded during the proceedings of the *Maritime Dispute* (*Peru* v. *Chile*), cannot be overlooked. In its oral arguments Peru claimed:

> [i]t is clear that even in a geographic situation where the principle set out in the second sentence of point IV of the Santiago Declaration applied – that is, as between Peru and Ecuador because of the presence of islands – the Declaration did not delimit the boundary. That was only done in the 2 May 2011 Exchange of Notes. Still less did the Santiago Declaration delimit a maritime boundary in a geographic situation where the second sentence of point IV did not apply – namely, as between Peru and Chile. That is the boundary that remains to be determined by your Court.[164]

In the agreement of 2 May 2011, Ecuador and Peru, taking into account paragraph IV of the Santiago Declaration, applied the method of the geographical parallel so as to establish their maritime boundary. Moreover, the 2011 agreement contained a specification of the maritime spaces being delimited (i.e. the water column, seabed and subsoil); a precise location of the starting point of the maritime boundary; the course of the maritime boundary seaward of its starting point; the end of the maritime boundary; and even the course of the line delimiting the internal waters adjacent to the Parties' coasts lying landward.[165]

Later on, on 23 November 2012, taking into account their historic exercise of sovereignty and jurisdiction over the area of the Gulf of Guayaquil, as well as the importance that Ecuadorean and Peruvian populations have granted to it as a place of exploitation of natural resources, trade and navigation, Ecuador and Peru made a Joint Declaration on the International Recognition of the Gulf of Guayaquil as a historic bay.[166] The Joint Declaration made reference to the 2011 Agreement and no reference whatsoever to the 1952 Santiago Declaration.

Bahamas/Cuba – 2011

Concluded after 15 years of negotiations, this agreement[167] constitutes the Bahamas' first maritime delimitation agreement. The Bahamas concluded it by following its archipelagic baseline claim that took effect on 8 December 2008.[168] It remains for the Bahamas to establish its maritime boundaries with Haiti, with the US and with the UK (with respect to the Turks and Caicos Islands). Towards the northeast, however, it does not need to effect any maritime delimitation whatsoever.[169]

In its preamble, the agreement considers the right of the Bahamas, as an archipelagic State, to declare archipelagic baselines in a manner consistent with UNCLOS, as well as Cuba's similar right mutatis mutandis relating to its own baselines. Furthermore, it appears that after the conclusion of this treaty, a Norwegian company has started prospecting in the Bahamas' EEZ.

The maritime delimitation is defined by geodesic lines joining 69 coordinates, using as a reference system the World Geodetic System 1984 (WGS 84). It delimits, as applicable, the territorial seas, contiguous zones, exclusive economic zones and continental shelves of the Parties, either declared or "as may be declared at any time in the future".

The maritime boundary, following a northwest-southeast direction, starts in/towards the north at the Cuba/US/Bahamas tripoint (point 1: 20°22′24.8″N and 73°34′56.5″W) and ends in/towards the south at the Cuba/Haiti/Bahamas tripoint (point 69: 23°55′30.0″N and 81°12′55.0″W).[170]

Cuba/Honduras – 2012

After several rounds of negotiations, Cuba and Honduras – two countries that face a number of maritime boundary situations – concluded a maritime delimitation agreement in August 2012. They established, on the basis of "the principle of equity", an adjusted equidistance line between their islands in the Caribbean Sea, in relation to their EEZs and continental shelves.[171]

The agreement also includes the duty to cooperate mutually on the development and implementation of several programmes, including navigation safety, maritime search and rescue, hydrographic surveys, marine scientific research, preservation and protection of the marine environment, and responses to illicit acts against the safety of maritime navigation and the illegal trafficking of drugs and migrants by sea.

The maritime delimitation, which applies to the EEZs and continental shelves of the two countries, is defined by four points following geodetic coordinates indicated in Article II of the treaty.

Costa Rica/Ecuador – 2014

Costa Rica and Ecuador signed a treaty in 2014, which entered into force in 2016. Although the first part of the agreement was signed on 12 March 1985,[172] an additional agreement was concluded in 2014 in which the maritime boundary coordinates were identified. It is important to note that the boundary divides the maritime spaces between Costa Rica's Island of Coco and the Galápagos Islands.

As mentioned before, the maritime boundary established in 1985 aimed at delimiting the overlapping maritime spaces of the Parties in the Pacific Ocean, namely, the maritime zones generated by Costa Rica's Island of Coco and Ecuador's Galápagos Islands. According to Ecuador, the line signed in 1985, though non-ratified, has been respected ever since.[173]

Later, in a bilateral meeting that took place in February 2012, both delegations agreed to start negotiations about a maritime delimitation agreement concerning their marine and submarine areas in the Pacific Ocean, and even about the possibility of a collaboration with the aim of extending their respective continental shelves corresponding to the Island of Coco and Galápagos Islands.[174]

On 16 December 2020, Ecuador made a Joint Partial Submission with Costa Rica regarding the limits of the continental shelf beyond 200 nautical miles from which the breadth of the territorial sea is measured in the Panama Basin. The Joint Submission was made within the period of ten years established by the Convention. It is known that by March 2022, Ecuador will submit a second partial submission for the delineation of the outer limit of its continental shelf in the southern region of the Carnegie Ridge.

France (Saint Martin)/The Netherlands (Sint Maarten) – 2016

The delimitation of the land boundary of Saint Martin Island was made pursuant to a treaty concluded in 1648, the Treaty of Concordia,[175] whereby the Dutch and the French decided upon rules to divide and share the island. That treaty is still in force.

With respect to the maritime boundary, negotiations started in 1996. The first informal meeting took place in Sint Maarten on 24–25 February 1999, followed by a second informal meeting held in Saint Martin on 7–8 June 2000. After a rather long lull, negotiations were re-launched by means of a bilateral informal meeting held in Paris on 12 February 2009.

It was then agreed that, on the east side of this Caribbean island, all issues concerning Oyster Pond (l'Etang aux Huîtres) would be left aside so that negotiations could follow. On the west side, however, the Parties have already expressed their agreement on a line drawn joining three clearly defined points.[176] Negotiations continued, and the parties signed a maritime boundary agreement on 6 April 2016.[177]

France (French Guyana)/Suriname – 2017

Prior to the signature of the 2017 treaty, there was an understanding ("Draft Treaty of 1999")[178] between those two coastal States whereby the said boundary reflects a straight equidistance line, drawn from the middle (midpoint) of the closing line of the estuary of the Maroni River,[179] with a single constant azimuth of 24°30′E.[180] The closing line joins Kwerieman (Suriname) and a point placed in the northeast of the Isere Cape (French Guyana).[181]

The Draft Treaty of 1999 was successfully negotiated following commencement in 1998,[182] yet Suriname expressed to France that they could not sign the agreement immediately. In fact, while negotiating with France, Suriname was having difficulties reaching an agreement with its other neighbour, Guyana. The latter considered the equidistance method as the applicable one, but Suriname rejected it by reason of the coastal configuration which, in its view, rendered the resulting line non-equitable.

The two parties signed a maritime delimitation agreement on 8 November 2017.[183] The line starts in the estuary of River Maroni, which forms the border between French Guyana and Suriname, and continues in two segments. The first segment is constituted by loxodrome 24.5°, from point C1 (5°48′04″N and 53°56′50″W) to point C2 (6°01′55″N and 53°50′32″W). The definitive establishment of this maritime boundary was all the more important because of these CLCS-issued recommendations.[184]

France (Saint Barthélemy and Guadeloupe)/Antigua and Barbuda – 2017

Antigua and Barbuda and France signed an agreement on the delimitation of their maritime spaces on 15 March 2017,[185] on the basis of the principle of good neighbourliness and conscious of the importance of the marine environment for their peoples. Pursuant to Article 1, paragraph 2 of the Agreement, the lines of delimitation "are based on equidistance which is considered and equitable solution in this case".[186]

With regards to the delimitation between Saint Barthélemy and Antigua and Barbuda, it comprises loxodromes joining a set of points indicated in Article 3, paragraph 1 of the agreement.

As per the delimitation between Guadeloupe and Antigua and Barbuda, it comprises loxodromes joining a set of points identified by geographical coordinates indicated in Article 4, paragraph 1 of the treaty.

UK (Anguilla)/Antigua and Barbuda – 2021

On 27 July 2021, the UK (in respect of Anguilla) and Antigua and Barbuda signed their maritime delimitation treaty,[187] establishing an all-purpose maritime boundary on the basis of the principle of good neighbourliness and the importance of the marine environment for their peoples.

The line of delimitation, which is based on equidistance (which is considered an equitable solution in this case), is formed by geodesic lines connecting the points indicated in Article 1, paragraph 2 of the agreement.

As has been the case in other agreements, the parties to this treaty declared in Article 2 that

> the maritime boundary established by this Treaty shall not affect or prejudice in any manner either Party's position with respect to the rules of international law relating to the law of the sea, including those concerned with the exercise of sovereignty, sovereign rights, or jurisdiction with respect to the water column, seabed or subsoil.

With this agreement, Antigua and Barbuda – with the support of the Commonwealth technical assistance since 2014 – has delimited three of its five maritime boundaries. It still needs to conclude the agreements with Saint Kitts and Nevis and with the UK (Montserrat).

Notes

1 The Glossary of this book also includes a classification of all agreements according to the method or methods of maritime delimitation employed. The following categories have been considered in the Glossary: strict equidistance, simplified equidistance, modified equidistance, simplified and modified equidistance, perpendicular to the general direction of the coast, coastal length comparison, parallels and meridians, and composite delimitations, which includes the so-called pragmatic lines.

2 *North Sea Continental Shelf, Judgment, I.C.J. Reports 1969*, p. 3.

3 See also a reference to the "alleged" attempt by Latin American countries to influence the pre-negotiation and negotiation at UNCLOS III, in: Remiro Brotóns (1993), *ibid.*, pp. 120–121. There, the author mentioned a number of national laws, the case of Colombia and Ecuador concerning outrageous baselines, as well as the 1961 closing of Río de la Plata by the 1973 agreement between Argentina and Uruguay.

4 *Case Concerning the Delimitation of the Continental Shelf between the United Kingdom of Great Britain and Northern Ireland, and the French Republic, RIAA*, Vol. 18, pp. 3–413.

5 Note however that during this same period, judicial and arbitral decisions on maritime delimitation were numerous; see: *Continental Shelf* (*Tunisia/Libyan Arab Jamahiriya*)*, Judgment, I.C.J. Reports 1982*, p. 18; *Delimitation of the Maritime Boundary in the Gulf of Maine Area, Judgment, I.C.J. Reports 1984*, p. 246; *Continental Shelf* (*Libyan Arab Jamahiriya/Malta*)*, Judgment, I.C.J. Reports 1985*, p. 13; and *Maritime Delimitation in the Area between Greenland and Jan Mayen, Judgment, I.C.J. Reports 1993*, p. 38. See also: *Case concerning the delimitation of the Maritime Boundary between Guinea and Guinea-Bissau* (*Republic of Guinea v. Republic of Guinea-Bissau*)*, ILR*, Vol. 77, p. 635; *Affaire de la délimitation de la frontière maritime entre la Guinée-Bissau et le Sénégal. Sentence du 31 juillet 1989, RIAA*, Vol. 20, p. 121; and *Case Concerning the Delimitation of Maritime Areas between Canada and France* (*St. Pierre and Miquelon*), award of 10 June 1992, *ILM*, Vol. 31, 1992, p. 1145.

6 *Dispute between Argentina and Chile concerning the Beagle Channel. 18 February 1977, RIAA*, Vol. 21, pp. 53–264.

7 Colson, David A. and Robert W. Smith (eds.), *International Maritime Boundaries*, Vol. VI, pp. 4213–4222.

8 For a discussion on "rocks" as a subcategory of islands, see for instance: *I.C.J. Pleadings, Maritime Delimitation in the Black Sea* (*Romania* v. *Ukraine*). Romania's first round of oral argument (Counsel: Vaughan Lowe), 4 September 2008 (CR 2008/20), pp. 40–54, especially paras. 9–14; and *The South China Sea Arbitration* (*The Republic of the Philippines v. The People's Republic of China*)*, Award of 12 July 2016*, paras. 473 *et seq*., in particular, paras. 478–520 See also, generally: Jayewardene, Hiran W. (1990), *The Regime of Islands in International Law* (Dordrecht: Martinus Nijhoff), and more recently: Guillaume, Gilbert, "Rocks in the Law of the Sea: Some comments on the South China Sea Arbitration Award", (25 February 2021), *EJIL Talk*. Blog of the European Journal of International Law.

9 For instance, 2005 Honduras/Mexico.

10 For instance, 2010 Trinidad and Tobago/Grenada.

11 *Maritime Delimitation and Territorial Questions between Qatar and Bahrain, Merits, Judgment, I.C.J. Reports 2001*, p. 40.

12 *North Sea Continental Shelf, Judgment, I.C.J. Reports 1969*, p. 3.

13 Text of the agreement available at DOALOS' website. For an account of this agreement written by a British author see for instance: Anderson, David (2008), *Modern Law of the Sea. Selected Essays*. Leiden: Martinus Nijhoff, p. 438. For a different approach, which in a certain way restricts the impact of the agreement see: Pulvenis, Jean-François (1985), "Le plateau continental, definition et régime", in: Dupuy, René-Jean and Daniel Vignes, *Traité du Nouveau Droit de la Mer*, Paris: Economica, pp. 284–285. See also generally: Nweihed, Kaldone (1993), in: Charney, J.J. and L.M. Alexander (eds.), *International Maritime Boundaries*, Vol. I, Dordrecht: Martinus Nijhoff, pp. 639–654; and Labrecque, Georges (2004), *Les frontières maritimes internationales. Géopolitique de la délimitation en mer*, Paris: L'Harmattan, pp. 196–200.

14 *Limits in the Seas No. 11 – Continental Shelf Boundary: Trinidad and Tobago – Venezuela*, Issued by the Geographer; and *Limits in the Seas No. 131, Trinidad and*

Tobago: Archipelagic and other Maritime Claims and Boundaries. US Department of State, 31 January 2014.

15 Churchill, Robin and Vaughan Lowe (1988), *The Law of the Sea*, Second Edition Revised and Enlarged, p. 155. This was also recalled by Tullio Treves in a recent pleading before the International Court of Justice, when he stated that at the time of the Santiago Declaration one of the two precedents "concerning delimitation of maritime areas wider than the territorial sea", was the Gulf of Paria Treaty (the other being the 1945 Truman Proclamation on the continental shelf). Treves then added that the treaty "purports to define the respective interests of the contracting parties in the oil-rich bed of the Gulf of Paria. In fact, it draws a line that today can be classified as a delimitation one"; see: *I.C.J. Pleadings, Maritime Dispute* (*Peru* v. *Chile*). Peru's first round of oral argument (Counsel: Tullio Treves), 3 December 2012 (CR 2012/27), para. 35 *et seq*.

16 Nweihed, *ibid*., pp. 641–642.

17 However, the delimitation method can be described as "sui generis"; see: Nweihed, *ibid*., p. 640.

18 Anderson (2008), *ibid*., p. 438.

19 Nweihed, *ibid*., p. 648.

20 Reference be made to agreements concluded in 1970, 1978, 2001 and 2017 (not yet in force). See: www.state.gov/u-s-maritime-boundaries-agreements-and-treaties/ (accessed on 22 March 2022).

21 Treaty of Peace, Friendship, Limits, and Settlement with Republic of Mexico, 2 February 1848. US Congress.

22 Treaty to Resolve pending Boundary Differences and Maintain the Rio Grande and Colorado River as the International Boundary between the United States of America and the United Mexican States (Signature: 23 November 1970; entry into force: 18 April 1972). Text of the treaty available at DOALOS' website. See generally: Smith, Robert and David Colson (1993), in: Charney, J.J. and L.M. Alexander (eds.), *International Maritime Boundaries*, Vol. I, Dordrecht: Martinus Nijhoff, pp. 427–445; and Labrecque, Georges (2004), *ibid*., pp. 211–212.

23 In this regard, see also: *The Chamizal Case* (*Mexico, United States*), *Award 15 June 1911, RIAA*, Vol. 11, pp. 309–347.

24 Smith, Robert and David Colson (1993), in: Charney, J.J. and L.M. Alexander (eds.), *International Maritime Boundaries*, Vol. I, Dordrecht: Martinus Nijhoff, pp. 428–429.

25 Smith and Colson (1993), *ibid*., pp. 432 and 434. In a certain way, this example of State practice seems to be in line with the solution given by the International Court of Justice in the 2007 *Nicaragua* v. *Honduras* judgment in as much as it decided to establish the starting point of the maritime boundary three miles out to sea (15°00′52″N and 83°05′58″W). As it is known, in that case the Parties agreed that the starting point of the boundary should be located some distance from the mouth of the river Coco due to its alluvial deposits causing eastward accretion of Cape *Gracias a Dios*; see: *Territorial and Maritime Dispute between Nicaragua and Honduras in the Caribbean Sea* (*Nicaragua* v. *Honduras*), *Judgment, I.C.J. Reports 2007*, paras. 307 and 311.

26 Mexico and the US were bound by all four 1958 Geneva Conventions, although Mexico only acceded to them in 1966. In terms of jurisdiction, Mexico – apart from its 1946 Presidential Declaration – claimed a 12-nautical-mile territorial sea in 1969. The US, in turn, had claimed a three-nautical-mile territorial sea in 1793. On the other hand, Mexico ratified the Law of the Sea Convention on 18 March 1983.

27 Agreement between the Government of Brazil and the Government of Uruguay Relating to the Maritime Delimitation between Brazil and Uruguay (Signature: 21 July 1972; entry into force: 12 June 1975). Text available at DOALOS' website and DOALOS (1987), *The Law of the Sea: Maritime Boundary Agreements* (*1970–1984*), New York: United Nations, p. 103. See also generally: Jiménez de Aréchaga, Eduardo

(1993), in: Charney and Alexander (eds.), *ibid.*, pp. 785–792; and Labrecque, Georges, *ibid.*, p. 191.

28 Boundary Treaty between Brazil and Uruguay, 12 October 1851.

29 Jiménez de Aréchaga, Eduardo, *ibid.*, p. 786.

30 See, for instance: *Case concerning delimitation of the maritime boundary in the Gulf of Maine Area* (*Canada/United States of America*), Vol. III, Counter-Memorial of Canada, para. 637.

31 *Case concerning delimitation of the maritime boundary in the Gulf of Maine Area* (*Canada/United States of America*), Counter-Memorial of Canada, para. 640.

32 Ortolland and Pirat, *ibid.*, p. 61. Neither of the States was a Party to the 1958 Geneva Conventions while both, at the time, had claimed a 200 nautical mile territorial sea. For a commentary on Brazil's maritime claims, see: Kwiatkowska, Barbara (1993), "Brazil's 1993 Law . . ." *IJMCL*, Vol. 8, pp. 497–506.

33 Treaty between Uruguay and Argentina concerning the Río de la Plata and the Corresponding Maritime Boundary (Signature: 19 November 1973; entry into force: 12 February 1974). Text available at DOALOS' website and also at: DOALOS (1987), *The Law of the Sea: Maritime Boundary Agreements* (*1970–1984*), New York: United Nations, p. 106. See also generally: Jiménez de Aréchaga, Eduardo (1993), in: Charney and Alexander (eds), *ibid.*, pp. 757–776; *Limits in the Seas No. 64, Continental Shelf Boundary: Argentina-Uruguay*. US Department of State, Issued by the Geographer, 24 October 1975; Gros Espiell, Hector (1975), "Le Traité relative au Rio de la Plata et à sa façade maritime", *AFDI*, Vol. 21, pp. 241–249; and Labrecque, Georges (2004), *ibid.*, pp. 191–192.

34 Joint Declaration of the Governments of Argentina and Uruguay, 30 January 1961.

35 *North Atlantic Coast Fisheries Case*. Grounds for the Dissent to the Award on Question V by Dr Luis M. Drago, pp. 203 *et seq*.

36 Note that some countries, including France, the Netherlands, the UK and the US sent notes of protest against that Joint Declaration; see for instance: Roach, J. Ashley and Robert W. Smith (2012), *ibid.*, pp. 38–39; and Remiro Brotóns (1993), pp. 122 and 123. See also Symmons' "List of Alleged Historic Bays"; Symmons, Clive (2008), *Historic Waters in the Law of the Sea. A Modern Re-Appraisal*, Leiden: Martinus Nijhoff, pp. 301 *et seq*. It seems that according to Argentina and Uruguay they would not agree with the interpretation whereby only those rivers flowing directly into the sea were subject to closure; see: Remiro Brotóns (1993), *ibid.*, p. 123.

37 This point is, at the same time, point 23 of the line dividing the river and established pursuant to Article 41 of the Treaty. Note that the 1973 Agreement was thought to be complemented, pursuant to its Articles 66 and 46, by an Exchange of Notes of 11 June 1988 concerning the delimitation of the boundary between Martín García and Timoteo Domínguez Islands. It seems that, so far, there has not been a conclusion of the work of the Commission set up by this Exchange of Notes. The Exchange of Notes constituting an agreement between the Argentine Republic and the Eastern Republic of Uruguay entrusting the Río de la Plata Administrative Commission with the delimitation of the boundary between Martín García and Timoteo Domínguez Islands, of 10 June 1988, is available at DOALOS' website.

38 According to *Limits in the Seas*, this first segment is a bisector. *Limits in the Seas No. 64, ibid.* and *Limits in the Seas No. 123, Uruguay's Maritime Claims and Boundaries*. US Department of State, 27 November 2000.

39 Jiménez de Aréchaga, *ibid.*, p. 761. Pursuant to Article 73 *et seq.*, the Parties established a common fishing zone straddling the boundary; see in this regard: Churchill and Lowe, *ibid.*, p. 200. Note that both Argentina and Uruguay had claimed a 200-nautical-mile territorial sea, and that both countries are Parties to UNCLOS. Argentina ratified it on 1 December 1995 and Uruguay on 10 December 1992.

40 Agreement Concerning Delimitation of Marine and Submarine Areas and Maritime Co-operation between the Republics of Colombia and Ecuador (Signature:

23 August 1975; entry into force: 22 December 1975). Text of the agreement available at DOALOS' website. See also generally: Jiménez de Aréchaga, Eduardo (1993), in: Charney, J.J. and L.M. Alexander (eds.), *ibid.*, pp. 809–817; and Labrecque, Georges (2004), *ibid.*, pp. 184–185. See sketch-map No. 5. Following Latin America tradition, this treaty is also known as "Tratado Liévano-Lucio, 1975". Note that it is Chile's position, in the *Maritime Dispute* (*Peru* v. *Chile*) currently before ICJ's jurisdiction, that the maritime boundary between those two Southeast Pacific coastal States was established by the 1952 Declaration of Santiago. The decision of the Court of 27 January 2014 is analysed *infra*.

41 Colombia has concluded agreements with almost all of its neighbours, namely: with Ecuador (1975); Panama (1976); Costa Rica (1977); Dominican Republic (1978); Haiti (1978); Honduras (1986); and Jamaica (1993). See also: *Territorial and Maritime Questions* (*Nicaragua* v. *Colombia*), *I.C.J. Reports 2012*, paras. 224 *et seq*.

42 Nweihed, p. 618.

43 Note however that the two countries broke diplomatic relations between March 2008 and November 2010 following a cross border incursion into Ecuador by Colombian forces.

44 Tratado Muñoz Vernaza-Suárez of 1916.

45 Colombia was Party to the 1958 Geneva Convention on the Continental Shelf and had claimed a 12-nautical-mile territorial sea, while Ecuador did not ratify the Continental Shelf Convention and had already claimed a 200-nautical-mile territorial sea. Ecuador acceded to UNCLOS on 24 September 2012.

46 Remiro Brotóns criticises this practice whereby, in his view, certain States interpret international law to their own convenience and sign agreements recognising these exorbitant claims to each other; see: Remiro Brotóns, Antonio (1993), *ibid.*, p. 123.

47 The Joint Declaration by the Ministers of Foreign Affairs of Ecuador and Colombia approved studies conducted by the Permanent Commission of Ecuador and Colombia on Limits, and by the Bi-national Technical Commission of the mouth of River Mataje, whereby it was determined that at the mouth of River Mataje, on the Pacific Ocean, the coordinates 1°28′10.49″N and 78°52′07.27″W (WGS 84) was the point at which the land boundary between Ecuador and Colombia reached the sea, in accordance with the 1975 maritime delimitation treaty. See: Ministry of Foreign Affairs of Ecuador.

48 Exchange of Notes constituting an agreement on the delimitation of the exclusive economic zone of Mexico in the bordering area with Cuban waters (Signature: 26 July 1976; entry into force: 26 July 1976). Text available at: DOALOS (1987), *The Law of the Sea: Maritime Boundary Agreements* (*1970–1984*), New York: United Nations, pp. 168–169. See also generally: Nweihed, Kaldone (1993), in: Charney and Alexander (eds), *Ibid.*, pp. 565–576; *Limits in the Seas No. 104, Maritime Boundary: Cuba-Mexico*. US Department of State, Issued by the Geographer, 10 September 1985; and Labrecque, Georges, *ibid.*, pp. 210–211. Note that Cuba has signed maritime delimitation agreements with Mexico (1976), Haiti (1977), the US (1977), Jamaica and the Bahamas (2011).

49 Remiro Brotóns, Antonio (1993), *ibid.*, p. 134.

50 While Cuba had not ratified any of the 1958 Geneva Conventions on the Continental Shelf, Mexico had ratified all of them in 1966. Mexico, in turn, had just adopted a 200-nautical-mile EEZ whereas Cuba had only claimed a three-nautical-mile territorial sea in 1936–1942 and a ten-nautical-mile fishery conservation zone in 1955.

51 Nweihed, *ibid.*, p. 520.

52 Treaty on the Delimitation of Marine and Submarine Areas and Related Matters between the Republic of Panama and the Republic of Colombia (Signature: 20 November 1976; entry into force: 30 November 1977). Text of the treaty available at DOALOS' website and also at *UNTS*, Vol. 1074, p. 221. See also generally: Nweihed, Kaldone (1993), in: Charney, J.J. and L.M. Alexander (eds.), *Ibid.*, pp. 519–535;

Limits in the Seas No. 79, Maritime Boundaries: Colombia-Panama. US Department of State, Issued by the Geographer, 3 November 1978; and Labrecque, Georges (2004), *ibid.*, p. 186. Following the Latin American practice, this treaty is also known as "Tratado Liévano-Boyd, 1976".

53 See, in this regard: *Territorial and Maritime Dispute* (*Nicaragua* v. *Colombia*), *I.C.J. Reports 2012, Declaration of Judge ad hoc Cot*, para. 10: "To be more specific, the Court decided to end the line delimiting the Parties' maritime spaces where that line reached an area delimited by an agreement concluded with a third State. The problem is that those treaty-based delimitations no longer exist, since their object disappears with the substitution of Nicaragua for Colombia as the holder of sovereignty or sovereign rights in the spaces concerned"; and para. 12: "As a result of the disappearance of those agreements, none of the provisions contained therein, particularly those relating to the delimitation of maritime spaces, can be binding on Nicaragua in its relations with third States. Equally, no third State is bound by those provisions in its relations with Nicaragua. In particular, those States' maritime delimitation claims cannot be subject to an agreement, which has become null and void or ceased to exist, that was agreed on the basis of different political and geographical information, and, in particular, on different baselines, with Colombia." See also: *Territorial and Maritime Dispute* (*Nicaragua* v. *Colombia*), *I.C.J. Reports 2012, Declaration of Judge Xue*, para. 15: "The boundary line in the south would virtually produce the effect of invalidating the existing agreements on maritime delimitation that Colombia has concluded with Panama and Costa Rica respectively and drastically changing the maritime relations in the area. Even supposing that these agreements might have indeed infringed upon the maritime entitlements of Nicaragua in the area, it would be much better off for the maintenance of regional stability and public order if the Court just pointed out the direction of the boundary between the Parties in this area, allowing enough space for the States concerned to first draw up their respective boundaries and then readjust their maritime relations."

54 Note however that the ICJ seems to have considered the step-line boundary as a simplified form of equidistance; see: *Territorial and Maritime Dispute* (*Nicaragua* v. *Colombia*), *I.C.J. Reports 2012*, para. 160. Similarly, Colombia stated, in its Counter-Memorial, that it was a median line averaged through the use of parallels and meridians; see: Counter-Memorial of the Republic of Colombia, Vol. I, 11 November 2008, para. 4.143.

55 Nweihed, *ibid.*, p. 527.

56 Remiro Brotóns, Antonio (1993), *ibid.*, p. 123. Panama declared the Gulf of Panama as historic bay in 1956; see for instance: Bouchez, Leo (1964), *ibid.*; Goldie, L.F. (1984), "Historic bays in international law – An impressionistic overview", *Syracuse Journal of International Law and Commerce*, Vol. 11, pp. 211–273; and Symmons, Clive (2008), *ibid.* Note that Colombia was a Party to the 1958 Geneva Convention on the Continental Shelf since 1962, while Panama did not ratify any of the Geneva conventions. Similarly, Colombia had claimed a 12-nautical-mile fishing zone in 1922, and Panama had claimed a 200-nautical-mile territorial sea in 1967.

57 Agreement between the Republic of Haiti and the Republic of Cuba Regarding the Delimitation of the Maritime Boundaries between the Two States (Signature: 27 October 1977; entry into force: 6 January 1978). Text (and commentaries) available at: Nweihed, Kaldone (1993), in: Charney and Alexander, *ibid.*, pp. 551–563. See also: Labrecque, Georges, *ibid.*, pp. 212–213.

58 Nweihed (1993), *ibid.*, p. 553.

59 Nweihed, p. 557. Note, as pointed out earlier, that Cuba did not sign any of the 1958 Geneva Conventions while Haiti was Party to all of them. Yet, both, Cuba, and Haiti, had claimed a 200-nautical-mile EEZ in 1977.

60 Agreement on delimitation of marine and submarine areas and maritime cooperation between the Republic of Colombia and the Dominican Republic (Signature:

13 January 1978; entry into force: 15 February 1979). Text available at DOALOS' website and also at: DOALOS (1987), *The Law of the Sea: Maritime Boundary Agreements (1970–1984)*, New York: United Nations, p. 150. See also generally: Nweihed, Kaldone (1993), in: Charney and Alexander, *ibid.*, pp. 477–490; *Limits in the Seas No. 130, Dominican Republic: Archipelagic and other Maritime Claims and Boundaries*. US Department of State, 31 January 2014; and Labrecque, Georges (2004), *ibid.*, pp. 206–207. Tratado Liévano-Jiménez.

61 Ortolland and Pirat (2010), *ibid.*, p. 102.

62 Nweihed, *ibid.*, p. 477. Note that while Colombia declared its jurisdiction in August 1978, the Dominican Republic had already done so in 1977.

63 A/CONF.62/WP.8/PART I, 7 May 1975.

64 For Nweihed, the agreement constituted "another link in a chain of maritime delimitation treaties concluded in the Caribbean area during the second half of the 1970s." See: Nweihed, *ibid.*, pp. 484–485.

65 It seems that this issue, to a certain extent, was one of the drivers of the beginning of negotiations between Venezuela and the Dominican Republic.

66 Both States were Parties to the Fishing and Continental Shelf Conventions of 1958. Similarly, while Colombia had only claimed a three-nautical-mile territorial sea, in 1977 the Dominican Republic had already claimed a 200-nautical-mile EEZ. See also: Kopela, Sophia (2009), "2007 Archipelagic Legislation of the Dominican Republic: An assessment", *IJMCL*, Vol. 24, pp. 501–533. Colombia has not yet ratified UNCLOS, while the Dominican Republic did so on 10 July 2009.

67 Agreement on Delimitation of the Maritime Boundaries between the Republic of Colombia and the Republic of Haiti (Signature: 17 February 1978; entry into force: 16 February 1979). Text of the agreement available at DOALOS' website and also at: DOALOS (1987), *The Law of the Sea: Maritime Boundary Agreements (1970–1984)*, New York: United Nations, p. 147. See also generally: Nweihed, Kaldone (1993), in: Charney and Alexander, *ibid.*, pp. 491–502; and Labrecque, Georges, *ibid.*, p. 207. In Latin America, (boundary) treaties are usually known by the names of the plenipotentiaries who signed them; in this regard, this treaty is also known as "Tratado Liévano-Brutus, 1978".

68 Note that while Haiti is a Party to all Geneva Conventions, Colombia ratified the Convention on Fishing and on the Continental Shelf. Haiti ratified UNCLOS on 31 July 1996.

69 1975 Colombia/Ecuador; 1976 Colombia/Panama; 1978 Colombia/Dominican Republic; 1978 Colombia/Haiti; and non-ratified 1977 Colombia/Costa Rica.

70 Churchill and Lowe, *ibid.*, p. 197.

71 Maritime Boundary Treaty between the United States of America and the Republic of Venezuela (Signature 28 March 1978; entry into force 24 November 1980). Text of the agreement available at DOALOS' website and also at: DOALOS (1987), *The Law of the Sea: Maritime Boundary Agreements (1970–1984)*, New York: United Nations, p. 126. For an account of the negotiation written by American authors see for instance: Feldman and Colson (1981), *ibid.*, pp. 746–748. See also generally: Nweihed, Kaldone (1993), in: Charney and Alexander (eds.), *ibid.*, pp. 691–703; *Limits in the Seas No. 91, Maritime Boundary: United States–Venezuela*. US Department of State, 21 February 1990; and Labrecque, Georges, *ibid.*, pp. 200–201.

72 Feldman and Colson (1981), *ibid.*, pp. 746 747.

73 Nweihed (1993), *ibid.*, p. 692. It should be recalled that there was a dispute over Aves Island between Venezuela and the Netherlands in the nineteenth century, following the enactment of the US Guano Act in 1856. The dispute was settled by arbitration; see: *Arbitral Award relating to the issue of control and sovereignty over Aves island, raised between Venezuela and the Kingdom of the Netherlands, Decision of 30 June 1865, RIAA*, Vol. 28, pp. 115–124. For an analysis of the so-called guano rush in US history; see: Skaggs, Jimmy M. (1994), *The Great Guano Rush: Entrepreneurs*

and American Overseas Expansion, New York: St. Martin's Press, 352 pp. Under Article 123 of the United Nations Convention on the Law of the Sea, Aves is a rock incapable of sustaining human habitation or economic activity of its own and hence cannot project more than 12 nautical miles of territorial sea. It seems Article 123 of UNCLOS was Venezuela's main concern during UNCLOS III and, eventually, the reason why it decided not to host the closure of the conference in Caracas and to reject the Convention. However, with this agreement, together with agreements concluded by the Netherlands and France with Venezuela, Aves has been recognised full or almost full weight, a move that is contested by the small States of the region.

74 It seems important to emphasise here that both the US and Venezuela share the same approach to drawing maritime boundaries, in the sense that those two States view each case on its own merits and reject any mandatory method to be applied as a "theory" (*sic*) of international law; see: Nweihed, *ibid.*, p. 696.

75 Legault and Hankey (1993), *ibid.*, p. 210.

76 Note that both States were Parties to all four Geneva Conventions, while only the US had already claimed a 200-nautical-mile fishery conservation zone. Venezuela would only follow in July 1978, that is, four months after the conclusion of this treaty. None of them has ratified UNCLOS.

77 Boundary Delimitation Treaty between the Republic Venezuela and the Kingdom of the Netherlands (Signature: 31 March 1978; entry into force: 15 December 1978). Text of the treaty available at DOALOS' website. See also generally: Nweihed, Kaldone (1993), in: Charney, J.J. and L.M. Alexander (eds.), *ibid.*, pp. 615–637; and Labrecque, Georges (2004), *ibid.*, p. 201–202. See also: Molenaar, Erik (2003), "Netherlands Antilles and Aruba", *IJMCL*, Vol. 18, pp. 127–144.

78 Nweihed, *ibid.*, p. 617.

79 Nweihed, *ibid.*, p. 616.

80 *Arbitral award relating to the issue of control and sovereignty over Aves island, raised between Venezuela and the Kingdom of the Netherlands, RIAA*, Vol. 28, pp. 115–124.

81 For a comparison between the treatment given by the Parties to the ABC islands and the situation of Malta in the case Libya/Malta, see: *Continental Shelf* (*Libyan Arab Jamahiriya/Malta*), *Judgment, I.C.J. Reports 1985, Separate Opinion of Judges Ruda, Bedjaoui and Jiménez de Aréchaga*, para. 8.

82 Note that both, the Netherlands and Venezuela were Parties to all four 1958 Geneva Conventions. The Netherlands claimed a three-nautical-mile territorial sea, whereas Venezuela claimed one of 12 nautical miles. Concerning the continental shelf, both the Netherlands and Venezuela claimed one 200 metres deep. Yet, although the Netherlands had already established a 200-nautical-mile fishery zone in 1977, it was only in 1993 that it claimed jurisdiction in matters of fisheries off the Netherland Antilles; see: Molenaar, Erik (2003), "Netherlands Antilles and Aruba", *IJMCL*, Vol. 18, pp. 130–131. The Netherlands ratified UNCLOS on 28 June 1996.

83 Maritime boundaries agreement effected by Exchange of Notes between the United States of America and Mexico (Signature: 24 November 1976; entry into force: 24 November 1976). Text of the Exchange of Notes available at DOALOS' website and also at: DOALOS (1987), *The Law of the Sea: Maritime Boundary Agreements (1970–1984)*, New York: United Nations, p. 258.

84 Treaty on Maritime Boundaries between the United Mexican States and the United States of America (Caribbean Sea and Pacific Ocean) (Signature: 4 May 1978; entry into force: 13 November 1997). Text of the agreement available at DOALOS website. For an account of the treaty from the US point of view see for instance: Feldman and Colson (1981), *ibid.*, pp. 743–745. See also generally: Smith, Robert and David Colson (1993), in: Charney, J.J. and L.M. Alexander, *ibid.*, pp. 427–445; and Labrecque, Georges, *ibid.*, pp. 211–212.

85 Legault and Hankey (1993), *ibid.*, p. 207.

86 Feldman and Colson (1981), *ibid.*, p. 743.

87 Mexico and the US acceded to all four Geneva LOS Conventions. Both States had also claimed a 200-nautical-mile fishing zone.

88 Treaty on the delimitation of marine and submarine areas between the Republic of Venezuela and the Dominican Republic (Signature: 3 March 1979; entry into force: 15 January 1982). Text available at DOALOS' website and also at DOALOS (1987), *The Law of the Sea: Maritime Boundary Agreements (1970–1984)*, New York: United Nations, p. 135. See generally: Nweihed (1993), in: Charney and Alexander (eds.), *ibid.*, pp. 577–590; *Limits in the Seas No. 130, Dominican Republic: Archipelagic and other Maritime Claims and Boundaries*. US Department of State, 31 January 2014; and Labrecque, Georges (2004), *ibid.*, pp. 202–203.

89 While Dominican Republic was Party to all Geneva Conventions except the one on the Territorial Sea, Venezuela was Party to all. Both States had already claimed a 200-nautical-mile economic zone.

90 Treaty concerning Delimitation of Marine Areas and Maritime Cooperation between the Republic of Costa Rica and the Republic of Panama (Signature: 2 February 1980; entry into force: 11 February 1982). Text of the treaty available at DOALOS' website. See also generally: Nweihed, Kaldone (1993), in: Charney, J.J. and L.M. Alexander (eds.), *Ibid.*, pp. 537–549; *Limits in the Seas No. 97, Maritime Boundaries: Costa Rica–Panama*. US Department of State, Issued by the Geographer, 6 December 1982; and Labrecque, Georges (2004), *Ibid.*, p. 209–210. Following the Latin American practice, this treaty is also known as "Tratado Calderón-Ozores, 1980".

91 Nweihed (1993), *ibid.*, p. 543. Note however that in its Application for Permission to Intervene, Costa Rica considered that it had delimited its maritime boundary in the Caribbean with Panama "with an equidistant line"; see: *Territorial and Maritime Dispute* (*Nicaragua* v. *Colombia*), Application for Permission to Intervene by the Government of Costa Rica, 25 February 2010, p. 6.

92 Remiro Brotóns, A., *ibid.*, p. 123. Note that while Panama was not a Party to any of the Geneva Conventions, Costa Rica was, since 1972, Party to the Geneva Convention on the High Seas and to the Convention on the Continental Shelf. Panama, in turn, proclaimed a 200-nautical-mile territorial sea in 1967 whereas Costa Rica claimed in 1975 an EEZ (formerly known as patrimonial sea). Panama ratified UNCLOS on 1 July 1996.

93 Delimitation Treaty between the Government of the French Republic (Martinique and Guadeloupe) and the Government of the Republic of Venezuela (Signature: 17 July 1980; entry into force: 28 January 1983). Text of the treaty available at DOALOS' website and also: DOALOS (1987), *The Law of the Sea: Maritime Boundary Agreements (1970–1984)*, New York: United Nations, p. 132. For an account of this agreement written by a French author, see for instance: Guillaume, Gilbert (1983), "Les accords de délimitation maritime passés par la France", *Colloque de Rouen: Perspectives du droit de la mer à l'issue de la 3e conférence des nations unies*, Paris: Pedone, pp. 276 *et seq*. See also generally: Nweihed, Kaldone (1993), in: Charney, J.J. and L.M. Alexander (eds.), *ibid.*, pp. 603–614; and Labrecque, Georges (2004), *ibid.*, pp. 203–204.

94 It started with Martinique and Guadeloupe (1980) to continue then with French Guyana (1981). More recently, it concluded treaties with the Netherlands, concerning Sint Maarten (2016), and with Suriname (2017). France still has the following pending delimitations in the Caribbean: Antigua and Barbuda and Saint Kitts and Nevis.

95 Guillaume, Gilbert (1983), *ibid.*, p. 278. In this regard, one author has referred to a "universal policy" of the French Republic to provide all of its overseas territories with maritime boundaries; see: Nweihed (1993), p. 604.

96 Gilbert Guillaume, at the time Legal Adviser to the Quai d'Orsay, put it this way: "dans le domaine de la pêche, la pratique ancestrale des pêcheurs martiniquais et

guadeloupéens d'exercer leurs activités à proximité des côtes des Etats voisins, dans des eaux qui ont longtemps appartenu à la haute mer avant de passer sous juridiction nationale, conduit à négocier dans le meilleurs délais des accords de délimitation"; see: Guillaume, Gilbert (1983), *ibid.*, p. 278.

97 Nweihed, p. 609. *Cf.* Guillaume, Gilbert (1983), *ibid.*, p. 283. It has also been claimed that the strict equidistance method was not applied but rather adjusted, giving a reduced effect to the economic zone of that Venezuelan rock; that is, approximately an 11% reduction in relation to what the equidistance method would have given it. See also *supra* US (Puerto Rico and Virgin Islands)/Venezuela.

98 Note that both States were Parties to the 1958 Geneva Convention on the Continental Shelf, and formulated Declarations affecting Article 6. In 1978, France adopted legislation to create economic zones off the coasts of Guadeloupe and Martinique; see: *Décret 78–277 du 6 mars 1978 portant création d'une zone économique au large des côtes du département de la Martinique*; and *Décret 78–276 du 6 mars 1978 portant création d'une zone économique au large des côtes du département de la Guadeloupe*. Venezuela, on the other hand, had a 12-nautical-mile territorial sea and a 200-nautical-mile EEZ in 1978.

99 Agreement between the Government of Brazil and the Government of France Relating to the Maritime Delimitation between Brazil and French Guyana (Signature: 30 January 1981; entry into force: 19 October 1983). Text of the agreement available at DOALOS' website and also at DOALOS (1987), *The Law of the Sea: Maritime Boundary Agreements* (*1970–1984*), New York: United Nations, p. 87. For an account of the treaty from a French point of view see for instance: Guillaume (1983), *ibid.*, pp. 276 *et seq*. See also generally: Jiménez de Aréchaga, Eduardo, (1993), in: Charney and Alexander (eds), *ibid.*, pp. 777–783; and Labrecque, Georges (2004), *ibid.*, p. 193. It is interesting to note that this agreement takes into account the provisions of the Treaty of Utrecht of 11 April 1713, as well as the Arbitral Tribunal of the Swiss Federal Council of 1 December 1900 (see preamble of the agreement).

100 Guillaume, Gilbert (1983), *ibid.*, p. 278.

101 Ortolland and Pirat (2010), *ibid.*, p. 109.

102 Guillaume, Gilbert (1983), *ibid.*, p. 283.

103 Brazil was not a Party to any of the 1958 Geneva Conventions, whereas France was Party to the 1958 Geneva Convention on the Continental Shelf. Later, Brazil ratified UNCLOS on 22 December 1988. Similarly, while Brazil had claimed a 200-nautical-mile territorial sea, France, by means of Decree 77–170 of 25 February 1977, had created an exclusive economic zone in French Guyana.

104 Convention on delimitation between the Government of the French Republic (Martinique) and the Government of Saint Lucia (Signature: 4 March 1981; entry into force: 4 March 1981). Text of the agreement available at DOALOS' website and also at: DOALOS (1987), *The Law of the Sea: Maritime Boundary Agreements* (*1970–1984*), New York: United Nations, p. 129. For an account of the treaty written by a French author, see for instance: Guillaume (1983), *ibid.*, p. 282. See also generally: Nweihed, Kaldone (1993), in: Charney and Alexander, *ibid.*, pp. 591–601; and Labrecque, *ibid.*, p. 204.

105 Guillaume (1983), *ibid.*, p. 282.

106 It seems that this point that does no coincide entirely with point 1 in the France-Barbados agreement of 2009.

107 While Saint Lucia had not acceded to any of 1958 Conventions, France was a Party to the 1958 Geneva Convention on the Continental Shelf (with a Declaration effecting Article 6). France, by Decree 78–277 of 3 June 1978, had created an exclusive economic zone for Martinique. Saint Lucia had an assumed three-nautical-mile territorial sea. Saint Lucia ratified UNCLOS on 27 March 1985.

108 Note however that during this same period, judicial and arbitral decisions on maritime delimitation were numerous; see: *Continental Shelf* (*Tunisia/Libyan Arab*

Jamahiriya), Judgment, I.C.J. Reports 1982, p. 18; *Delimitation of the Maritime Boundary in the Gulf of Maine Area, Judgment, I.C.J. Reports 1984*, p. 246; *Continental Shelf (Libyan Arab Jamahiriya/Malta), Judgment, I.C.J. Reports 1985*, p. 13; and *Maritime Delimitation in the Area between Greenland and Jan Mayen, Judgment, I.C.J. Reports 1993*, p. 38. See also: *Case concerning the delimitation of the Maritime Boundary between Guinea and Guinea-Bissau* (*Republic of Guinea v. Republic of Guinea-Bissau*), *ILR*, Vol. 77, p. 635; *Affaire de la délimitation de la frontière maritime entre la Guinée-Bissau et le Sénégal. Sentence du 31 juillet 1989, RIAA*, Vol. 20, p. 121; and *Case Concerning the Delimitation of Maritime Areas between Canada and France* (*St. Pierre and Miquelon*), award of 10 June 1992, *ILM*, Vol. 31, 1992, p. 1145.

109 *Dispute between Argentina and Chile concerning the Beagle Channel. 18 February 1977, RIAA*, Vol. 21, pp. 53–264.

110 Treaty of Peace and Friendship between Chile and Argentina (Signature: 29 November 1984.; entered into force: 2 May 1985). Text of the treaty available at DOALOS' website. See also generally: Jiménez de Aréchaga, Eduardo (1993), in: Charney, J.J. and L.M. Alexander (eds.), *ibid.*, pp. 719–755; and Labrecque, Georges (2004), *ibid.*, pp. 186–191.

111 *Case concerning a dispute between Argentina and Chile concerning the Beagle Channel. Award of 18 February 1977. RIAA*, Vol. 21, pp. 53–264.

112 Jiménez de Aréchaga, *ibid.*, p. 721.

113 Note that at the time, neither Argentina nor Chile had ratified the Law of the Sea Convention, although Argentina would sign it shortly after, in October 1984, and Chile on 25 August 1997. Neither did either of them sign the 1958 Geneva Conventions on the Continental Shelf. Argentina, on the one hand, had claimed a 200-nautical-mile territorial sea, whereas Chile, while having declared a three-nautical-mile territorial sea, also claimed a 200-nautical-mile zone of exclusive sovereignty.

114 See: position of Chile, contained in Note by Chile, dated 26 May 2020, and Note dated 11 May 2020; and the position of Argentina contained in the Note of the Permanent Mission of the Argentine Republic to the United Nations in New York, dated 3 September 2021; both available at United Nations DOALOS website.

115 Treaty on the Delimitation of Marine and Submarine Areas and Maritime Cooperation between the Republic of Colombia and the Republic of Costa Rica, in addition to the Treaty signed at San José on 17 March 1977 (Signature: 6 April 1984; entry into force: 20 February 2001). Text of the treaty available at DOALOS' website. See generally: Nweihed (1993), in: Charney and Alexander (eds.), *ibid.*, pp. 801–808 (although there is a mistake in the text of the publication, because it shows the 1977 agreement), and Charney and Smith (eds.), Vol. IV, pp. 2641–2643; and Labrecque, *ibid.*, pp. 185–186. See also: *Nicaragua* v. *Colombia*, Counter-Memorial of the Republic of Colombia, 11 November 2008, para. 4.162.

116 Colombia is a Party to the Geneva Conventions on Fishing and on the Continental Shelf and, as Costa Rica, has claimed a 200-nautical-mile EEZ. Similarly, Costa Rica ratified UNCLOS on 21 September 1992, but Colombia has not.

117 One should also take into account the statement by the International Court of Justice in its 2012 judgment *Nicaragua* v. *Colombia*: "the treaties which Colombia has concluded with Jamaica and Panama and the treaty which it has signed with Costa Rica cannot confer upon Colombia rights against Nicaragua and, in particular, can not entitle it, vis-à-vis Nicaragua, to a greater share of the area in which its maritime entitlements overlap with those of Nicaragua than it would otherwise receive"; para. 227. The same clause seems to apply to the treaties that Colombia has concluded with Jamaica and Panama.

118 Treaty concerning Maritime Delimitation between the Republic of Colombia and the Republic of Honduras (Signature: 2 August 1986; entry into force: 20 December 1999). Text of the treaty available at DOALOS' website and at *UNTS*, Vol. 2093,

p. 295. See also generally: Nweihed, Kaldone (1993), in: Charney, J.J. and L.M. Alexander (eds.), *ibid.*, pp. 503–518; and Labrecque, Georges (2004), *ibid.*, p. 207–208. Following the Latin American practice, this treaty is also known as "Tratado Ramírez-López, 1986" or "Tratado López-Ramírez, 1986".

119 The Court, in its 2007 Judgment on *Nicaragua* v. *Honduras*, did not rely on the 1986 Treaty as an appropriate endpoint for the maritime delimitation at stake. It held that "any delimitation between Honduras and Nicaragua extending east beyond the 82nd meridian and north of the 15th parallel . . . would not actually prejudice Colombia's right because Colombia's rights under this Treaty do not extend north of the 15th parallel"; see: *I.C.J. Reports 2007*, para. 316. In this regard, Honduras claimed "an actual, present, direct and concrete interest of a legal nature in the delimitation of the maritime areas in the zone to the north of the boundary line deriving from the 1986 Treaty". It hence raised, according to the Court, mainly two issues concerning its interest of a legal nature: "whether the 2007 Judgment has settled the entire maritime boundary between Honduras and Nicaragua in the Caribbean Sea and what effect, if any, the decision of the Court in the pending proceedings will have on the rights that Honduras enjoys under the 1986 Treaty", see: Application for Permission to Intervene by Honduras, 10 June 2010, para. 12 and *Territorial and Maritime Dispute* (*Nicaragua* v. *Colombia*)*, Application for Permission to Intervene, Judgment, I.C.J. Reports 2011*, p. 420, para. 59. The Court thus held that Honduras had failed to satisfy it that it had an interest of a legal nature that could be affected by its decision in the main proceedings, and hence found that the Application for permission to intervene could not be granted; see: *Territorial and Maritime Dispute* (*Nicaragua* v. *Colombia*)*, Application for Permission to Intervene, Judgment, I.C.J. Reports 2011*, p. 420, paras. 64–65 and 76.

120 Application for Permission to Intervene by Honduras, 10 June 2010, para. 12: "The 1986 Treaty between Honduras and Colombia vests rights in Honduras in that maritime zone. Thus, any claim by Nicaragua to maritime zones north of the 15th parallel is liable to affect the rights and interests of Honduras as a third State, as the Court recognised in its Judgment in October 2007."

121 In a diplomatic Note to Honduras dated 8 September 1986, Nicaragua said that the treaty divided between Honduras and Colombia "extensive zones that include insular territories, adjacent seas and continental shelf that historically, geographically and legally correspond to the sovereignty of Nicaragua"; see: *I.C.J. Reports 2007*, para. 59.

122 Counter-Memorial of the Republic of Honduras, p. 2.

123 As stated earlier, Colombia was a Party to the 1958 Convention and has not yet signed the LOS Convention. Honduras, in turn, as stated before signed the Law of the Sea Convention in 1993. Colombia and Honduras had claimed a 200-nautical-mile EEZ.

124 Agreement on Maritime Delimitation between the Government of the French Republic and the Government of Dominica (Signature: 7 September 1987; entry into force: 23 December 1988). The text of the agreement is available at DOALOS' website. See also generally: Nweihed (1993), in: Charney and Alexander (eds.), *ibid.*, pp. 705–715; and Labrecque, *ibid.*, pp. 204–205.

125 Dundas, Carl W. (1991), *Practical steps in negotiating maritime boundary agreements: a guide to small states*, London: Commonwealth Fund for Technical Assistance, Technical Assistance Group, 282 pp.

126 CARICOM, Delimitation of Maritime Boundaries within CARICOM, Background Paper for Report. On the origins of the negotiation, see: Guillaume, Gilbert (1983), *ibid.*, p. 284. "nous serions prêts à accroître la zone économique dominicaine dans le secteur Atlantique par rapport à l'équidistance, en nous inspirant des solutions dégagées dans l'affaire de délimitation maritime du plateau continental en mer du Nord." See also in this regard the reference to Bangladesh's claims of State practice, where a

State would have been cut off if the equidistance method had been used: *Delimitation of the maritime boundary in the Bay of Bengal (Bangladesh/Myanmar), Judgment, ITLOS Reports 2012*, para. 285. Together with this example, Bangladesh mentioned, in the region, the 1990 agreement between Venezuela and Trinidad and Tobago, see: *Barbados/Trinidad and Tobago, Award of 11 April 2006, RIAA*, Vol. 27, para. 342.

127 While Dominica had not ratified any of the Geneva Conventions it did sign the Law of the Sea Convention, like France did. By an Act of 1981 Dominica had established a 200-nautical-mile EEZ while France did the same for its overseas territories, as pointed out earlier. Dominica ratified UNCLOS on 24 October 1991.

128 Treaty between the Republic of Trinidad and Tobago and the Republic of Venezuela on the delimitation of marine and submarine areas (Signature: 18 April 1990; entry into force: 23 July 1991). Text of the treaty available at DOALOS' website. See generally: Nweihed (1993), Charney and Alexander (eds.), *ibid.*, pp. 655–673; *Limits in the Seas No. 131, Trinidad and Tobago: Archipelagic and other Maritime Claims and Boundaries*. US Department of State, 31 January 2014; and Labrecque, *ibid.*, pp. 196–200. On 12 May 2009 Trinidad and Tobago presented a submission to the Commission on the Limits of the Continental Shelf.

129 Churchill and Lowe, *ibid.*, p. 197.

130 In this first segment, an author has claimed that, towards the north, the boundary could also meet "the potential tri-junction with Grenada"; see: Nweihed, *ibid.*, p. 665.

131 This last issue was discussed upon in the arbitration between Barbados and Trinidad and Tobago; see *Award*, para. 341. Note that Trinidad and Tobago was a Party to all Geneva Conventions and ratified UNCLOS on 25 April 1986. Venezuela, although also a Party to all Geneva Conventions, has refused so far to ratify UNCLOS. Similarly, Trinidad and Tobago claimed a 200-nautical-mile EEZ in 1986, as did Venezuela in 1978.

132 Agreement between the Government of the United Kingdom of Great Britain and Northern Ireland and the Government of the United States of America on the Delimitation in the Caribbean of a Maritime Boundary between Puerto Rico/US Virgin Islands and the British Virgin Islands (Signature: 5 November 1993; entry into force: 1 June 1995). Text of the agreement available at DOALOS' website. See also generally: Smith, Robert W. and David A. Colson (2004), in: Charney and Alexander, *International Maritime Boundaries*, Vol. III, pp. 2161–2170; *Limits in the Seas No. 115, United States–United Kingdom Maritime Boundaries in the Caribbean*. US Department of State, 11 April 1994; and Labrecque, Georges (2004), *ibid.*, pp. 214–215. For the second agreement see *infra* section 3.2.6. See also: Carleton, C.M. (1994), "The British Virgin Islands/Puerto Rico and US Virgin Islands – Anguilla/US Virgin Islands, *IJMCL*, Vol. 9, pp. 253–260.

133 *Limits in the Seas No. 115*, pp. 2–3.

134 *Limits in the Seas No. 115*, pp. 4–5.

135 While the US has not so far ratified UNCLOS, the UK only acceded to it on 25 July 1997. Concerning national jurisdiction, on 1 March 1977 the US enacted the Fishery Conservation and Management Act which included the waters around Puerto Rico and the US Virgin Islands. The Governor of the British Virgin Islands, in turn, established on 9 March 1977 a 200-nautical-mile fisheries zone. For a political analysis of how the UK acceded to UNCLOS, see an article by a former UK Foreign Minister, available at: www.project-syndicate.org/commentary/the-law-of-the-sea-s-next-wave-by-david-miliband.

136 Treaty between the Government of the United Kingdom of Great Britain and Northern Ireland and the Government of the United States of America on the Delimitation in the Caribbean of a Maritime Boundary between the US Virgin Islands and Anguilla (Signature: 5 November 1993; entry into force: 1 June 1995). Text of the agreement available at DOALOS' website. See also generally: Smith, Robert W. and David A. Colson (2004), *ibid.*, pp. 2171–2178; *Limits in the Seas No. 115, United*

States–United Kingdom Maritime Boundaries in the Caribbean. US Department of State, 11 April 1994; and Labrecque, Georges (2004), *ibid*., pp. 214–215.

137 Treaty on Maritime Delimitation between Jamaica and the Republic of Colombia (Signature: 12 November 1993; entry into force: 14 March 1994). Text of the agreement available at DOALOS' website and also at *UNTS*, Vol. 1776, p. 27. See also generally: Nweihed, Kaldone G. (2004), in Vol. III, pp. 2179–2204; *Limits in the Seas No. 125, Jamaica's Maritime Claims and Boundaries*. US Department of State, 5 February 2004; Labrecque, Georges (2004), *ibid*., p. 208.

138 See for instance: *Nicaragua* v. *Colombia, I.C.J. Reports 2012*, paras. 152 and 160.

139 For the construction of the Joint Regime Area according to Colombia see: Counter-Memorial of the Republic of Colombia, Vol. I, 11 November 2008, paras. 4.184 *et seq*.

140 See generally: Ortolland and Pirat (2010), *ibid*., pp. 106–107.

141 Agreement between the Government of Jamaica and the Government of Republic of Cuba on the delimitation of the maritime boundary between the two States (Signature: 18 February 1994; entry into force: 18 July 1995). Text of the agreement available at DOALOS' website. See also generally: Nweihed, Kaldone G. (2004), in *International Maritime Boundaries*, Vol. III, pp. 2205–2218; *Limits in the Seas No. 125, Jamaica's Maritime Claims and Boundaries*. US Department of State, 05 February 2004; and Labrecque, Georges (2004), *Les frontières maritimes internationales. Géopolitique de la délimitation en mer*, Paris: L'Harmattan, p. 209.

142 At the time of signature, Cuba and Jamaica were Parties to UNCLOS, which would enter into force on 16 November 1994. Cuba ratified UNCLOS on 15 August 1984, while Jamaica did so on 21 March 1983.

143 Agreement on maritime delimitation between the Government of the French Republic and the Government of the United Kingdom of Great Britain and Northern Ireland concerning Guadeloupe and Montserrat (Signature: 27 June 1996; entry into force 15 January 1997). Text of the agreement available at DOALOS' website. See also generally: Anderson, David H. (2004), in Vol. III, pp. 2227–2233; Labrecque, Georges (2004), *ibid*., p. 215.

144 Agreement on maritime delimitation between the Government of the French Republic and the Government of the United Kingdom of Great Britain and Northern Ireland concerning Saint Martin and Saint Barthélemy (Signature: 27 June 1996; entry into force: 15 January 1997). Text of the agreement available at DOALOS' website. See also generally: Anderson, David H. (2004), in Vol. III, pp. 2219–2225; Labrecque, Georges (2004), *ibid*., p. 215.

145 Agreement between the Government of the Dominican Republic and the Government of Great Britain and Northern Ireland regarding the Delimitation of the Maritime Limit between the Dominican Republic and the Turks and Caicos Islands (Signature: 2 August 1996). See also generally: Anderson, David H. (2004), in Vol. III, pp. 2235–2243; *Limits in the Seas No. 130, Dominican Republic: Archipelagic and other Maritime Claims and Boundaries*. US Department of State, 31 January 2014; and Labrecque, Georges (2004), *ibid*., p. 215.

146 Ortolland and Pirat, *ibid*. p. 102.

147 *Limits in the Seas No. 130, ibid*., pp. 2–3.

148 The UK had not yet ratified UNCLOS; it would do so the following year. The Dominican Republic only ratified UNCLOS on 10 July 2009.

149 Treaty between the Government of the United States of America and the Government of the United Mexican States on the Delimitation of the Continental Shelf in the Western Gulf of Mexico beyond 200 Nautical Miles (Signature: 9 June 2000; entry into force: 17 January 2001). Text of the agreement available at DOALOS' website. See: Smith, Robert W. (2002), in Vol. IV, pp. 2621–2633; Labrecque, Georges (2004), *ibid*., p. 212. See also: Baldet-Ladan, G. (2000), "Le traité concernant la délimitation du plateau continental conclu entre les Etats-unis et le Mexique le 9 juin 2000", *Annuaire du Droit de la Mer*, Vol. 5, pp. 45–54.

150 McLaughlin, Richard G. (2008), "Hydrocarbon Development in the Ultra-Deepwater Boundary Region of the Gulf of Mexico: Time to Reexamine a Comprehensive U.S.-Mexico Cooperation Agreement", *Ocean Development and International Law*, Vol. 39, pp. 1–31.

151 Treaty between the Government of the Republic of Honduras and the Government of the United Kingdom of Great Britain and Northern Ireland concerning the delimitation of the maritime areas between the Cayman Islands and the Republic of Honduras (Signature: 4 December 2001; entry into force: 1 March 2002). Text of the agreement available at DOALOS' website. See also generally: López Contreras, Carlos and Michael Wood (2005), Colson, David A. and Robert W. Smith, *International Maritime Boundaries*, Vol. V, pp. 3564–3574; Labrecque, Georges (2004), *ibid*., p. 216.

152 *Limits in the Seas No. 124, Straight Baseline Claim: Honduras*. US Department of State, 28 June 2001.

153 Ortolland and Pirat (2010), *ibid*., p. 103.

154 Maritime Delimitation Treaty between the Government of the United Mexican States and the Government of the Republic of Honduras (Signature: 18 April 2005; entry into force: 30 November 2006). See for instance: Meese, Richard (2005), "Le traité du 18 avril 2005 entre le Honduras et les Etats-Unis du Mexique sur la délimitation maritime", *Annuaire du droit de la mer*, Vol. 10, pp. 237–243; and also López Contreras, Carlos (2011), in: Colson, David A. and Robert W. Smith (eds.), *International Maritime Boundaries*, Vol. VI, pp. 4202–4212.

155 Ortolland and Pirat (2010), *ibid*., p. 103. The author goes on to compare this situation with the situation in the *North Sea* cases; see: *North Sea Continental Shelf, Judgment, I.C.J. Reports 1969*, p. 3. On the other hand, as mentioned before, Mexico ratified UNCLOS in 1983, whereas Honduras did so only ten years later, on 5 October 1993.

156 Agreement between the Government of the French Republic and the Government of Barbados on the delimitation of the maritime space between France and Barbados (Signature: 15 October 2009; entry into force: not available). See also: Dundas, Carl W. (2011), in: Colson, David A. and Robert W. Smith (eds.), *International Maritime Boundaries*, Vol. VI, pp. 4223–4231.

157 By means of Decree No. 99–324 of 21 April 1999, France determined the baselines from which the breadth of the territorial sea of France (Martinique and Guadeloupe) was to be measured. Barbados ratified UNCLOS on 12 October 1993 and France, in turn, did so on 11 April 1996.

158 This point seems to be the triple point (tripoint) with Santa Lucia, according to the 1981 agreement between France and Santa Lucia.

159 In this regard, it seems that the Parties are envisaging the possibility of presenting both submissions to the CLCS. In the case of France, however, that is to be followed by the French Programme for the Extension of the Continental Shelf (*Programme français d'extension du plateau continental* – EXTRAPLAC). Since it appears that the extension of the French continental shelf in the Antilles could cover an area of around 5000 km^2 and that Barbados could claim exactly the same arguments, the cooperation between these two countries should be straightforward.

160 Treaty between the Republic of Trinidad and Tobago and Grenada on the Delimitation of Marine and Submarine Areas (Signature: 21 April 2010). Text of the treaty available at www.gov.gd/egov/docs/other/delimitation_treaty_trinidad_tobago_grenada.pdf. See also: *Limits in the Seas No. 131, Trinidad and Tobago: Archipelagic and other Maritime Claims and Boundaries*. US Department of State, 31 January 2014. For the French version see: INDEMER (2010), *Annuaire du Droit de la Mer*, Tome XV, pp. 573–577.

161 Grenada ratified UNCLOS on 25 April 1991.

162 Agreement by Exchange of notes of identical content between the Republic of Peru and the Republic of Ecuador (Signature: 2 May 2011; entry into force: 20 May 2011). See: Note (GAB) No. 6–12-YY/01 of 2 May 2011 from the Minister of Foreign Affairs of Peru to the Minister of Foreign Affairs of Ecuador; and Note No. 9428 GMRECI/CGJ/2011

of 2 May 2011 from the Minister of Foreign Affairs of Ecuador to the Minister of Foreign Affairs of Peru. Certificate of Registration with the Secretary-General of the United Nations No. 60913. *UNTS* 48631. This agreement and the annexed map were registered with the United Nations jointly by both countries.

163 As a matter of fact, this was confirmed by Peru's president in a letter addressed to the president of Ecuador on 9 June 2010. See: Letter of 9 June 2010, from His Excellency Alan García, President of the Republic of Peru to His Excellency Rafael Correa, President of the Republic of Ecuador; *Maritime Dispute* (*Peru* v. *Chile*), Reply by the Government of Peru, Vol. II, Annex 81.

164 *I.C.J. Pleadings, Maritime Dispute* (*Peru* v. *Chile*). Peru's first round of oral argument (Counsel: Rodman Bundy), 4 December 2012 (CR 2012/29), p. 15, para. 60. See also Chile's pleading titled "L'attitude de l'Equateur": *I.C.J. Pleadings, Maritime Dispute* (*Peru* v. *Chile*). Chile's first round of oral argument (Counsel: Pierre-Marie Dupuy), 7 December 2012 (CR 2012/32), pp. 12–28, especially paras. 5, 8, 9, 10–64; and also: *I.C.J. Pleadings, Maritime Dispute* (*Peru* v. *Chile*). Chile's second round of oral argument (Counsel: Pierre-Marie Dupuy), 14 December 2012 (CR 2012/36), pp. 24 *et seq*.

165 The agreement was jointly registered with the United Nations on 27 June 2011 (Certificate of Registration No. 60913). Ecuador acceded to UNCLOS on 24 September 2012. Peru, in turn, made a declaration in the context of the judicial proceedings before the ICJ against Chile – the *Maritime Dispute* (*Peru* v. *Chile*) – that the term "maritime domain" used in Peru's Constitution is applied in a manner consistent with the maritime zones established in UNCLOS. More importantly, this was noted by the Court in its Judgment of 27 January 2014; see: *Maritime Dispute* (*Peru* v. *Chile*), *Judgment of the I.C.J. of 27 January 2014*, para. 178.

166 Declaración Conjunta sobre el Reconocimiento Internacional del Golfo de Guayaquil como Bahía Histórica, available at: www.un.org/Depts/los/LEGISLATIONANDTREATIES/PDFFILES/TREATIES/ECU_PER_03102016.pdf (accessed on 1 March 2022).

167 Agreement between the Commonwealth of the Bahamas and the Republic of Cuba for the delimiting line between their maritime zones (Signature: 3 October 2011; entry into force: 9 March 2012). The text of the agreement is available at DOALOS' website. See also: *Limits in the Seas No. 128, The Bahamas: Archipelagic and other Maritime Claims and Boundaries*. US Department of State, 31 January 2014. The agreement also established a frame clause concerning cooperation in the following areas: navigational safety and safety of life at sea, including search and rescue; hydrographic surveys; marine scientific research; preservation and protection of the marine environment, dealing with illegal acts affecting the safety of navigation, illegal trafficking in narcotic drugs and psychotropic substances and the smuggling of migrant by sea; conservation and management of living resources which occur within the EEZ of both parties, as provided for in the United Nations Convention on the Law of the Sea; management and exploitation of common hydrocarbon reserves which extend across the maritime boundary defined in this Agreement; and such other areas of common interest as the Parties may agree.

168 Archipelagic Waters and Maritime Jurisdiction Order, in: *Limits in the Seas No. 128, ibid.*

169 It should also be noted that the Government of Bahamas has submitted preliminary information concerning the extension of its continental shelf to the United Nations. It appears that this will have to be negotiated with the US.

170 The Bahamas and Cuba ratified the 1982 Law of the Sea Convention on 29 July 1983 and on 15 August 1984, respectively.

171 Maritime delimitation treaty between the Republic of Honduras and the Republic of Cuba It appears that this treaty was ratified by the two governments on 11 December 2013 (Signature: 21 August 2012; entry into force: 11 December 2013). The text of the agreement is available at DOALOS' website.

172 Agreement between the Government of Costa Rica and the Government of Ecuador relating to the Delimitation of the Maritime Areas between Costa Rica and Ecuador (Signature: 12 March 1985). While Ecuador ratified this treaty on 27 March 1990, Costa Rica has not so far.

173 Press releases of both Ministries of Foreign Affairs: for Costa Rica, available at www.rree.go.cr/index.php?sec=servicios%20al%20publico&cat=servicios%20de%20informacion&cont=593&noticia=929; and for Ecuador, available at www.mmrree.gob.ec/2012/bol0108.asp. It seems that the agreement will soon be signed by the two governments: www.eluniverso.com/2013/03/04/1/1355/ecuador-costa-rica-ultiman-acuerdo-limites-maritimos.html.

174 See: Statement by Ecuador, at the 29th Meeting of States Parties to the Law of the Sea Convention (SPLOS 29), June 2019.

175 Treaty of Concordia or Partition Treaty of 1648 signed on 23 March 1648 between the Kingdom of France and the Dutch Republic, which divided the island of Saint Martin.

176 Point A: 18°03′10″N and 63°08′20″W; Point B: 17°52′22″N and 63°17′14″W; and Point C: 17°57′06″N and 63°37′52″W. Source: French Ministry of Foreign Affairs.

177 Accord entre le gouvernement de la République française et le gouvernement du Royaume des Pays-Bas relative à la delimitation maritime dans la region des Caraïbes, signed in Philipsburg, on 6 April 2016.

178 Ministry of Foreign Affairs of France. For a discussion of this treaty as an expression of "conduct of the Parties", see: *Guyana/Suriname Arbitration*. Suriname Counter-Memorial, para. 2.20; and also, *Guyana/Suriname Arbitration, Award of 17 September 2007 ILM*, Vol. 47, paras. 391 *et seq*.

179 Note that according to the Agreed Minutes of May 1999, the closing line of the estuary is located beyond the confluence of the Maroni River and the Mana River. According to Draft Article 1, point A from which the line is drawn is composed of the following coordinates: 5°47′25″N and 53°57′10″W.

180 *Guyana/Suriname Arbitration*. Memorial of Guyana, para. 2.15. See also Annex 55 and Annex 96 of the Memorial of Guyana.

181 According to Draft Article 1, the line closing the mouth of the Maroni River is a loxodrome joining points C1 (5°49′43″N and 54°01′01″W) and C2 (5°45′07″N and 53°53′19″W).

182 Negotiations took in fact place in Cayenne on 22 July 1998 and in Saramacca on 5 and 6 May 1999.

183 Maritime Delimitation Agreement between the Government of the French Republic and the Government of the Republic of Suriname, signed in Paris on 8 November 2017.

184 CLCS Recommendation adopted on 2 September 2009 for France; and CLCS Recommendation adopted on 30 March 2011 for Suriname; see DOALOS' website.

185 Agreement between the Government of the Republic of France and the Government of Antigua and Barbuda on the delimitation of maritime space between France and Antigua and Barbuda in the Caribbean region (with map). Saint John's, 15 March 2017. Entry into force: 1 October 2018.

186 Note also the relevance of the Agreement in the form of an Exchange of Notes between the Government of the United Kingdom of Great Britain and Northern Ireland in respect of Anguilla and the Government of the French Republic concerning Arrangements relating to the Tripoint between the Maritime Areas Under the Jurisdictions of the United Kingdom of Great Britain and Northern Ireland (in respect of Anguilla), Antigua and Barbuda, and the French Republic (in respect of Saint-Martin and Saint-Barthélemy) (The "Tripoint"), Paris, 29 January and 4 March 2021; entered into force on 4 March 2021.

187 Treaty between the Government of the United Kingdom of Great Britain and Northern Ireland and the Government of Antigua and Barbuda establishing a maritime boundary between Anguilla and Antigua and Barbuda. Signed 27 July 2021. Not yet in force.

8 Case Law in Latin America and the Caribbean

This chapter deals with maritime boundary delimitation case law concerning Latin America and the Caribbean. It includes two Annex VII Arbitral Tribunals, *Barbados/Trinidad and Tobago* and *Guyana/Suriname*; two cases filed by Nicaragua, one against Honduras and the other against Colombia; the case of *Maritime Dispute* (*Peru* v. *Chile*); and the case of *Costa Rica* v. *Nicaragua*.

Before delving into the aforementioned cases, a short reference will be made to the *El Salvador/Honduras* judgment, although it did not imply the actual drawing of a maritime delimitation whatsoever.[1]

The case between *El Salvador/Honduras*, brought to a Chamber of the ICJ, was divided into three main elements, namely, (1) a dispute over the land boundary, (2) a dispute over the legal situation of the islands and (3) a dispute over the legal situation of the maritime spaces, in respect of both the waters within and outside the Gulf of Fonseca. In relation to the latter, there was another dispute over the role of the Chamber, that is, on whether it had or had not been requested to delimit those waters.[2] The Chamber noted that there was a fundamental disagreement between the Parties in relation to the interpretation of the 1986 *compromis*.[3] Whereas El Salvador contended that the Chamber had no jurisdiction to effect any delimitation, Honduras pleaded for the delimitation of the maritime boundary inside and outside the Gulf of Fonseca.[4] The Chamber came to the conclusion that it had no jurisdiction to effect any such delimitation.[5] It therefore follows that this is not a *typical* case of maritime delimitation, even though the question of whether the Chamber of the Court had been entrusted with that task was touched upon. On the other hand, the Chamber considered the Gulf as a condominium, and declared that Honduras is not locked out from rights in respect of ocean waters outside the bay (Pacific Ocean).[6]

Barbados/Trinidad and Tobago – Arbitral Award 2006

Following nine rounds of negotiations spanning July 2000 and November 2003, which included questions associated with access for Barbadian fisherfolk to certain fish stocks, Barbados in February 2004 invoked Part XV of UNCLOS and decided to make use of the compulsory arbitration procedures in accordance with Annex VII of the United Nations Convention on the Law of the Sea. After written

DOI: 10.4324/9781003290452-11

and oral proceedings had taken place, the Arbitral Tribunal went on to carry out the delimitation of the overlapping maritime spaces (exclusive economic zones and continental shelves) of the Parties in three different areas (western, central and eastern segments).

In the western segment, while Trinidad and Tobago maintained that the provisional equidistance line should be the definitive line to be laid down by the Tribunal, Barbados claimed that the provisional line was to be adjusted so as to encompass the area of Barbadian artisanal fishing in the waters off Tobago (flying-fish fishery),[7] a centuries-old activity on which it was argued that Barbadian fisherfolk, unlike those of Trinidad and Tobago, were critically dependent. In its assessment, the Arbitral Tribunal could not sustain Barbados' contention, for the evidence submitted was considered distinctly fragmentary and inconclusive; neither could it accept that the lack of access by Barbados fisherfolk to the waters in issue would be catastrophic. It then went on to conclude that the equidistance line in the west was to be the line of delimitation between the Parties.[8]

In the central segment, extending only 16 nautical miles, the Parties agreed that no adjustment was necessary. Hence, the Tribunal decided that the equidistance line as agreed by the otherwise contending Parties was to be established as the maritime boundary without any modification.

In the eastern segment, the Arbitral Tribunal identified two relevant circumstances, namely, the broad coastal frontages of Trinidad and the disparity in coastal lengths between the Parties.[9] The Tribunal then explained that "[t]his particular frontage abuts directly upon the area subject to delimitation and it would be inequitable to ignore its existence." As for the question of where the adjustment was to take place, the Arbitral Tribunal concluded that the point of deflection was to be situated where the provisional equidistance line meets the geodetic line that joins the archipelagic baseline turning point on Little Tobago Island with the point of intersection of Trinidad and Tobago's southern maritime boundary with its 200-nautical-mile EEZ limit. That point, called point 10, is situated at the coordinate 11°03.70′N and 57°58.72′W. The maritime boundary then ran in a straight line towards the southeast until it reached point 11, with approximate geographic coordinates of 10°58.59′N and 57°07.05′W. The Tribunal then applied the test of proportionality so as to avoid any gross disproportion in the outcome of delimitation, and thus justified the previous adjustment.[10]

The Arbitral Tribunal noted that the Parties were in agreement in as much as the governing rule on maritime delimitation was expressed in the equidistance/relevant circumstances approach and hence proceeded to look at any relevant circumstances that justified departures from that general rule based on the equidistance line so as to achieve an equitable solution. The Tribunal, however, noted also that between the Parties there were "fundamental differences" about "what the relevant circumstances" were and the "extent and location of any adjustments" to be effected. Furthermore, by looking at the Parties' domestic legislation, one could claim that they had also different views about the method to be used in case of maritime overlap. While Barbados' Marine Boundaries and Jurisdiction Act of 1978 made reference to the median line, Trinidad and Tobago's Archipelagic

Waters Act referred to the agreement-based-on-international-law formula in order to achieve an equitable solution.[11]

Finally, the Arbitral Tribunal opted for the equidistance method in two out of three segments of the maritime boundary, whereas in the third segment it proceeded to adjust the provisional equidistance line due to the existence of two relevant circumstances (relevant coasts and proportionality). As for the methodology used, the Arbitral Tribunal referred to a "two-step approach"[12] rather than the currently named "standard method" in three stages.[13] It is to be noted that said approach was not followed subsequently.

Guyana/Suriname – Arbitral Award 2007

Guyana and Suriname, two South American countries located on the northeast coast of the subcontinent, both Parties to UNCLOS and former British and Dutch colonies, respectively,[14] had their maritime boundary settled by an Arbitral Award in 2007.[15] The Arbitral Tribunal was constituted in accordance with Annex VII of UNCLOS after Guyana initiated arbitration proceedings in 2004.

Concerning the method, it can be said that equidistance prevailed, albeit with slight variations, between miles 3 and 12. In the exclusive economic zone and the continental shelf, an unadjusted equidistance line was established by the tribunal.

With regards to the territorial sea, Guyana, seeing no reason to depart from the rule of Article 15 of UNCLOS, contended that an equidistance line should be drawn along an azimuth of N34°E from Point 61 out to a distance of 12 nautical miles.[16] Yet, Suriname argued that it should be delimited along an azimuth of N10°E from the 1936 Point/Point 61 (the so-called 10-degree line),[17] on the basis of a tacit or de facto agreement, acquiescence or estoppel, between the UK and the Netherlands.[18]

In its appraisal, the Arbitral Tribunal held that the 10-degree line claimed by Suriname was to be restricted to a three-nautical-mile limit. It also accepted the 1936 Point/Point 61 as a reference point for drawing the line. From that point to the 12-nautical-mile limit, the Arbitral Tribunal decided that the line should be drawn "diagonally by the shortest distance to meet the line adopted later in this Award to delimit the Parties' continental shelf and exclusive economic zone." In other words, it held that the boundary line should be joined to the point at which the equidistance line applied to the EEZ and continental shelf intersects the outer limit of the territorial sea.[19]

With respect to the delimitation of the EEZs and the continental shelves, the Arbitral Tribunal, after considering the relevant coasts (nearly the same ratio of relevant areas), the coastal geography (which does not bring about any distortion), the provisional equidistance line (in its three sections, as claimed by Suriname), and the conduct of the Parties (oil and gas concessions as well as the "material significance" of the draft agreement between Suriname and France),[20] came to the conclusion that there were no relevant circumstances in the continental shelf or EEZ calling for an adjustment of the above-mentioned provisional equidistance line.

The Arbitral Tribunal followed generally established case law by the International Court of Justice, although it referred to a two-stage methodology.[21] It eventually found no reason, that is to say no relevant circumstance, that could justify the adjustment of the provisional equidistance line dividing the EEZs and the continental shelves of the Parties.

Nicaragua v. *Honduras* – ICJ Judgment 2007

This maritime dispute had as antecedents a long land boundary dispute whose origins date back to an Arbitral Award rendered by the King of Spain in 1906.[22] The award settled the territorial delimitation of Nicaragua and Honduras towards the Atlantic, which had been left incomplete by a Mixed Boundary Commission established pursuant to the 1894 Gámez-Bonilla Treaty.[23] Other antecedents include a judgment of the ICJ in the 1950s, which related to the validity of the 1906 Award,[24] and a number of Mixed Commissions which in 1962 completed the demarcations on the Atlantic coast at the mouth of the river Coco.[25] Some years of friendly relations came along after that (1963–1979), but only until the arrival of the Sandinista Government and its alleged clean slate approach towards relations with other countries.[26]

It was under this new approach that a Honduran fishing vessel was attacked in 1979 by Nicaragua eight miles north of the 15th parallel,[27] which according to Honduras served as the limit between the two countries.[28] Nicaragua responded with no reference whatsoever to the alleged limit. In 1982 a second Honduran fishing vessel was captured by Nicaragua. This time Nicaragua responded, by Note of 14 April 1982, stating that it had not recognised any maritime frontier with Honduras in the Caribbean Sea,[29] bringing about a non-friendly period, principally during the 1980s and 1990s.[30]

In 1986, Honduras and Colombia concluded a maritime boundary treaty.[31] This was strongly protested by Nicaragua and was followed by efforts made both by Nicaragua and Honduras to overcome this impasse.[32] In 1997 a Memorandum of Understanding was signed by the two countries seeking the settlement of their maritime delimitation differences. This marked the revival of bilateral negotiations. However, following Honduras' ratification in December 1999 of the 1986 Treaty, Nicaragua decided to break off negotiations.[33]

Shortly after that, on 29 November 1999, an application before the CACJ was filed by Nicaragua against Honduras, requesting that the Court declare that Honduras, by ratifying the 1986 Treaty, had acted in violation of the Tegucigalpa Protocol to the Charter of OAS. Nicaragua also requested provisional measures from the Court so as to establish the suspension of the ratification procedure.[34] By way of a Judgment of 27 November 2001, the CACJ held that Honduras had infringed the fundamental principles of the Central American Integration System, including the so-called territorial patrimony of Central America.[35]

Against these circumstances, on 8 December 1999 Nicaragua brought an Application before the ICJ asking the Court to determine the course of the single maritime boundary between the areas of territorial sea, continental shelf and EEZ appertaining to Nicaragua and Honduras, respectively, in accordance with equitable principles and relevant circumstances recognised by general international law.[36] Yet, a second claim was introduced by Nicaragua "by the back door"[37] at an "unprecedentedly late stage".[38] According to this new claim made as late as in the final oral submissions on 20 March 2007, "Without prejudice of the foregoing, the Court is requested to decide the question of the sovereignty of the islands and cays within the area in dispute."[39] It can therefore be seen that there were actually two disputes, one concerning sovereignty over islands[40] and the other maritime delimitation. Only the latter will be treated here in detail.

With respect to the maritime delimitation itself, Nicaragua claimed that there was no maritime boundary agreement with Honduras and therefore, in the absence of such an agreement, the law of maritime delimitation should be applied. More specifically, Nicaragua put forward the application of a particular method, the bisector,[41] in light of geomorphological features present at the mouth of the river Coco that constitute a special circumstance within the meaning of Article 15 of UNCLOS.[42] This would justify a departure from the equidistance rule applicable to the territorial sea. As for the critical date for this dispute, Nicaragua considered the same one as for the islands' dispute: 11 May 1977.

Honduras, for its part, considered that there was (and had existed for a long time) a traditional boundary line along the 15th parallel that constituted the maritime boundary between the Parties. Nicaragua referred to this as "*de facto* delimitation". The basis for Honduras' claim was thought to be the application of a maritime *uti possidetis juris* and, on the other hand, a tacit agreement.[43]

With regards to the dispute over the delimitation of the maritime area between the Parties, the Court declared that the critical date was 14 April 1982, when Nicaragua denied for the first time the existence of a tacit maritime boundary agreement with Honduras.[44]

Concerning delimitation of maritime areas, the Court analysed first the argument proposed by Honduras whereby there existed a traditional maritime boundary based on either *uti possidetis juris* or a tacit agreement. As for the former, the Court observed that this principle might in certain circumstances (e.g. connection with historic bays and territorial seas) play a role in a maritime delimitation. Yet, in the circumstances of the instant case, the *uti possidetis juris* principle could not be said to have provided a basis for a maritime division along the 15th parallel. With respect to the tacit agreement argument, the Court recalled that evidence of the tacit agreement must be compelling. In other words, one could not infer from a timid and ambiguous expression of will a tacit agreement to establish a legally binding maritime boundary.[45] Accordingly, the Court concluded that there was no maritime boundary agreement in force between the Parties and therefore it had to look at the law of maritime delimitation applicable in the absence of agreement. This is to be found in Articles 15, 74 and 83 of UNCLOS.

The Court then found that the coastal geomorphological problems present in the mouth of the river Coco (which constitutes the point at which the land boundary reaches the sea) amounted to special circumstances that justified the non-application of the equidistance rule established in Article 15 of UNCLOS. It therefore went on to say that the adequate method applicable in this case was to be the bisector method.[46]

The bisector method, one of the so-called *méthodes de lissage* as stated earlier, amounts to the general direction of the coasts of two adjacent States to straight lines. Hence, the bisector of the angle formed by such lines will constitute the maritime boundary.[47] In order to construct the bisector, one line was drawn from the 1962 Mixed Commission Point,[48] both to the Punta Patuca Lighthouse on the coast of Honduras and to a point called Wouhnta on the Nicaraguan coast. The ICJ then drew a line bisecting the angle formed by the two simplified coastlines on an azimuth[49] of 70°14′41.25′ that formed the basis of the maritime boundary.

With respect to the islands, the Parties agreed that the four islands in dispute north of the 15th parallel, as well as Edinburgh Cay south of the 15th parallel, generated territorial seas. That being said, the Court found that all four islands shall be accorded a territorial sea of 12 nautical miles.[50]

The Court upheld Honduras' submission concerning the starting point of the maritime boundary. Since the mouth of the river Coco is shifting seawards due to a continuous process of accretion, the terminal point of the land boundary cannot remain fixed at the same point. In this sense, Honduras proposed that the starting point of the maritime boundary be a point off the coast that does not touch the land boundary terminus. The Court, recalling judicial practice showing that a delimitation line may begin at some distance out at sea,[51] established that the starting point will be located three nautical miles out to sea. The Court then urged the Parties to agree on a line that would link the end of the land boundary and the point of departure of the maritime delimitation in accordance with this Judgment.

Concerning the endpoint of the maritime boundary, the Court did not specify a precise endpoint[52] beyond the 82nd meridian but claimed that such a projection would not cross the 1928 Treaty line between Nicaragua and Colombia and therefore could not affect Colombia's rights or, for that matter, the rights of any other third State.[53]

In its operative clause, the Court unanimously found that Honduras had sovereignty over the (four) islands. By 15 votes to 2, the Court decided that the starting point of the single maritime boundary was 15°00′52″N and 83°05′58″W (three nautical miles seawards of the 1962 point). Similarly, by 14 votes to 3, the Court decided the course of the maritime delimitation around the islands; and finally, by 16 votes to 1, the Court found that the Parties were under the obligation to negotiate in good faith the delimitation of the portion of the territorial sea located between the land boundary terminus and the starting point of the single maritime boundary determined by the Court.[54]

Nicaragua v. *Colombia* – ICJ Judgment (Merits) 2012

The delimitation of the maritime boundary between Nicaragua and Colombia in the Caribbean Sea was the result of a long judicial process that started in 2001, included a long preliminary phase, and ended in 2012, although with additional ongoing implications. On 6 December 2001, Nicaragua submitted an Application instituting proceedings against Colombia and requesting the Court to determine that it had sovereignty over the islands of Providencia, San Andrés and Santa Catalina and all the appurtenant islands and keys, and also over the Roncador, Serrana, Serranilla and Quitasueño keys.[55] Similarly, it asked the Court to determine the course of the single maritime boundary between the areas of continental shelf and EEZ appertaining to Nicaragua and Colombia, respectively, in accordance with equitable principles and relevant circumstances recognised by general international law.

On 21 July 2003, Colombia filed certain preliminary objections to the jurisdiction of the Court, which, according to Article 79, paragraph 5 of the Rules of Court, suspended the proceedings on the merits. Colombia requested the Court to declare that, under Article VI and Article XXXIV of the Pact of Bogotá, it lacked jurisdiction to hear the dispute and that the dispute had ended. It maintained, referring specifically to Article VI of the Pact, that the matters raised by Nicaragua were duly settled by a treaty in force (the Barcenas-Esguerra Treaty) on the date on which the Pact was concluded. Nicaragua, in turn, requested the Court to reject Colombia's preliminary objections. Alternatively, Nicaragua contended that, pursuant to Article 79, paragraph 9 of the Rules of Court, Colombian objections did not have an exclusively preliminary character.[56]

Hence, Nicaragua claimed that the 1928 Treaty and its 1930 Protocol did not settle the whole dispute between the Parties within the meaning of Article VI of the Pact of Bogotá and, even if that was not the case, that the 1928 Treaty did not comprise all the matters at stake. Furthermore, Nicaragua claimed that the Court could not deal with these issues at this stage of the proceedings since that would require an examination of the merits.

Invalidity of the 1928 Treaty was also advanced by Nicaragua, as an argument confirming that the dispute was not settled. First, because it had been concluded "in manifest violation of the Nicaraguan Constitution of 1911 that was in force in 1928".[57] Second, because at the time of the conclusion of that Treaty, Nicaragua was under US military occupation and was therefore precluded from entering into agreements that could harm the interests of the occupying power.

Nicaragua even claimed that Colombia "took advantage of the US occupation of Nicaragua to extort from her the conclusion of the 1928 Treaty". Colombia, in this regard, claimed that even assuming that the 1928 Treaty was against the 1911 Constitution of Nicaragua or that Nicaragua's will was undermined due to US occupation, such claims were not raised during the ratification process in 1930, or during the following 50 years. Therefore, Colombia considers that Nicaragua was precluded from challenging the validity of the 1928 Treaty and its 1930 Protocol. The Court found that the 1928 Treaty was valid and in force on the date of the conclusion of the Pact of Bogotá in 1948.[58]

With respect to the scope of application of the 1928 Treaty, the Court had a very important finding. It held that the terms of that treaty did not answer the question of which maritime features apart from the islands of San Andrés, Providencia and Santa Catalina formed part of the San Andrés Archipelago over which Colombia had sovereignty. It thus considered that the matter had *not* been settled within the meaning of Article VI of the Pact of Bogotá and therefore the Court *did* have jurisdiction under Article XXXI of the Pact of Bogotá in so far as it concerned the question of sovereignty over the maritime features, except for the islands of San Andrés, Providencia and Santa Catalina.[59]

As regards maritime delimitation, the Court concluded that the 1928 Treaty and the 1930 Protocol did not establish a general delimitation of the maritime boundary between the Parties and that the dispute was therefore not settled within the meaning of Article VI of the Pact of Bogotá. In other words, it did not uphold Colombia's first preliminary objection concerning the Court's jurisdiction on the issue of maritime delimitation. Thus, on 13 December 2007, the Court ruled unanimously that it had jurisdiction on the basis of Article XXXI of the Pact of Bogotá to adjudicate upon the dispute concerning sovereignty over the maritime features claimed by the Parties other than the islands of San Andrés, Providencia and Santa Catalina, and upon the dispute concerning maritime delimitation.[60]

By the time the Court was able to address the merits of this case,[61] the two central elements at stake were sovereignty over certain maritime features and the maritime delimitation between the continental shelf and EEZ of Nicaragua and the continental shelf and EEZ projected by Colombian islands.

Regarding sovereignty over disputed maritime features, the Court came to the conclusion that no title over them could be found on the basis of the 1928 Treaty or on the principle of *uti possidetis juris*. Regarding the latter, the Court concluded that "nothing clearly indicated whether these features were attributed to the colonial provinces of Nicaragua or of Colombia prior to or upon independence".[62]

Before dealing with the question of *effectivités*, the Court established as the critical date 12 June 1969, that is, the date of a note by Nicaragua in response to Colombia's Note of 4 June 1969.[63] Once it did so, it went on to assess the arguments put forward by Colombia on the basis of *effectivités*, since Nicaragua did not provide any evidence that it had acted *à titre de souverain* in relation to the disputed maritime features.[64]

After assessing the evidence submitted by Colombia – which included several categories of *effectivités*, such as public administration and legislation, regulation of economic activities, public works, law enforcement measures, naval visits and search and rescue operations, and consular representation, with regard to the seven maritime features in dispute – the Court concluded that such activities *à titre de souverain* continued after the critical date. For that reason, the ICJ held that Colombia's claim of sovereignty over the maritime features in dispute had strong support from the facts reviewed.[65] In light of the foregoing, the Court concluded that Colombia, and not Nicaragua, had sovereignty over the islands of Albuquerque, Bajo Nuevo, East-Southeast Cays, Quitasueño,[66] Roncador, Serrana and Serranilla.[67]

In the absence of a maritime boundary agreement, the Court proceeded to apply the three-stage methodology discussed earlier. In so doing, the Court identified two relevant circumstances: the disparity in the lengths of the relevant coasts, with a ratio of 1:8.2 between Colombia's relevant coast and Nicaragua's relevant coast; and the overall geographical context, because the coast of Colombia consists of a series of islands, most of them very small and located far from each other.

These circumstances called for the provisional median line being shifted eastwards to reach an equitable solution.[68] Besides that first adjustment, the Court decided to give a different weighting to the base points of the Parties. Hence, it gave a weighting of one to each of the base points of Colombia and a weighting of three to each of Nicaragua's base points, that is a 3:1 ratio between Nicaraguan and Colombian base points. The resulting line seemed to be too convoluted for a good practical application and therefore the Court simplified it to five points.

The Court went on to state that extending the line north of point 1 or south of point 5 would not be equitable and hence, in an unexpected turn, drew a line westwards along a parallel of latitude, from point 1, until it reached the 200-nautical-mile limit from the baselines from which the territorial sea of Nicaragua is measured. As for point 5, in the south, after considering the 12 nautical mile envelope of arcs surrounding South Cay of Albuquerque Cays and East-Southeast Cays, it held that it would follow the same method, running along a parallel of latitude until it reached the 200-nautical-mile limit from Nicaragua's baselines. As for the grounds on which this process was founded, concern has been expressed.[69] In any case, the decision to follow a "parallel of latitude" does not seem to be the adjustment of an equidistance line. Rather, it appears that a different result was founded by the Court and that, at the same time, it wanted to affirm its jurisprudence.

With Quitasueño and Serrana ending up on "the wrong side of the boundary" but being entitled to a 12-nautical-mile territorial sea,[70] the Court finally tested the result achieved and found that the Judgment did not "entail such a disproportionality as to create an inequitable result".[71]

With respect to the continental shelf beyond 200 nautical miles, Nicaragua maintained that its entitlement extended into areas within Colombia's 200 nautical miles, and that "an entitlement to continental shelf based on the distance criterion does not take precedence over an entitlement based on the criterion of natural prolongation". Inversely, Colombia claimed that Nicaragua had not established any entitlement to an extended continental shelf and that the information furnished by it was "rudimentary and incomplete". In this regard, the Court concluded that Nicaragua had not established that it had a continental margin extending far enough within Colombia's 200-nautical-mile zone, and so it found itself in no position to delimit the continental shelf boundary between Nicaragua and Colombia.[72]

As it is known, in the aftermath of that 2012 ICJ judgment, Nicaragua asked the Court to declare "the precise course of the maritime boundary between Nicaragua and Colombia in the areas of the continental shelf which appertain to each of them beyond the boundaries determined by the Court in its Judgment of 19 November 2012".[73]

Indeed, in the 2012 *Nicaragua* v. *Colombia* judgment the Court had not been in a position to delimit the continental shelf boundary between the Parties, as requested by Nicaragua, because Nicaragua had not established that it possessed a continental margin extending far enough to overlap with Colombia's 200-nautical-mile entitlement to the continental shelf.[74]

On 16 September 2013, Nicaragua hence filed a new Application before the ICJ instituting proceedings against Colombia, whereby it requested the Court to adjudge and declare "the precise course of the maritime boundary between Nicaragua and Colombia in the areas of the continental shelf which appertain to each of them beyond the boundaries determined by the Court in its judgment of 19 November 2012". Nicaragua claimed that, having submitted its final information to the Commission on the Limits of the Continental Shelf of 24 June 2013, it was possible to demonstrate that its continental margin extended more than 200 nautical miles from the baselines from which the breadth of the territorial sea of Nicaragua had been measured.[75]

As a result, in 2016 the ICJ (following ITLOS *Bangladesh/Myanmar*) corrected its own jurisprudence of 2007 and 2012 and concluded that

> since the delimitation of the continental shelf beyond 200 nautical miles can be undertaken independently of a recommendation from the CLCS, the latter is not a prerequisite that needs to be satisfied by a State party to UNCLOS before it can ask the Court to settle a dispute with another State over such a delimitation.[76]

This is how this thorny issue was settled. The question on the merits, however, still remains under consideration by the Court.

Peru v. *Chile* – ICJ Judgment 2014

The historical background of the dispute between Peru and Chile can be traced back to the War of the Pacific (declared by Chile on Peru and Bolivia in 1879). In this respect, it should be recalled that before the hostilities Peru and Chile were not neighbouring States, yet after the war, the entire Bolivian coast became Chilean and Peru lost possession of certain provinces in its southern region.[77] In 1929, Peru and Chile signed the Treaty for the Settlement of the Dispute regarding Tacna and Arica,[78] whereby they agreed that Tacna would be returned to Peru and Arica would remain a part of Chile.[79] While the land boundary was fully delimited and demarcated in 1929 and 1930, the maritime boundary was not agreed upon at the time. In line with the development of the modern law of the sea, and after more than 20 years of fruitless attempts to enter into negotiations with Chile so as to agree on a maritime boundary delimitation,[80] Peru instituted proceedings against Chile before the International Court of Justice on 16 January 2008.

On 27 January 2014 the ICJ delivered its judgment on the *Maritime Dispute* (*Peru* v. *Chile*), putting an end to a six-year judicial process. The decision, while allowing Peru to gain sovereign rights and jurisdiction over an area of the Pacific Ocean amounting to more than 50,000 square kilometres, also accepted partially Chile's argument that a maritime boundary ran along a parallel of latitude.

The core of the dispute was the fundamentally different positions adopted by the Parties. Peru argued that no agreed maritime boundary existed between the two countries and requested the Court to establish a boundary using the equidistance method.[81] Chile, in turn, contended that the 1952 Declaration of Santiago established an international maritime boundary along the parallel of latitude passing through Boundary Marker No. 1 (Hito No. 1),[82] and that, in general, "a boundary line ha[d] been in place for many decades and observed in the Parties' bilateral practice without incidents or reservation of position".[83]

To settle the dispute, the Court therefore had to ascertain whether an agreed maritime boundary already existed. It began by examining the 1947 Proclamations.[84] The Court concluded, contrary to Chile's arguments, that they could not be interpreted as reflecting any shared understanding of the Parties concerning maritime delimitation.[85]

In relation to the 1952 Santiago Declaration, the Court applied the rules of interpretation as reflected in the Vienna Convention on the Law of Treaties. It hence considered, *inter alia*, the ordinary meaning given to the terms of the Declaration, its object and purpose, and especially the terms of paragraph IV. The Court concluded, contrary to Chile's submission, that Peru and Chile had not, by adopting the 1952 Santiago Declaration, agreed to the establishment of a lateral maritime boundary between them. However, the Court at the same time reached another preliminary conclusion, namely, that "various factors suggest that there might have been some sort of shared understanding concerning maritime boundaries".[86]

Following on from this analysis, the Court considered then the 1954 Agreements invoked by Chile in support of its claim that the parallel constitutes the maritime boundary with Peru. Attention was given to the 1954 Special Maritime Frontier Zone Agreement (SMFZA) which established a zone of tolerance, starting at a distance of 12 nautical miles from the coast, "of 10 nautical miles on either side of the parallel which constitutes the maritime boundary". In this regard, Chile claimed that the "basic predicate" of that agreement was that the States Parties already had lateral boundaries between them. Peru's position was that the agreement was only applicable as a delimitation criterion to its northern border (with Ecuador), that the Parties were claiming a limited functional jurisdiction, and in any case that it was a practical arrangement of a technical nature, and of limited geographical scope. Yet, in the view of the Court, the terms of the 1954 SMFZA are clear: "[t]hey acknowledge in a binding international agreement that a maritime boundary already exists."[87] The Court, in the following paragraph, went on to add:

> The 1954 Special Maritime Frontier Zone Agreement does not indicate when and by what means that boundary was agreed upon. The Parties' express acknowledgment of its existence can only reflect a *tacit agreement* which they had reached earlier. . . . In this case, the Court has before it an Agreement which makes clear that the maritime boundary along a parallel already existed between the Parties. The 1954 Agreement is decisive in this respect. That Agreement *cements* the tacit agreement [emphasis added].[88]

The Court later examined the 1968–1969 lighthouse arrangements and confirmed its previous conclusion: that the said arrangements proceeded on the basis that a maritime boundary extending along the parallel beyond 12 nautical miles already existed.[89]

Having reached this conclusion, the Court further noted that the 1954 SMFZA gives no indication of the nature of the maritime boundary or of its extent. It restricts itself to mentioning that it has effects beyond 12 nautical miles from the coast. On the nature of the agreed maritime boundary, the Court considered that the tacit agreement acknowledged in the 1954 SMFZA is to be understood in the context of the 1947 Proclamations and the 1952 Santiago Declaration, which expressed claims to the seabed and to the waters above the seabed. The Court therefore concluded that the maritime boundary is an all-purpose one.[90]

To determine the extent of the tacitly agreed maritime boundary, the Court examined the relevant practice of the Parties, both before and after 1954. Recalling that the purpose of the 1954 SMFZA was narrow and specific (to establish a zone of tolerance for fishing activity operated by small vessels), the Court took special account of the fishing activities undertaken by the Parties at the time and concluded that the agreed maritime boundary along the parallel could not extend beyond 80 nautical miles from its starting point.[91]

With respect to the starting point of the agreed maritime boundary (not of the land boundary, identified as "Concordia" in the 1929 Treaty),[92] the Court considered that with the 1968–1969 lighthouse arrangements the Parties intended to signal the parallel passing through Boundary Marker No. 1.[93] Consequently, in the view of the Court "[t]he 1968–1969 lighthouse arrangements . . . serve as *compelling evidence* that the agreed maritime boundary follows the parallel that passes through Boundary Marker No. 1" (emphasis added). The ICJ concluded that "the starting-point of the maritime boundary between the Parties is the intersection of the parallel of latitude passing through Boundary Marker No. 1 with the low-water line."[94] In no way does that point affect the so-called land triangle (*triángulo terrestre*), which according to the 1929 Treaty is on Peru's side of the land boundary. The "land triangle" is formed by the joining of three points: Boundary Marker No. 1, the intersection of the parallel of latitude passing through Boundary Marker No. 1 with the low water line, and "Point Concordia", defined as the with the low-water mark (seashore) of a 10-kilometre-radius arc having as its centre the first bridge over the River Lluta of the Arica-La Paz railway. In this respect, the Court added that it was possible that the starting point of the maritime boundary did not coincide with the starting point of the land frontier.

The first segment, from the starting point of the maritime boundary until Point A, situated at 80 nautical miles from the coast, follows the parallel of latitude.

As for the course of the maritime boundary from Point A (beyond 80 nautical miles), the Court proceeded according to its "standard method" (three-stage methodology).[95] The line, therefore, runs in a general southwest direction (from Point A) until it reaches the 200-nautical-mile limit measured from Chilean baselines (Point B). Since beyond Point B the 200-nautical-mile limits of the Parties' entitlements no longer overlap, the last segment of the maritime boundary runs in a generally southward direction (until Point C).[96]

It is important to mention that Peru's second submission (concerning the so-called Outer Triangle)[97] became moot, therefore the Court did not need to rule on it since it had already concluded that the agreed boundary line running along the parallel of latitude ended at 80 nautical miles from the coast. In other words, it rejected Chile's argument that a single lateral limit had been established by the 1952 Santiago Declaration to "a minimum distance of 200 nautical miles" and that Peru could not claim any maritime are south of the parallel, which Chile considered *Alta Mar* (the high seas). When the Court rejected this line of argument, the basis for Chile's position in this regard no longer existed.[98]

In conclusion, the maritime boundary between Peru and Chile starts at the intersection of the parallel of latitude passing through Boundary Marker No. 1 with the low-water line, and extends for 80 nautical miles along that parallel of latitude to Point A. From this point, the maritime boundary runs along the equidistance line to Point B, and then along the 200 nautical mile limit measured from the Chilean baselines to Point C.[99]

While the Court defined the course of the maritime boundary between the Parties, it did not determine precise geographical coordinates. It nevertheless requested the Parties to determine those coordinates in accordance with the Judgment, "in the spirit of good neighbourliness", which they did in a timely manner.[100]

As has been set out, the main subject-matter of the dispute was related to answering the question: "is there an agreed maritime boundary between Peru and Chile?" In this regard, to a large extent the *Maritime Dispute* (*Peru* v. *Chile*) was not a typical maritime delimitation case but rather a case focused on the interpretation of several instruments (the 1947 Proclamations, the 1952 Santiago Declaration, the various 1954 Agreements, specially the 1954 SMFZA, and even the 1968–1969 lighthouse arrangements) and hence in the application of the law of treaties, a kind of task that the Court had already undertaken, for instance, in the *Qatar* v. *Bahrain* second judgment on preliminary objections.[101]

One of the main features of this case appears to be the reasoning employed by the Court in support of the existence of a tacit agreement on maritime delimitation, a legal reasoning over which two judges expressed "serious reservations".[102] As set out above, the Court came to the conclusion that neither of the 1947 Proclamations established an international maritime boundary, nor did the 1952 Santiago Declaration make any express reference to delimitation of maritime boundaries. And yet, the ICJ was of the view that the terms of the 1954 SMZFA were "clear" and that they "acknowledge[d] in a binding international agreement that a maritime boundary already exist[ed]".[103] In this regard, a more detailed analysis of the evidence as to the Parties' intentions could have been more adequate.[104] This is especially apt because the legal threshold established by the Court in its 2007 *Nicaragua* v. *Honduras* judgment had been set very high: "[e]vidence of a tacit agreement must be compelling. The establishment of a permanent maritime boundary is a matter of grave importance and agreement is not easily to be presumed".[105] Peru's counsel referred to paragraph 253 of that judgment several times, which reflects its reliance on that "stringent standard of proof".[106] However, the Court opted to come along with the tacit agreement argument. This could crystallise the danger of transforming provisional (tacit) lines into definitive ones, hence deterring States from seeking partial accommodations for specific purposes.[107]

Another aspect related to this is that, unlike the maritime delimitation case between Nicaragua and Honduras, in which the latter pleaded the existence of a tacit agreement,[108] in the instant case Chile did not put forward the existence of a tacit agreement as a legal argument, and yet the Court considered it the best solution. This could also bring about a discussion on the Court's procedural approaches when dealing with issues not entirely addressed by the Parties.[109]

On the question of the length of the maritime boundary established by the tacit agreement, so declared by the Court to have existed in 1954, the distance of 80 nautical miles also seems problematic. Despite biological considerations supported by information provided by the UN Food and Agriculture Organization (FAO), it appears difficult to establish an 80-nautical-mile maritime boundary at a time when no more than 12 nautical miles were accepted by international law and any space beyond that distance was considered part of the high seas. This means that a legal event must be assessed in light of the law in force at the time of its occurrence (intertemporal law). In other words, an agreement could not delimit those maritime spaces which did not exist at the time – in this case, the exclusive economic zone.

A final remark relates to the issue of the starting point of the maritime boundary. As mentioned earlier, the Court established that point as "the intersection of the parallel of latitude passing through Boundary Marker No. 1 with the low-water line."[110] However, it did not settle – as it could not, because of its lacking jurisdiction over the Treaty that delimited the land boundary – the Parties' disagreement on the exact location of the starting point of the land boundary, identified as "Concordia" in Article 2 of the 1929 Treaty of Lima. The judgment is clear in this respect:

> The Court is not called upon to take a position as to the location of Point Concordia, where the land frontier between the Parties starts. It notes that it could be possible for the aforementioned point not to coincide with the starting-point of the maritime boundary, as it was just defined.[111]

As rightly pointed out by Judge ad hoc Guillaume, this resulted in a situation where "[t]he coast between the starting-point of the maritime boundary and Point Concordia falls under the sovereignty of Peru, whilst the sea belongs to Chile".[112] Put differently, this is another case of what is known as "dry coast". Point Concordia thus remains a new example of coast without sea, and where the land does not necessarily "dominate the sea".[113] Be it as it may, any disagreement as to the interpretation of any of the provisions of the 1929 Treaty shall be settled, pursuant to Article 12 of the treaty, by the president of the US.

All in all, it appears that the *Maritime Dispute* (*Peru* v. *Chile*) will be remembered as the first case, after the 1982 Tunisia/Libya modus vivendi, where the conduct of the Parties, in this case the acknowledgement of a maritime boundary in a treaty, confirmed the existence of a maritime boundary of 80 nautical miles.

It should be recalled that in the 1982 Judgment, the ICJ considered that in the relations between France and Italy during the period when they were responsible for the external relations of present-day Tunisia and Libya, "there came into existence a *modus vivendi* concerning the lateral delimitation of fisheries jurisdiction expressed in *de facto* respect for a line drawn from the land frontier at approximately 26° to the meridian".[114] That modus vivendi on its own was considered by the Court to fall short of proving the existence of a recognised maritime boundary between the two Parties. However, "the respect for the *tacit modus vivendi*, which was never formally contested by either side throughout a long period of time", together with the conduct of the parties, was considered by the Court to have great relevance for the delimitation of the continental shelf.[115] It seems likely that in future maritime delimitation disputes contending Parties could consider placing more efforts in proving the existence of tacit agreements, in line with the Court's reasoning *Peru* v. *Chile*.[116]

Costa Rica v. *Nicaragua* – ICJ Judgment 2018

On 25 February 2014 Costa Rica initiated proceedings against Nicaragua with regards to a "dispute concerning maritime delimitation in the Caribbean Sea and the Pacific Ocean".[117] Following the site visits of experts, by an Order of the Court dated 2 February 2017 it decided to join the proceedings in this case and the *Land Boundary in the Northern Part of Isla Portillos* case, which had been brought to the Court also by Costa Rica in January 2017. Indeed, the Court considered that the *Land Boundary* case put forward issues of territorial sovereignty which should be examined first because of their potential implications for the delimitation of the relevant maritime boundaries. After public hearings held in July 2017, the Court handed down its ruling in February 2018.

Regarding the jurisdiction of the Court, Costa Rica invoked Article XXXI of the Pact of Bogotá and Nicaragua did not contest it. The Court found that it had jurisdiction over both cases. The Court also held that the question of sovereignty over the coast of Isla Portillos on the Caribbean Sea had not been decided in its 2015 Judgment. Moreover, pursuant to its own interpretation of the 1858 Treaty of Limits between the Parties, "the territory under Costa Rica's sovereignty extended to the right bank of the Lower San Juan River as far as its mouth in the Caribbean Sea". The Court then established that Costa Rica had sovereignty over the whole of Isla Portillos, except with regards of Harbor Head Lagoon and the sandbar separating it from the Caribbean Sea, which fall under Nicaragua's sovereignty.

As for issues concerning territorial sovereignty (the land boundary in the northern part of Isla Portillos), the Court determined that Costa Rica has sovereignty over the whole of Isla Portillos up to where the river reaches the Caribbean Sea. Also, it found that the starting point of the land boundary is the point at which the right bank of the San Juan River reaches the low-water mark of the coast of the Caribbean Sea – the end of the sandpit bordering the San Juan River where the river reaches the Caribbean Sea.[118]

As for maritime areas, a sub-commission was established by the two Parties in May 1997 to conduct preliminary technical studies regarding possible maritime delimitations in the Pacific Ocean and the Caribbean Sea. After having held five meetings, between 2002 and 2005, negotiations between the two States stalled.

In the Caribbean Sea, because of the great instability of the coastline in the area of the mouth of the San Juan River, the Court found that it was preferable to select a fixed point at sea as starting point for the delimitation, at a distance of two nautical miles from the coast on the median line.[119]

In the territorial sea, the Court then proceeded to apply Article 15 of UNCLOS and its own jurisprudence, in two stages. First, it drew a provisional median line, and then it assessed whether any special circumstances existed which justified an adjustment of the line. In this regard, the Court considered that the instability of the sandbar separating Harbor Head Lagoon and its situation as a small enclave within Costa Rica's territory required a special solution. The Court hence held that the delimitation of the territorial sea between Costa Rica and Nicaragua would not take into account any entitlement generated by the enclave.[120]

In relation to the EEZ and the continental shelf, after identifying the relevant coasts and relevant area, the Court proceeded in accordance with its three-stage methodology. It hence drew a provisional equidistance line based on base points along the Parties' natural coasts, but also considering the Corn Islands. Second, the Court, after examining any relevant circumstances, found that given their limited size and significant distance from the mainland coast, said Corn Islands shall be given only half effect. Finally, it concluded there was no marked disproportionality in the result.[121]

Regarding maritime delimitation in the Pacific Ocean, the Court found that the starting point of the maritime boundary shall be, as had been agreed by the Parties, the midpoint of the closing line of Salinas Bay (coordinates 11°03′56.3″N and 85°44′28.3″W [WGC 84 datum]).

For the territorial sea, the Court pursued its two-stage approach (regarding the Caribbean Sea) and concluded that in the Pacific Ocean it would be delimited between the Parties by means of a median line which would follow a series of geodetic lines connecting the points set out in the Judgment.[122]

As for the EEZ and the continental shelf, the Court again conducted its three-stage methodology. After defining the relevant coasts, the Court checked for relevant circumstances and decided to give half effect to the Santa Elena peninsula on Costa Rica's coast so as to avoid a cut-off effect on Nicaragua's coastal projections. Then, upon the disproportionality test, the Court also found that no significant disproportion existed.[123]

In this way, the International Court of Justice defined the maritime boundaries of Costa Rica and Nicaragua, using modified and simplified equidistance in both the Caribbean Sea and Pacific Ocean.

One issue that was raised, as had been the case in the 2012 ICJ Judgment regarding *Nicaragua* v. *Colombia*, was the claims made by third States. In this regard, the Court concluded that its Judgments may only address the maritime boundaries between the Parties. It added that while the Judgment may refer to such claims, "it cannot determine whether they are well founded". Similarly, "a judgment rendered by the Court between one of the Parties and a third State or between two third States cannot *per se* affect the maritime boundary between the Parties."[124] In other words, a Judgment of the ICJ cannot override previously established maritime boundaries involving States that are not party to the dispute at hand.

Notes

1 See for instance: Scovazzi, Tullio (2009), "Maritime Delimitation Cases before International Courts and Tribunals", *Max Planck Encyclopedia of Public International Law*.

2 For a general introduction of the case, see: *Land, Island and Maritime Frontier Dispute* (*El Salvador/Honduras: Nicaragua intervening*), *Judgment, I.C.J. Reports 1992*, para. 27. For the Chamber's assessment of the "Legal situation of the Islands", see: *I.C.J. Reports 1992*, paras. 323 *et seq*.

3 Special Agreement of 24 May 1986.

4 *Land, Island and Maritime Frontier Dispute* (*El Salvador/Honduras: Nicaragua intervening*), *Judgment, I.C.J. Reports 1992*, para. 372. See also discussion about equating the word "delimitation" with the word "determination", *I.C.J. Reports 1992*, para. 373.

5 *Land, Island and Maritime Frontier Dispute* (*El Salvador/Honduras: Nicaragua intervening*), *Judgment, I.C.J. Reports 1992*, para. 378. For a reference to cases where a clear agreement was spelled concerning the task of the Court, see *I.C.J. Reports 1992*, para. 380. Another interesting aspect of the judgment is the reference to a 1900 Agreement between Honduras and Nicaragua whereby "a partial maritime boundary between the two States had been delimited". It, however, stopped well short of the waters of the main entrance to the bay; see *I.C.J. Reports 1992*, para. 389. That delimitation line is treated as one of the two exceptions to the area of joint sovereignty recognised by the 1917 Judgment; see *I.C.J. Reports 1992*, para. 413 and the 1917 Judgment, *ibid*., p. 710. The Chamber later touched upon the use of the term "condominium" by the Judgment of 1917, *I.C.J. Reports 1992*, paras. 400–401; and finally to the waters outside the Gulf; *I.C.J. Reports 1992*, paras. 415–420.

6 *Land, Island and Maritime Frontier Dispute* (*El Salvador/Honduras: Nicaragua intervening*), *Judgment, I.C.J. Reports 1992*, paras. 404, 405 and 418.

7 *Barbados/Trinidad and Tobago* Arbitration. Memorial of Barbados, paras. 142 *et seq*.

8 *Barbados/Trinidad and Tobago, Award of 11 April 2006, RIAA*, Vol. 27, paras. 250, 266, 267, 271, and 294.

9 In this respect, note that Trinidad and Tobago had claimed that the relevant circumstances were: the relevant coasts and their projection, proportionality and regional considerations. See: *Barbados/Trinidad and Tobago, Award of 11 April 2006, RIAA*, Vol. 27, paras. 321–349. See also, Kwiatkowska, Barbara (2007), "The 2006 *Barbados/Trinidad and Tobago* Award: A Landmark in Compulsory and Equitable Maritime Boundary Delimitation", *IJMCL*, Vol. 22, pp. 7–60, at pp. 48–49.

10 *Barbados/Trinidad and Tobago, Award of 11 April 2006, RIAA*, Vol. 27, paras. 372, 373–374, and 379–380.

11 *Ibid*., paras. 300–302.

12 *Ibid*., paras. 321, 335 and 242.

13 *Territorial and Maritime Dispute* (*Nicaragua* v. *Colombia*), *Judgment, I.C.J. Reports 2012*, para. 199.

14 Guyana ratified the Convention on 16 November 1993 and Suriname on 9 July 1998.

15 For a comment on the case, see for instance: Akhavi, Narges (2007), "La sentence arbitrale du 17 septembre 2007: la délimitation de la frontière maritime entre le Guyana et la Suriname", *Annuaire du droit de la Mer*, Vol. 12, pp. 89–99.

16 *Guyana/Suriname Arbitration*, Reply of the Republic of Guyana, Vol. I, 1 April 2006, paras. 6.23 *et seq*.
17 *Guyana/Suriname Arbitration*, Rejoinder of the Republic of Suriname, Vol. I, 1 September 2006, para. 3.259. See also: *Arbitral Tribunal Constituted Pursuant to Article 287, and in Accordance with Annex VII, of the United Nations Convention on the Law of the Sea in the Matter of an Arbitration Between Guyana and Suriname, Award of 17 September 2007, ILM*, Vol. 47, para. 281.
18 *Guyana/Suriname Arbitration, Award of 17 September 2007 ILM*, Vol. 47, para. 282.
19 *Ibid*., paras. 307, 323 and 295–329.
20 *Ibid*., Vol. 47, paras. 343–352, 353–357, 358–377, and 378–391. With regards to oil practice, the Arbitral Tribunal stated "The cases reveal a marked reluctance of international courts and tribunals to accord significance to the oil practice of the parties in the determination of the delimitation line"; *Guyana/Suriname Arbitration, Award of 17 September 2007 ILM*, Vol. 47, para. 390. Concerning the "material significance" of the French-Suriname agreement, see: *Ibid*., para. 391.
21 *Ibid*., para. 342.
22 The operative part of the Award is reproduced in the ICJ Judgment of 1960, see: *Arbitral Award Made by the King of Spain on 23 December 1906, Judgment, I.C.J. Reports 1960*, p. 202. The Award drew the boundary from the mouth of the river Coco, also known as Segovia or Wanks. Subsequently, Nicaragua challenged several times the validity and binding character of the Award, which ended up in a special agreement or *compromis* between Nicaragua and Honduras in order to submit that new dispute to the ICJ. Nicaragua claimed that the award was invalid by reason of its "omissions, contradictions and obscurities".
23 The Gámez-Bonilla Treaty, as translated from the Spanish and revised by the ICJ's Registry, is reproduced in: *Arbitral Award Made by the King of Spain on 23 December 1906, Judgment, I.C.J. Reports 1960*, pp. 199–204. It enshrined between the Parties the principle of *uti possidetis*. Article I of that treaty provided for the establishment of a Mixed Boundary Commission to demarcate the land boundary between Nicaragua and Honduras. The said Mixed Boundary Commission, which functioned between 1900 and 1904, effected the delimitation of the land boundary towards the Pacific Ocean but it failed to do so towards the Atlantic coast, that is the Caribbean Sea. Therefore, pursuant to the terms of Articles III and V of the Treaty, Nicaragua and Honduras submitted their dispute over the remaining portion of boundary to the King of Spain.
24 The Court found that the Award made by the King of Spain was valid and binding and that Nicaragua was under an obligation to give effect to it; see: *Arbitral Award Made by the King of Spain on 23 December 1906, Judgment, I.C.J. Reports 1960*, p. 217.
25 It was hence established that the land boundary in the Atlantic coast would begin at the mouth of the river Coco, at 14°59.8′N and 83°08.9′W.
26 It was in this context that the Sandinista Revolution overthrew the Government of Nicaragua on 19 July 1979 and brought a radical change in Nicaraguan Foreign Policy. For instance, it declared null and void the 1928 Treaty concerning Territorial Questions at issue between Colombia and Nicaragua. See: *Territorial and Maritime Dispute between Nicaragua and Honduras in the Caribbean Sea* (*Nicaragua* v. *Honduras*), *Judgment, I.C.J. Reports 2007*, para. 48. Similarly, see: *Declaración de la Junta de Gobierno de Reconstrucción Nacional de Nicaragua* of 4 February 1980 and Counter-Memorial of the Republic of Honduras, p. 41.
27 Note that the allusion to the 15th parallel is made for the sake of simplicity, since the actual parallel is constituted by the coordinate: 14°59.8′00″, see: *Nicaragua* v. *Honduras*, Counter-Memorial of the Republic of Honduras, p. 2.
28 *Territorial and Maritime Dispute between Nicaragua and Honduras in the Caribbean Sea* (*Nicaragua* v. *Honduras*), *Judgment, I.C.J. Reports 2007*, para. 49.
29 *Ibid*., para. 53.

30 *Ibid.*, para. 58.

31 Treaty concerning Maritime Delimitation between the Republic of Colombia and the Republic of Honduras; see *supra* and also: *Territorial and Maritime Dispute between Nicaragua and Honduras in the Caribbean Sea* (*Nicaragua* v. *Honduras*), *Judgment, I.C.J. Reports 2007*, paras. 59–60.

32 *Territorial and Maritime Dispute between Nicaragua and Honduras in the Caribbean Sea* (*Nicaragua* v. *Honduras*), *Judgment, I.C.J. Reports 2007*, paras. 61–66.

33 *Ibid.* para. *67*.

34 *Ibid.*, paras. 68–69.

35 *Demanda por violación de normativa y principios comunitarios centroamericanos del Sistema de Integración Centroamericana* (*SICA*), available online at www.ccj.org.ni/.

36 Nicaragua put forward two bases of the Court's jurisdiction: Article XXXI of the Pact of Bogotá, and the Declarations made by both countries under Article 36, paragraph 2, of the ICJ Statute. Neither the Jurisdiction of the Court nor the admissibility of the claims was challenged by the Respondent. In this regard, one of the points of agreement alluded to by Nicaragua's Reply was that there had not been any contradiction with respect to the jurisdiction of the Court or the admissibility of the Application, see: Reply of the Government of Nicaragua of 13 January 2003, p. 5. On a more general comment, it seems that this claim, as contended by Honduras, was premised in large part on the Applicant's unstated invitation to the Court to ignore entirely the islands, reefs and banks which are located north of the 15th parallel, features that are critical for Honduras; see Counter-Memorial of the Republic of Honduras, p. 8. Such strategy, in Honduras' view, had been chosen to denude the features of the legal status accorded to them under Article 121 of UNCLOS. Hence, for Honduras, each of these features notwithstanding its denomination as "cays" is an island in accordance with international law. *Cf.* Nicaragua claimed that it had overlooked the importance of the cays due, among other reasons, to their size; see Reply of Nicaragua, p. 31.

37 This expression has been borrowed from Honduras' Rejoinder, p. 1.

38 *I.C.J. Pleadings, Territorial and Maritime Dispute between Nicaragua and Honduras in the Caribbean Sea.* Honduras' first round of oral argument (Counsel: Christopher Greenwood), 12 March 2007 (CR 2007/6), p. 11, para. 8.

39 *I.C.J. Pleadings, Territorial and Maritime Dispute between Nicaragua and Honduras in the Caribbean Sea.* Nicaragua's second round of oral argument, 20 March 2007 (CR 2007/12), Final submissions, p. 53.

40 The islands identified as the subject matter of this dispute were Bobel Cay, Savanna Cay, Port Royal Cay and South Cay, all located north of the 15th parallel. Nicaragua put forward as its title to the islands the principle of adjacency. At the same time, it invoked as critical date 11 May 1977, when a Nicaraguan Diplomatic Note expressed to Honduras its will to initiate negotiations leading to the determination of the maritime boundary. This fact, according to Nicaragua by implication encompassed the dispute over the islands; see: *Nicaragua* v. *Honduras Judgment, I.C.J. Reports 2007*, para. 121. Honduras, in turn, claimed that its title over the islands was formed by two independent arguments: the application of the principle of *uti possidetis juris* which had been subsequently confirmed by several *effectivités*; and failing the former, it claimed to have put forward superior claims than Honduras anyway, through its many *effectivités* (i.e. historical, uninterrupted, and unchallenged exercise of sovereignty over the islands and waters which lie north of the 15th parallel, which has even been acknowledged by third States). It also claimed that Nicaragua had provided the Court with no evidence that it had ever applied or ought to apply any of its laws or regulations to the area north of the 15th parallel, and that neither had it ever sought to regulate oil, gas and fisheries activities in that area; see: Counter-Memorial of the Republic of Honduras, p. 130. Similarly, for Honduras the critical date could not be other than 2001, the date of the filing of Nicaragua's Memorial. Concerning the

attribution of the sovereignty over the islands, the Court upheld Honduras' assertion establishing as the critical date for this dispute 21 March 2001, the date of the filing of the Memorial; see: *ibid.*, para. 129. The Court, after rejecting the principle of adjacency put forward by Nicaragua, went on to analyse the *uti possidetis juris* argument advanced by Honduras as well as subsequent *effectivités*. In so doing, the Court rejected the former as well as colonial *effectivités*; see: *ibid.*, para. 167; but after dealing with post-colonial *effectivités* found that Honduras had evidenced an "intention and will to act as sovereign" and that that constitutes "a modest but real display of authority over the islands in dispute"; see: *ibid.*, para. 208. Similarly, in view of the Court Nicaragua failed to provide evidence of intention and will to act as sovereign and of any actual exercise or display of sovereign authority; see: *ibid.*

41 Nicaragua refers to the benefits of the bisector method in its Memorial, p. 96; as well as in its first round of oral arguments, see: *I.C.J. Pleadings, Territorial and Maritime Dispute between Nicaragua and Honduras in the Caribbean Sea*. Nicaragua's first round of oral argument (Counsel: Ian Brownlie), 6 March 2007 (CR 2007/2), p. 16, paras. 31 *et seq*. Honduras pointed out the inadequacy of such method in its Rejoinder of 13 August 2003, p. 3.

42 Both Parties have ratified UNCLOS, Nicaragua ratified in on 3 May 2000 whereas Honduras did on 5 October 1993.

43 *Territorial and Maritime Dispute between Nicaragua and Honduras in the Caribbean Sea* (*Nicaragua* v. *Honduras*), Counter-Memorial of the Republic of Honduras, p. 2, pp. 74–75 and pp. 85–86.

44 *Territorial and Maritime Dispute between Nicaragua and Honduras in the Caribbean Sea* (*Nicaragua* v. *Honduras*), *Judgment, I.C.J. Reports 2007*, paras. 123 and 131.

45 *Ibid.*, paras. 236, 253 and 258.

46 *Ibid.*, paras. 283–287. For a reference to cases where the bisector method was utilised see: *Continental Shelf* (*Tunisia/Libyan Arab Jamahiriya*), *Judgment, I.C.J. Reports 1982*, p. 18 (applied to the second segment); *Delimitation of the Maritime Boundary in the Gulf of Maine Area, Judgment, I.C.J. Reports 1984*, p. 246 (applied to the first segment); and *Case concerning the delimitation of the Maritime Boundary between Guinea and Guinea-Bissau* (*Republic of Guinea v. Republic of Guinea-Bissau*), *ILR* 77, p. 635 (applied to the outer stretch of the boundary).

47 Antunes, Nuno (2003), *ibid.*, p. 163.

48 That is to say the starting point of the land boundary at the mouth of the river Coco. For the coordinates see: *Territorial and Maritime Dispute between Nicaragua and Honduras in the Caribbean Sea* (*Nicaragua* v. *Honduras*), *Judgment, I.C.J. Reports 2007*, para. 99.

49 Azimuth is a mathematical concept defined as the angle, usually measured in degrees between a reference plane and a point, see: IHB (2006), *ibid.*

50 *Territorial and Maritime Dispute between Nicaragua and Honduras in the Caribbean Sea* (*Nicaragua* v. *Honduras*), *Judgment, I.C.J. Reports 2007*, para. 302.

51 *Ibid.*, para. 311.

52 *Territorial and Maritime Dispute between Nicaragua and Honduras in the Caribbean Sea* (*Nicaragua* v. *Honduras*), *Judgment, I.C.J. Reports 2007*, para. 319.

53 *Ibid.*, para. 315. *Cf. Opinion dissidente de M. le Juge Torres Bernárdez*, para. 155.

54 *Territorial and Maritime Dispute between Nicaragua and Honduras in the Caribbean Sea* (*Nicaragua* v. *Honduras*), *Judgment, I.C.J. Reports 2007*, para. 321.

55 As in the case against Honduras, Nicaragua put forward two bases for the jurisdiction of the Court. On the one hand, Article 36, paragraph 1, of the ICJ Statute, in combination with Article XXXI of the Pact of Bogotá. On the other hand, Article 36, paragraph 2, of the Statute whereby jurisdiction would also exist by way of the Declarations made by the Parties. With respect to the Declarations made by the Parties, the Court noted that they were: "made . . . under Article 36 of the Statute of the

Permanent Court of International Justice, which are deemed, for the period which they still have to run, to be acceptances of the compulsory jurisdiction of the present Court pursuant to Article 36, paragraph 5, of its Statute." See: *Territorial and Maritime Dispute* (*Nicaragua* v. *Colombia*), *Preliminary Objections, Judgment, I.C.J. Reports 2007*, p. 832, para. 1.

56 *Territorial and Maritime Dispute* (*Nicaragua* v. *Colombia*), *Preliminary Objections, Judgment, I.C.J. Reports 2007*, paras. 6 and 12.

57 Nicaragua considered that the conclusion of the 1928 Treaty violated Articles 2 and 3 of its 1911 Constitution in force until 1939. Article 2 stipulated, *inter alia*, that "treaties may not be reached that oppose the independence and integrity of the nation or that in some way affect her sovereignty"; Article 3, that "[p]ublic officials only enjoy those powers expressly granted to them by Law. Any action of theirs that exceeds these [powers] is null."

58 *Territorial and Maritime Dispute* (*Nicaragua* v. *Colombia*), *Preliminary Objections, Judgment, I.C.J. Reports 2007*, para. 81.

59 *Territorial and Maritime Dispute* (*Nicaragua* v. *Colombia*), *Preliminary Objections, Judgment, I.C.J. Reports 2007*, paras. 104 and 97.

60 *Ibid.*, paras. 120 and 142.

61 After having also considered two Applications to Intervene, both by Costa Rica and by Honduras, see: Application for Permission to Intervene by the Government of Costa Rica, 25 February 2010; and Application for Permission to Intervene by the Government of Honduras, 10 June 2010.

62 *Territorial and Maritime Dispute* (*Nicaragua* v. *Colombia*), *Judgment, I.C.J. Reports 2012*, para. 65.

63 *Territorial and Maritime Dispute* (*Nicaragua* v. *Colombia*), *Judgment, I.C.J. Reports 2012*, para. 71. According to the *Indonesia/Malaysia* judgment the critical date is the date on which the dispute between the Parties crystallised, that is, when conflicting claims were actually advanced, see: *Sovereignty over Pulau Ligitan and Pulau Sipadan* (*Indonesia/Malaysia*), *Judgment, I.C.J. Reports 2002*, para. 135. Similarly, in the *Nicaragua* v. *Honduras* case, the Court held that "[a] critical date will be the dividing line after which the Parties' acts become irrelevant for the purpose of assessing the value of effectivités" see: *Territorial and Maritime Dispute between Nicaragua and Honduras in the Caribbean Sea* (*Nicaragua* v. *Honduras*), *Judgment, I.C.J. Reports 2007*, para. 117.

64 *Territorial and Maritime Dispute* (*Nicaragua* v. *Colombia*), *Judgment, I.C.J. Reports 2012*, para. 72.

65 *Territorial and Maritime Dispute* (*Nicaragua* v. *Colombia*), *Judgment, I.C.J. Reports 2012*, para. 84.

66 Note that concerning Quitasueño, the Court concluded that only one of its features, that is QS32 (a one-square-metre feature), qualified as an island within the definition set forth in Article 121, paragraph 1, of UNCLOS. Therefore, it held that it was entitled to a territorial sea of 12 nautical miles; see: *Territorial and Maritime Dispute* (*Nicaragua* v. *Colombia*), *Judgment, I.C.J. Reports 2012*, paras. 38, 181, 182 and 202.

67 *Territorial and Maritime Dispute* (*Nicaragua* v. *Colombia*), *Judgment, I.C.J. Reports 2012*, para. 103.

68 *Territorial and Maritime Dispute* (*Nicaragua* v. *Colombia*), *Judgment, I.C.J. Reports 2012*, para. 233.

69 About the way this line was adjusted, ICJ Judge Ronny Abraham expressed his disagreement; see: *Territorial and Maritime Dispute* (*Nicaragua* v. *Colombia*), *Judgment, Separate Opinion of Judge Abraham, I.C.J. Reports 2012*, paras. 21–34. See also *Territorial and Maritime Dispute* (*Nicaragua* v. *Colombia*), *Judgment, Declaration of Judge ad hoc Cot, I.C.J. Reports*, para. 14.

70 See "enclaving" as a method of maritime delimitation (Glossary).

71 *Territorial and Maritime Dispute* (*Nicaragua* v. *Colombia*), *Judgment, I.C.J. Reports 2012*, para. 247.

72 *Ibid.*, paras. 121, 122 and 129. In so doing, the Court made reference to the distinction made by the ITLOS judgment about the delimitation of the continental shelf made under Article 83 and the delineation of its outer limits under Article 76; see *Delimitation of the Maritime Boundary in the Bay of Bengal* (*Bangladesh/Myanmar*), *ITLOS Reports 2012*, para. 376. See also *supra* new case filed by Nicaragua against Colombia. In this context, reference should be made to another ICJ case, filed subsequently by Nicaragua against Colombia.

73 Application by Nicaragua dated 16 September 2013. See also: Martin, Lawrence and Yuri Parkhomenko (2018), "The Territorial and Maritime Dispute (Nicaragua v. Colombia) and Its Implications for Future Maritime Delimitations in the Caribbean Sea and Elsewhere", in: Sobenes, Edgardo and Benjamin Samson (eds.), *Nicaragua Before the International Court of Justice. Impacts on International Law*, Springer, pp. 113–139.

74 *Territorial and Maritime Dispute* (*Nicaragua* v. *Colombia*), *Judgment, I.C.J. Reports 2012*, paras. 129–131.

75 Note that the Court also concluded that even if Colombia is not a party to UNCLOS, that "does not relieve Nicaragua of its obligations under Article 76 of that Convention"; see: *Question of the Delimitation of the Continental Shelf between Nicaragua and Colombia beyond 200 nautical miles from the Nicaraguan Coast* (*Nicaragua* v. *Colombia*), *Preliminary Objections, Judgment, I.C.J. Reports 2016*, para. 81.

76 *Question of the Delimitation of the Continental Shelf between Nicaragua and Colombia beyond 200 nautical miles from the Nicaraguan Coast* (*Nicaragua* v. *Colombia*), *Preliminary Objections, Judgment, I.C.J. Reports 2016*, p. 100, in particular, para. 114. As noted earlier in this work, the Judgment is relevant because it contributes to settling the debate concerning admissibility of maritime rights beyond 200 nautical miles without exhaustion of the procedure in UNCLOS Article 76(8), including on the question of the independence of the functions of delimitation and delineation; see ICJ Rep. Judgment, paras. 108–113.

77 *Maritime Dispute* (*Peru* v. *Chile*), *Judgment of the I.C.J. of 27 January 2014*, para. 17.

78 Treaty for the Settlement of the Dispute regarding Tacna and Arica, with Additional Protocol, between Chile and Peru, Lima, 3 June 1929, *LNTS* 94 (1929): 401–411.

79 *Maritime Dispute* (*Peru* v. *Chile*), *Judgment of the I.C.J. of 27 January 2014*, para. 18.

80 The first presentation, by diplomatic channels, made by the Government of Peru to the Government of Chile so as to enter into negotiations to establish a maritime boundary was made by a memorandum of 23 May 1986. The so-called Bákula Memorandum (presented by Peru's Ambassador Juan Miguel Bákula) is said to have been an invitation to negotiate a maritime boundary. Chile's position, in this regard, was that the Bákula Memorandum was rather an attempt by Peru to renegotiate the existing maritime boundary, see: *Maritime Dispute* (*Peru* v. *Chile*), Chile's Rejoinder, para. 3.107. See also: *Maritime Dispute* (*Peru* v. *Chile*), *Judgment of the I.C.J. of 27 January 2014*, para. 142.

81 About Peru's second submission, see: *Maritime Dispute* (*Peru* v. *Chile*), *Judgment of the I.C.J. of 27 January 2014*, paras. 14–15.

82 *Maritime Dispute* (*Peru* v. *Chile*), *Judgment of the I.C.J. of 27 January 2014*, para. 22.

83 *Maritime Dispute* (*Peru* v. *Chile*), Chile's Rejoinder, para. 1.2.

84 The 1947 Proclamations refer to Chile's Presidential Declaration of 23 June 1947 and Peru's Supreme Decree No. 781 of 1 August 1947.

85 *Maritime Dispute* (*Peru* v. *Chile*), *Judgment of the I.C.J. of 27 January 2014*, paras. 31 and 43–44.
86 *Ibid.*, paras. 58, 55–56, 60, 69 and 70.
87 *Ibid.*, paras. 71, 82, 83, 89 and 90.
88 *Ibid.*, para. 91. The French version reads: "L'accord de 1954 est un élément décisif à cet égard. Il a pour effet de *consacrer* l'accord tacite en question" (emphasis added).
89 *Ibid.*, paras. 96 and 99.
90 *Ibid.*, para. 102.
91 *Ibid.*, paras. 117, 129 and 151. See also the consideration by the Court to the answers by the Parties to Judge Bennouna's question, *Maritime Dispute* (*Peru* v. *Chile*), *Judgment of the I.C.J. of 27 January 2014*, para. 116. At the end of Chile's first round of oral arguments, Judge Bennouna made the following question to both Parties: "Considérez-vous, en tant que signataires de la déclaration de Santiago en 1952, que vous pouviez à cette date, conformément au droit international général, proclamer et délimiter une zone maritime de souveraineté et de juridiction exclusive sur la mer qui baigne les côtes de vos pays respectifs jusqu'à 200 milles marins au minimum des dites côtes?"; see: *I.C.J. Pleadings, Maritime Dispute* (*Peru* v. *Chile*). Chile's first round of oral argument, 7 December 2012 (CR 2012/32), pp. 62–63.
92 *Maritime Dispute* (*Peru* v. *Chile*), *Judgment of the I.C.J. of 27 January 2014*, para. 175. It reads: "The Court is not called upon to take a position as to the location of Point Concordia, where the land frontier between the Parties starts. It notes that it could be possible for the aforementioned point not to coincide with the starting-point of the maritime boundary, as it was just defined. The Court observes, however, that such a situation would be the consequence of the agreements reached between the Parties." In this respect, it should be recalled that the land boundary between Chile and Peru was fully delimited by the 1929 Treaty of Lima, which provided that the frontier between the Parties starts from a point on the coast to be named Concordia. A Joint Commission, subsequently, demarcated the boundary in 1930, under the explicit instructions from the two Governments that the final portion of the land boundary was defined by a ten-kilometre radius arc measured from the bridge over the river Lluta, and that the starting point of the dividing line between the Parties' territories was the intersection of that arc with the seashore; see: *Maritime Dispute* (*Peru* v. *Chile*), Peru's Reply, para. 2.89.
93 *Maritime Dispute* (*Peru* v. *Chile*), *Judgment of the I.C.J. of 27 January 2014*, para. 165.
94 *Ibid.*, paras. 174 and 176.
95 *Ibid.*, para. 181. For a reference to practice in that sense, see: *Peru* v. *Chile*, para. 183. Note that, as the Court has done in previous cases, it applies customary rules of the Law of the Sea Convention concerning maritime delimitation even though Peru has not yet ratified it, see: *Peru* v. *Chile*, para. 179.
96 *Ibid.*, paras. 186, 190 and 195.
97 *Ibid.*, paras. 14–15 and 187. Peru's second submission reads: "Beyond the point where the common maritime border ends, Peru is entitled to exercise exclusive sovereign rights over a maritime area lying out to a distance of 200 nautical miles from its baselines." This is referred to by Peru as the "Outer Triangle", while Chile calls it "the *Alta Mar* area" (the high seas). It consists of an area located within the 200-nautical-mile limit from the Peruvian coasts and beyond 200 nautical miles from Chile's coasts.
98 *Ibid.*, para. 189.
99 *Ibid.*, para. 196.
100 *Ibid.*, para. 197. Peru and Chile have already started a process to comply with the Court's mandate contained in paragraph 197 (and also in paragraph 196) of the Judgment of 27 January 2014. On 6 February 2014, the Parties signed a Joint Declaration establishing, *inter alia*, a technical and cartographic working group in view to finalise

those works before the end of March 2014; see: "Declaración Conjunta de los Ministros de Relaciones Exteriores y Defensa de Perú y Chile con ocasión de la Reunión Extraordinaria del Comité Permanente de Consulta y Coordinación Política (2 + 2)", Santiago de Chile, 6 February 2014. Text available in Spanish at www.rree.gob.pe/Noticias/Paginas/DC-013-14.aspx (accessed on 1 March 2022).

101 *Maritime Delimitation and Territorial Questions between Qatar and Bahrain, Jurisdiction and Admissibility, Judgment, I.C.J. Reports 1995*, p. 6; and *I.C.J. Pleadings, Maritime Dispute* (*Peru* v. *Chile*). Peru's first round of oral argument (Counsel: Alain Pellet), 3 December 2012 (CR 2012/27), p. 24. See also: Horna, Angel V. (2009), "Maritime Dispute (Peru v. Chile): Background and Preliminary Thoughts", *Ocean Yearbook*, Vol. 23, p. 229.

102 The judges who expressed "serious reservations" were Judge Sepúlveda-Amor and Judge Owada, see: *Declaration of Vice-President Sepúlveda-Amor*, para. 1; and *Separate Opinion of Judge Owada*, para. 3, although Judge Owada proposed instead a "*de facto* delimitation", para. 26. Similarly, Judge Sebutinde was against this reasoning, see: *Dissenting Opinion of Judge Sebutinde*, para. 6. Even Judges Xue, Gaja, Bhandari and Judge ad hoc Orrego, were against the tacit agreement argument, see: *Joint Dissenting Opinion of Judges Xue, Gaja, Bhandari and Judge ad hoc Orrego Vicuña*, paras. 19–26. Cases in which the Court considered the existence of a *de facto* line include: *Continental Shelf* (*Tunisia/Libyan Arab Jamahiriya*), *Judgment, I.C.J. Reports 1982*, para. 96; *Delimitation of the Maritime Boundary in the Gulf of Maine Area, Judgment, I.C.J. Reports 1984*, para. 150; *Land and Maritime Boundary between Cameroon and Nigeria* (*Cameroon* v. *Nigeria: Equatorial Guinea intervening*), *Judgment, I.C.J. Reports 2002*, para. 304; and *Territorial and Maritime Dispute between Nicaragua and Honduras in the Caribbean Sea* (*Nicaragua* v. *Honduras*), *I.C.J. Reports 2007*, paras. 253, 256 and 258.

103 *Maritime Dispute* (*Peru* v. *Chile*), *Judgment of the I.C.J. of 27 January 2014*, para. 90.

104 *Declaration of Vice-President Sepúlveda-Amor*, para. 14.

105 *Territorial and Maritime Dispute between Nicaragua and Honduras in the Caribbean Sea* (*Nicaragua* v. *Honduras*), *I.C.J. Reports 2007*, para. 253.

106 See for instance: *I.C.J. Pleadings, Maritime Dispute* (*Peru* v. *Chile*). Peru's first round of oral argument (Counsel: Michael Wood), 3 December 2012 (CR 2012/27), p. 57; and *I.C.J. Pleadings, Maritime Dispute* (*Peru* v. *Chile*). Peru's first round of oral argument (Counsel: Vaughan Lowe), 4 December 2012 (CR 2012/29), p. 20.

107 In this regard see: Kolb, Robert (2003). *Case Law on Equitable Maritime Delimitation*. The Hague (etc.): Martinus Nijhoff, p. 455. Kolb discusses the solution of the ICJ to the *Jan Mayen* case when called upon to interpret a maritime delimitation agreement (concluded between Denmark and Norway on 8 December 1965). In so doing, the Court restricted its scope as much as it could. The ICJ then turned to the arguments based on the conduct of the parties (in particular of Denmark) and refused to apply lightly concepts such as tacit recognition, acquiescence or *estoppel*.

108 *Territorial and Maritime Dispute between Nicaragua and Honduras in the Caribbean Sea* (*Nicaragua* v. *Honduras*), Counter-Memorial of the Republic of Honduras, pp. 85–86.

109 See: *Declaration of Judge Donoghue*.

110 *Maritime Dispute* (*Peru* v. *Chile*), *Judgment of the I.C.J. of 27 January 2014*, para. 176.

111 *Maritime Dispute* (*Peru* v. *Chile*), *Judgment of the I.C.J. of 27 January 2014*, para. 175.

112 *Declaration of Judge ad hoc Guillaume*, para. 15.

113 *I.C.J. Pleadings, Maritime Dispute* (*Peru* v. *Chile*). Chile's first round of oral argument (Counsel: Jan Paulsson), 7 December 2012 (CR 2012/31), pp. 35–38.

114 *Continental Shelf* (*Tunisia/Libyan Arab Jamahiriya*), *Judgment, I.C.J. Reports 1982*, para. 119.

115 *Continental Shelf* (*Tunisia/Libyan Arab Jamahiriya*), *Judgment, I.C.J. Reports 1982*, para. 96. It is worth noting that the Italian authorities, "in order to avoid the danger of friction that might arise from the difficulty of establishing the precise position of a foreign vessel near the frontier, established two eight-mile buffer zones at the two ends of the Libyan coast, within which vessels flying foreign flags and not holding a license from the Italian authorities would be liable to be ordered away but not seized", para. 94. This formulation is similar to that established by the 1954 SMZFA.

116 See, for instance, *Delimitation of the Maritime Boundary in the Atlantic Ocean* (*Ghana/Côte d'Ivoire*), *Judgment, ITLOS Reports 2017*, p. 14, paras. 211–228; where the Special Chamber, however, did not accept the tacit agreement argument raised by Ghana; and *Maritime Delimitation in the Indian Ocean* (*Somalia* v. *Kenya*), *I.C.J. Reports 2021*, para. 52 *et seq*., and also para. 89.

117 *Maritime Delimitation in the Caribbean Sea and the Pacific Ocean* (*Costa Rica v. Nicaragua*) *and Land Boundary in the Northern Part of Isla Portillos* (*Costa Rica v. Nicaragua*), *Judgment, I.C.J. Reports 2018*, p. 139.

118 *Costa Rica v. Nicaragua, Judgment, I.C.J. Reports 2018*, paras. 59–73.

119 *Costa Rica v. Nicaragua, Judgment, I.C.J. Reports 2018*, paras. 80–89.

120 *Costa Rica v. Nicaragua, Judgment, I.C.J. Reports 2018*, paras. 90–106.

121 *Costa Rica v. Nicaragua, Judgment, I.C.J. Reports 2018*, paras. 135–145 and paras. 158–166.

122 *Costa Rica v. Nicaragua, Judgment, I.C.J. Reports 2018*, para. 175.

123 *Costa Rica v. Nicaragua, Judgment, I.C.J. Reports 2018*, paras. 177–185, and 201.

124 *Costa Rica v. Nicaragua, Judgment, I.C.J. Reports 2018*, para. 123 *et seq*.

9 Unresolved Maritime Boundaries

Before touching upon unresolved maritime boundaries in Latin America and the Caribbean, I will briefly discuss two cases relating to provisional arrangements. Then, reference will be made to ongoing negotiations and pending maritime boundaries.

Provisional Arrangements

Cuba/US – 1977

Despite the absence of diplomatic relations between Cuba and the US, the negotiation of a maritime boundary was at the centre of the agenda when these two countries resumed direct diplomatic discussions at the beginning of 1977. Hence, Cuba and the US concluded a modus vivendi concerning the delimitation of their maritime spaces in April 1977,[1] following the enactment by the two Governments of legislation establishing a 200-nautical-mile zone. Later that year, in December, after having carried out technical work, especially the coming into terms concerning a common datum,[2] the Parties reached a maritime delimitation agreement which was signed on 17 December 1977.[3] It appears that, even though it has not been ratified, it is the text of this latter agreement, and the line established therein which is used as the provisional agreement, that is renewed every two years pursuant to treaty provisions[4] governing the overlapping entitlements of the two countries.

The enactment of claims made by these two countries in 1977, and especially the need to enforce them – and following negotiations held in New York and Havana – Cuba and the US agreed on a line that would serve them both, pending the conclusion of a definitive agreement.[5]

The language used in the text of the Exchange of Letters proposed, "as a modus vivendi for 1977", that the line described by the 17 coordinates indicated therein be accepted as the maritime boundary between those States with opposite coasts. However, in the treaty itself, signed in December that year, the coordinates were no longer 17 but 27. Hence, the line joining the 27 coordinates, starting towards the east at 23°55′30″N and 81°12′55″W, and ending towards the west at 25°12′25″N and 86°33′12″W, was close to an equidistance line but, in the end, was negotiated

DOI: 10.4324/9781003290452-12

at every turning point. Therefore, it did not necessarily follow the initial approach of the US whereby the maritime boundary would be constructed according to the equidistance method, giving full effect to the Florida Keys and Dry Tortugas.

Concerning Cuba's straight baselines system, it seems that US negotiators established artificial straight baselines along Florida's coastline, from which a median line was drawn in order to compensate the utilisation of questionable straight baselines in the area affecting a US-Cuban equidistance line.[6]

It is interesting to note that the Parties used the formula put forward in the Gulf of Paria Treaty, and that has been used ever since in a number of treaties. The formula stipulates that "on the north side of the line Cuba would not, and on the south side of the line the United States would not, for any purpose, claim or exercise sovereign rights or jurisdiction over the waters or sea-bed and subsoil."

Colombia/Costa Rica – 1977 (Caribbean Sea)

Colombia, which carried out simultaneous negotiations with Panama, concluded a maritime delimitation agreement with Costa Rica concerning their overlapping areas in the Caribbean Sea in 1977.[7] It concerned Colombia's Albuquerque Cay (San Andrés Archipelago) and Costa Rica's rather brief mainland coast. As pointed out before, this agreement was left without object[8] with the 2012 ICJ Judgment on *Nicaragua* v. *Colombia*, because the object of this treaty-based delimitation "disappears with the substitution of Nicaragua for Colombia as the holder of sovereignty or sovereign rights in the spaces concerned."[9]

In addition to the foregoing, according to information released by the Ministry of Foreign Affairs of Honduras,[10] in May 2013 delegations of the two countries met for the second time after January 2013 in relation to the question of their maritime delimitation. Exchange of views concerning baselines and a general discussion about the nautical chart to be used took place.

The Bahamas and the US began negotiations in April 2012 in order to define their maritime borders.[11] The two governments held a second round of negotiations in December 2012 and a third round in June 2018. Discussions seem to have been based upon a preliminary proposal presented by the US during the first round of negotiations, which was followed by a counter-proposal presented by the Bahamas during the second round.[12] In the meantime, the Bahamas, pursuant to Act No. 37 of 1993, addressed the situation of undelimited boundaries. Section 8 of the Act states that if the median line is less than 200 miles from the nearest baseline, the outer limits of the EEZ of the Bahamas would extend to the median line.[13]

Similarly, it appears that the following negotiations are also taking place: Jamaica/UK (Cayman Islands); Cuba/UK (Cayman Islands); the Netherlands (Saba)/UK (Anguilla); and Bahamas/UK (Turks and Caicos Islands).[14] It is known that negotiations took place between Dominica and Venezuela and between Grenada and Venezuela but did not reach an outcome at that time.[15]

Other maritime boundary delimitations yet to be negotiated include US/UK (Bermuda); US/Cuba (Eastern Gap); US/Mexico (Eastern Gap); US (Puerto Rico)/Dominican Republic; and US (Virgin Islands)/the Netherlands (Saba).[16]

Similarly, UK (Monserrat)/Saint Kitts and Nevis; UK (Montserrat)/Antigua and Barbuda; UK (Montserrat)/Venezuela (Aves Island); and UK (Turks and Caicos Islands)/Haiti.[17] Also pending are France/Saint Kitts and Nevis; Antigua and Barbuda/Saint Kitts and Nevis; Dominican Republic/Haiti; Dominican Republic/the Netherlands (Aruba, Bonaire and Curaçao); and Jamaica/Haiti (with the added complication of US-claimed Navassa Island).

Concerning pending maritime delimitation issues between Belize and Honduras and between Guatemala and Honduras, their settlement seems difficult to reach due to their being related to disputes over land.[18] Similarly, the long-running maritime dispute between Belize and Guatemala was brought before the International Court of Justice on 7 June 2019, marking Guatemala's first reappearance before the Court since the *Nottebohm* case. It followed two referenda, one held by Guatemala on 15 April 2018 and the other by Belize on 8 May 2019.[19]

With respect to the maritime boundary between Guatemala and Mexico, recently voices have been raised, especially in Mexico, relating to the need to start negotiations to exploit resources – apparently oil and gas – that could be found in that region.[20]

Finally, in relation to South American coastal States, serious potential maritime disputes could result from the de facto situation concerning the Falkland Islands (Malvinas). Also, there does not seem to be a foreseeable solution for the pending delimitation between Colombia and Venezuela.

The Colombia/Venezuela dispute relates to a very sensitive issue for both States, the delimitation of the waters off the Gulf of Venezuela, situated between the Guajira Peninsula in Colombia and the Paraguaná Peninsula in Venezuela. The Gulf of Venezuela constitutes the natural exit from the Maracaibo "lake" for Caracas, whose claim to those waters is partially based on its possession of Los Monjes Islands.[21]

As for the Guyana/Venezuela dispute, it is anchored in Venezuela's claim to a large area known as the Essequibo Region. This dispute, although mainly related to land, was brought to the International Court of Justice in 2018 by Guyana. In its Application, Guyana requested the Court "to confirm the legal validity and binding effect of the Award Regarding the Boundary between the Colony of British Guiana and the United States of Venezuela, of 3 October 1899".[22]

To sum up, there are 43 maritime boundary agreements in Latin America and the Caribbean and at least 33 unresolved maritime boundaries. Two additional agreements were also concluded but never came into force. While there is no uniform delimitation method employed in maritime boundary agreements in Latin America and the Caribbean, a majority of them employ some form of equidistance.

Also, following a review of maritime delimitation treaties concluded in the region, it is possible to claim that while in the framework of UNCLOS III some coastal States advanced their views on certain principles and rules on maritime delimitation, in their maritime bilateral relations those States would put already into practice (i.e. enshrine in treaties), the views they were still defending in the conference.

Barbados/Guyana – 2003

This is the case of a provisional arrangement[23] concluded by Barbados and Guyana in December 2003, in application of Article 74, paragraph 3 of UNCLOS. It recognises explicitly that such arrangement shall be without prejudice to the final delimitation. The agreement established a co-operation zone for the exercise of joint jurisdiction, control, management, development, and exploration and exploitation of living and non-living natural resources in the area of overlap of their EEZs. The precise geographical extent of the co-operation zone was defined in Annex 1 to the treaty.[24] Note that Barbados and Guyana have expressed their concern about the 1990 maritime delimitation treaty between Trinidad and Tobago and Venezuela, as they consider that it infringes upon their EEZ or even on their potential outer continental shelf claims.

Notes

1 Modus vivendi effected by exchange of letters between the United States of America and the Republic of Cuba (Signature: 27 April 1977; entry into force: 27 April 1977). Text of the modus vivendi available at DOALOS' website; and also at: DOALOS (1987), *The Law of the Sea: Maritime Boundary Agreements* (*1970–1984*), New York: United Nations, p. 94. Note that although the Parties concluded a maritime boundary agreement on 16 December 1977, it never came into force, although the text of the treaty established 27 coordinates that should be joined by geodetic lines, whereas the Exchange of Letters established only 17. For an account of the negotiation from US authors, see: Feldman and Colson (1981), *ibid.*, p. 746. See also generally: Smith, Robert W. (1993), in: Charney, J.J. and L.M. Alexander (eds.), *Ibid.*, pp. 417–425; *Limits in the Seas No. 110, Maritime Boundary: Cuba–United States*. US Department of State, 21 February 1990; and Labrecque, Georges, *Ibid.*, pp. 213–214. For a discussion of the concept of *modus vivendi* in the framework of a maritime delimitation case see: *Continental Shelf* (*Tunisia/Libyan Arab Jamahiriya*)*, Judgment, I.C.J. Reports 1982*, paras. 95–96; and also: *Delimitation of the Maritime Boundary in the Gulf of Maine Area, Judgment, I.C.J. Reports 1984*, para. 151.

2 It seems that at the beginning of negotiations the two countries used different geodetic data; see: Feldman and Colson (1981), *ibid.*, p. 746.

3 Maritime Boundary Agreement Between the United States of America and the Republic of Cuba (Signature: 16 December 1977). Note, additionally, that on 18 January 2017 (shortly before Obama left office), the US signed a bilateral treaty with Cuba to delimit their maritime boundary in the eastern Gulf of Mexico. Before entering into force, the agreement will warrant the advice and consent of the US Senate; see: https://cu.usembassy.gov/united-states-cuba-sign-maritime-boundary-treaty/ (accessed on 22 March 2022).

4 The Cuba/US agreement is provisionally applied in accordance to Article V of the Treaty which reads: "The Parties agree to apply the terms of this Agreement provisionally from January 1, 1978, for a period of two years, and it will enter into force permanently on the date of exchange of instruments of ratification"; see: Roach and Smith, *ibid.*, p. 900.

5 As mentioned before, Cuba did not ratify any of the four Geneva Conventions on the Law of the Sea while the US is Party to all. In terms of national claims, the Government of Cuba, by means of Decree-Law No. 2 of 24 February 1977, and the US Government, by means of Public Law No. 94–265 of 13 April 1976, established a 200-nautical-mile EEZ. Cuba, on the other hand, ratified UNCLOS on 15 August 1984.

6 Feldman and Colson (1981), *ibid.*, p. 746. See also: Ortolland and Pirat (2010), *ibid.*, p. 102. For a comment and a reference to the US protest concerning a 69-mile segment of the Cuban system of straight baselines along the Bay of Cienfuegos, see: Roach and Smith (2012), *ibid.*, p. 118.

7 Treaty on Delimitation of Marine and Submarine Areas and Maritime Co-operation between the Republic of Colombia and the Republic of Costa Rica (Signature: 17 March 1977; entry into force: never). Costa Rica never ratified that instrument. While it was not approved by the Costa Rican Parliament, it seems to have been applied by both Parties, at least until November 2012. See in this regard, *inter alia*, Diplomatic Note No. DM. 172–96 from the Costa Rican Foreign Minister to the Colombian Foreign Minister, 14 May 1996; in: Annex 67 of Counter-Memorial of the Republic of Colombia. See also: *Application for Permission to Intervene by the Government of Costa Rica*, 25 February 2010, p. 6, where it is stated concerning this treaty that: "Costa Rica has, in good faith, refrained from acts which would defeat the object and purpose of this agreement". Text of the treaty available at DOALOS' website. See also generally: Nweihed, Kaldone (1993), in: Charney, J.J. and L.M. Alexander (eds.), *ibid.*, pp. 463–476; *Limits in the Seas No. 84, Maritime Boundaries: Colombia-Panama*. US Department of State, Issued by the Geographer, 1979; and Labrecque, Georges (2004), *ibid.*, p. 205–206. Following the Latin American practice, this treaty is also known as "the 1977 Tratado Facio-Fernández".

8 It became "null and void or ceased to exist", see: *Declaration of Judge ad hoc Cot, Territorial and Maritime Dispute* (*Nicaragua* v. *Colombia*), *Judgment, I.C.J. Reports 2012*, para. 10 *et seq*.

9 *Declaration of Judge ad hoc Cot, Territorial and Maritime Dispute* (*Nicaragua* v. *Colombia*), *Judgment, I.C.J. Reports 2012*, paras. 10 *et seq*., and *Declaration of Judge Xue, Territorial and Maritime Dispute* (*Nicaragua* v. *Colombia*), *Judgment, I.C.J. Reports 2012*, para. 15.

10 Available at www.sre.gob.hn/portada/2013/Enero/23_01_13/inician%20trabajos.pdf accessed on 1 March 2022).

11 Available at http://nassau.usembassy.gov/maritimeboundary.html (accessed on 1 March 2022)

12 Available at www.thebahamasweekly.com/publish/international/Bahamas_-_U_S_resume_maritime_boundary_delimitation_talks_in_Washington_D_C25707.shtml (accessed on 7 June 2020).

13 *Limits in the Seas No. 128*, 31 January 2014, *ibid.*, p. 4.

14 Dundas, Carl W. (2005-A), "Middle American and Caribbean Maritime Boundaries", in: Colson, David A. and Robert W. Smith (eds.), *ibid.*, p. 3406.

15 See: CARICOM Report, para. 60; and Dundas, Carl W. (2005-A), *ibid.*, p. 3406.

16 Roach and Smith (2012), *ibid.*, pp. 900–902.

17 Dundas, Carl W. (2005-A), *ibid.*, p. 3406. Note that the Organisation of Eastern Caribbean States (OECS) announced in November 2012 that its member States (Antigua and Barbuda, Dominica, Grenada, Montserrat, Saint Kitts and Nevis, Saint Lucia, and Saint Vincent and the Grenadines) will establish their maritime boundaries as of 2013 under the supervision of experts of that regional block; see www.oecs.org/media-center/press-releases/secretariat/60-authority/751-communiqu%C3%A9-fifty-seventh-meeting-of-the-oecs-authority (accessed on 1 March 2022).

18 According to statements by Honduran MFA, the issues of maritime boundaries with Guatemala and Belize are difficult due to their involving pending land and maritime disputes; see www.tiempo.hn/portada/item/5576-por-buen-camino-negociaci%C3%B3n-para-delimitaci%C3%B3n-mar%C3%ADtima-con-jamaica (accessed on 22 March 2022).

19 Lauterpacht, Elihu; Schwebel, Stephen; Rosenne, Shabtai; and Francisco Orrego Vicuña (2001), *Legal Opinion on Guatemala's Territorial Claim to Belize*. See also:

Special Agreement between Belize and Guatemala to submit Guatemala's territorial, insular and maritime claim to the International Court of Justice, 8 December 2008.

20 See www.noticiasnet.mx/portal/principal/81363-necesario-delimitar-frontera-maritima-guatemala-ericel (accessed on 1 March 2022).

21 Anderson, Thomas (1989), "The Gulf of Venezuela Sea Boundary: A Problem between Friends", *Yearbook of the Conference of Latin Americanist Geographers*, available at http://sites.maxwell.syr.edu/CLAG/yearbook1989/anderson.htm (accessed on 22 March 2022).

22 The case between Guyana and Venezuela, which involves a claim of Venezuela as far as the River Essequibo, was the object of United Nations Secretary-General mediation efforts; see: www.un.org/wcm/content/site/undpa/mediation_support. For a general account on South America's maritime boundaries, see: Colson, David A. and Robert W. Smith (2005), *ibid.*, pp. 3425–3428. Note that the ICJ (held) Public hearings by videoconference on 30 June 2020 concerning the case of the *Arbitral Award of 3 October 1899* (*Guyana* v. *Venezuela*).

23 Exclusive Economic Zone Co-operation Treaty between the State of Barbados and the Republic of Guyana concerning the exercise of jurisdiction in their exclusive economic zones in the area of bilateral overlap within each of their outer limits and beyond the outer limits of the exclusive economic zones of other States (with annex and figure) (Signature: 2 December 2003; entry into force, 5 May 2004). For a commentary, see: Dundas, Carl W. (2005), "Barbados-Guyana", in: Colson, David A. and Robert W. Smith, *ibid.*, pp. 3578–3597. See also: Nordquist, M.H. (ed.) (1993), *UNCLOS – A Commentary*, Vol. II, pp. 812–816 and 978–984; Galletti, Florence (2004), "Notion et pratique de 'l'arrangement provisoire' prévu aux articles 74 § 3 et 83 § 3 de la Convention sur le droit de la mer. Une contribution marginale du droit de la délimitation maritime", *Annuaire du droit de la Mer*, Vol. 9, pp. 115–141; and Klein, Natalie (2006), "Provisional Measures and Provisional Arrangements in Maritime Boundary Disputes", *IJMCL*, Vol. 21, pp. 423–460.

24 Guyana ratified UNCLOS on 16 November 1993. On 6 September 2011, Guyana submitted to the Commission on the Limits of the Continental Shelf information on the limits of the continental shelf beyond 200 nautical miles from the baselines from which the breadth of the territorial sea is measured. Barbados, on the other hand, ratified UNCLOS on 12 October 1993.

10 Impact of State Practice on the Law of Maritime Delimitation

This part discusses the possible impact of State practice, which consists of the conduct of the State, on the law of maritime delimitation. In so doing, it addresses State practice as an element in the formation of customary international law and State practice as an element in treaty interpretation. Additionally, it also includes some reflections on the impact of case law on regional State practice.

The law of maritime delimitation, due to its low normative density[1] and the "uninstructive" character of the fundamental norm governing it, that of the equitable result,[2] comprises essentially case law from the International Court of Justice, from the International Tribunal for the Law of the Sea, and decisions of arbitral tribunals, which is the reason why it is qualified as "judge-made law"[3] or praetorian law.[4]

Indeed, the weak contents of the rules enshrined in Articles 74 and 83 of the 1982 United Nations Convention on the Law of the Sea, and the fact that the equidistance method was neglected, contributed to the low normative density of the law of maritime delimitation. It did so, according to Prosper Weil, in the following terms:

> [T]hese provisions, the text of which stems from a last-minute compromise intended to save the conference, could only obtain a consensus . . . at the cost of maintaining silence both on equidistance and on equitable principles, in other words by eliminating the very issue of the controversy which had opposed two groups of States throughout the Third UN Conference: equitable principles disappeared in the turmoil at the same time as equidistance, and only survived the harmless mention of a just or equitable solution. Is it necessary to recall that these neutral provisions, far from stating a legal norm addressed to the judge or the arbitrator, formulate a directive addressed to the negotiators, moreover devoid of any scope or sanction? Should it be emphasized once again that apart from the prescription of equitable purpose, Articles 74 and 83 are silent, unlike Article 6 [of the 1958 Geneva Convention on the Continental Shelf], on the procedure to follow, on the modus operandi, making it possible to achieve this objective, whereas, precisely, it is on the problem of the means . . . that the difficulties and the controversies are concentrated?[5]

DOI: 10.4324/9781003290452-13

Similarly, for Judges Ruda, Bedjaoui and Jiménez de Aréchaga:

> the law governing maritime delimitation is still affected with a degree of indeterminacy, in the sense that the reasonings put forward do not invariably and automatically "produce" a delimitation line. Often, even, a regrettable but doubtless inevitable gap can be observed between the arguments expounded in a judicial decision and the concrete finding as regards the choice of delimitation line adopted. However well-founded, the reasoning does not necessarily, mathematically, "issue" in the conclusion adopted. This is, of course, because the law of the sea is still quite rudimentary and comprises few rules, and more especially because the entire process of maritime delimitation law is dominated by a "fundamental norm", that of the equitable result, which is as uninstructive as it is all-embracing. That being so, a judge can but anxiously, humbly, gauge and compare his crushing responsibility and the modest means at his disposal for assuming it. He undergoes what Verlaine called "l'extase et la terreur de celui qui a été choisi". He cannot see how to escape from the frustrating tyranny of a certain "praetorian subjectivism" when the very margin of indeterminacy responsible for it originated in a law still young and permeated with equity – which, though a highly respectable legal concept, is inevitably measured with a "human" yardstick. The finest legal dissertations on equity will never succeed in completely eliminating what is perhaps an irreducible core of the judicial subjectivism mentioned above. The utmost, in all honour, that a judge can then do is modest: to summon up all his resources with a view to reducing its scope and effects to a minimum. At the same time, in a situation where one intends to judge exclusively on a basis of law but finds that equity is the fundamental norm of the law concerned, it is impossible to ignore that while "few terms are as pleasing to mind and heart [as equity, and] few so deeply touch an ingrained expectancy of human nature, few, on the other hand, remain so mysterious."[6]

Against this background – where the applicable law has been categorised as highly subjective – this section will look into the actual legal impact that State practice in Latin America and the Caribbean, as discussed earlier in this work, has had on the law of maritime delimitation.[7] In so doing, it shall first touch upon the impact that State practice has had on the law of maritime delimitation, as an element in the formation of customary international law, and then upon the impact that State practice has had as an element in treaty interpretation.

State Practice as an Element in the Formation of Customary International Law

This section covers State practice as one of the two elements required for the formation of customary international law. In this sense, only certain forms of practice are being dealt with here: namely, national legislation on the one hand, and – even more foundationally – maritime delimitation agreements.

With regards to national legislation, the impact that Latin American and Caribbean practice has had on the extension of rights of coastal States, which eventually led them to enjoy sovereign rights and jurisdiction over a 200-nautical-mile zone, will be addressed. As will be seen, that extension constituted the ultimate cause that triggered the dramatic increase in the need to establish maritime boundaries, be they by negotiation or by international adjudication. On the other hand, as a result of that extension, I argue, there has been another kind of State practice, reflected in a number of maritime delimitation agreements, that contributed to the process resulting in the 1982 UNCLOS' provisions on delimitation of the EEZ and the continental shelf.

Unilateral Practice and the Extension of Maritime Areas to 200 Nautical Miles

Initiated in 1947, with unilateral proclamations made by Chile and Peru, and complemented in 1952 with the tripartite Santiago Declaration, signed by those two countries and Ecuador; the 200-nautical-mile zone (today "exclusive economic zone") is ultimately the result of Latin American and Caribbean State practice.[8] One author, regarding those claims, has described the process as "Latin American regionalism", since the nature of the claims reflected a regional approach of States defending their own interests.[9]

After the adoption and entry into force of the 1958 Geneva Conventions, the 200 nautical mile concept continued to develop progressively in the 1970s, when other States made fisheries jurisdiction claims, extending also to 200 nautical miles.[10] By the mid-1980s, before the entry into force of the 1982 Law of the Sea Convention, the ICJ stated that

> It is in the Court's view incontestable that . . . the institution of the exclusive economic zone, with its rule on entitlement by reason of distance, is shown by the *practice of States* to have become a part of customary law [emphasis added].[11]

This situation amounted to the crystallisation of a new rule of customary international law, the 200-nautical-mile zone, that emerged subsequent to the conclusion of a treaty, the 1958 Geneva Convention on the High Seas, that eventually replaced it.[12] In that regard, concerning the continental shelf the ICJ had already held in 1969 that the 1945 Truman Proclamation, together with claims made by other States, were considered by the Court as having given rise to a rule of customary law.[13] Similarly, Judge Alvarez, in his individual opinion in the *Anglo-Norwegian Fisheries* case, discussed these kinds of claims, stating in 1951 that they could carry a great weight "if established by a group of States, and specially by all the States of a continent."[14]

Be that as it may, this appears to be, as stated before, the case of a rule of customary international law emerging subsequent to the conclusion of a treaty, the 1958 Geneva Convention on the High Seas, that modified it while giving birth to a new treaty, the 1982 Law of the Sea Convention.

Another example of the same situation occurred a few years before. It was the case of States claiming, as of the Second United Nations Conference on the Law of the Sea, 12-nautical-mile exclusive fishing zones beyond their territorial seas. While this seemed to have been in violation of the 1958 High Seas Convention, it was acknowledged by the ICJ in the *Fisheries Jurisdiction* case.[15]

In any case, it seems possible to assert that the creation of the exclusive economic zone, together with the resulting dramatic enlargement of zones surrendered to national jurisdiction, is mainly attributable to Latin American and Caribbean coastal States, and that the sharp increase in maritime delimitation disputes (effective or potential) has been prompted by that expansion.[16] One may hence establish a relationship between the behaviour of those Latin American and Caribbean States and the development of the law of maritime delimitation.

Bilateral Practice and the Delimitation of Maritime Areas

Having stated that unilateral State practice in Latin America and the Caribbean was the driver of a process that contributed to the establishment of conventional rules concerning the breadth of the maritime area where coastal States could exercise a number of exclusive rights, I will now turn to the situation in which bilateral State practice, that is, the conduct of States in the form of maritime delimitation agreements, has influenced the provisions of the Law of the Sea Convention concerning the delimitation of the EEZ and the continental shelf.[17] This would amount to a rule of customary international law emerging either where there was no treaty, as is the case of the EEZ, or where there was a treaty with a similar subject matter, which is the case of the Convention on the Territorial Sea and the Convention on the Continental Shelf.[18]

By looking at State practice in Latin America and the Caribbean, particularly that taking place between 1970 and 1982, during which time 16 maritime delimitation agreements were concluded, one can find in at least seven agreements a reference to the "principle of equidistance", "equidistance line", "principle of median line", or simply "median line".[19] On the other hand, at least four agreements refer to some kind of "equitable principles".[20] Yet, more interestingly, in two agreements the boundary line is established either "on the basis of the principle of equidistance or equity, as the case requires",[21] or "considering that the application of the equidistance method provides an equitable means of delimitation".[22] These last two cases show clearly that equidistance and equity were not two opposing rules but that they could be used in the same situation in a harmonic manner.

It should be highlighted, at this point, that the last agreement mentioned was concluded by France after an Arbitral Tribunal had handed down its award on a dispute between that country and the UK. As has been pointed out elsewhere, one of the most conspicuous aspects of that award was to have tempered the opposition between equidistance and equity, stating that those two concepts had in fact the same object, namely, the delimitation of maritime boundaries with equitable principles. Another relevant finding is that at least in three of the agreements reviewed reference is made to the work of the Third United Nations Conference on the Law of the Sea.[23]

All in all, it seems that the agreements examined above did have an impact on the provisions enshrined in the 1982 Law of the Sea Conventions,[24] and perhaps even on its vagueness, showing delegations that, at the end of the day, concepts of equidistance and equity could be reconciled.

State Practice as an Element in Treaty Interpretation

Qualified in 1985 as a law "affected with a degree of indeterminacy",[25] the "uninstructive" character of the fundamental norm that governs maritime delimitation is not a new topic in international legal scholarship. Reference is made here to the expression "equitable result",[26] a variant of which ("equitable solution") was used in Articles 74 and 83 of the Law of the Sea Convention. Those "mysterious" provisions, which were the result of one of the most significant compromises reached in UNCLOS III, express the vagueness of the conventional law of maritime delimitation and have required an active interpretative role by international judges and arbitrators, and by States when confronted with the task of delimiting a maritime boundary.

In connection to this, an interpretation of the unclear provisions enshrined in Articles 74 and 83 of UNCLOS could also take into account the practice of States that are Parties to the treaty, in this case the 1982 Law of the Sea Convention.[27] This rule is contained in Article 31, paragraph 3, subparagraph (b) of the Vienna Convention on the Law of Treaties, which established that a treaty shall be interpreted taking into account, together with the context, "any subsequent practice in the application of the treaty which establishes the agreement of the parties regarding its interpretation".[28]

In any case, States willing to establish their maritime boundaries by agreement have had to interpret the available rules, presumably taking into account relevant case law,[29] so as to dispose of a certain methodology but bearing in mind that they are expected to reach an equitable solution.

In that context, Latin American and Caribbean States have concluded maritime delimitation agreements that make reference to equitable principles, to the rules and principles established in the Convention, to the equidistance method and other methods used together, in combination with or separated from equidistance. Tellingly, they have found a number of solutions which subsequently appear to have been taken into consideration by international courts and tribunals when interpreting UNCLOS' provisions dealing with maritime delimitation.[30]

For instance, the use of a point seawards, not on land, in order to effect the delimitation of the territorial sea because of the existence of certain geomorphologic circumstances was employed concerning the Rio Grande in the 1970 US/Mexico Treaty and the Bay of Oyapock in the 1981 Brazil/France Treaty. Also, this could have been in the mind of ICJ judges when settling the maritime dispute between Nicaragua and Honduras in 2007.[31]

Another example is furnished by the solution found by Dominica and France in their 1987 maritime delimitation agreement, a case where equidistance would have clearly led to inequity, which might have been considered by the arbitrators who settled the dispute between Canada and France in 1992.[32]

In the same vein, the U-shaped boundary found convenient in the 1978 Venezuela/Netherlands (on account of Aruba, Bonaire and Curaçao) treaty and the 1980 Venezuela/France treaty could have served as inspiration to the solution established by the Court in the 2012 *Nicaragua* v. *Colombia* judgment for the San Andrés Archipelago.

In light of the foregoing, it seems possible to assert that State practice, codified law and case law interacted for eight decades to bring about the existing law of maritime delimitation. State practice, in the form of unilateral claims and especially maritime delimitation agreements in Latin America and the Caribbean, were important elements, first in the codification of the law of the sea and later in the development of the law of maritime delimitation.

Impact of Case Law on Regional State Practice

This section relates to the assessment by Latin American and Caribbean State officials of case law on maritime delimitation. Although it would go beyond the scope of this research to properly measure that, I would claim that the evolution of the law of maritime delimitation through case law has strongly influenced the approaches to the subject matter in the region and beyond.

As I have pointed out before, the increase in coherence and predictability in the law of maritime delimitation has influenced positively the conduction of maritime boundary negotiations. Certainly, coastal States today have at their disposal a fully-fledged body of norms that regulate this subject-matter. It is therefore possible to affirm that case law on maritime delimitation, together with the development of State practice in the form of bilateral treaties, have shaped Latin American and Caribbean States negotiating policies.

On the other hand, on the basis of established case law on the matter, coastal States can reasonably argue for the establishment of maritime boundaries in order to achieve equitable results. However, I should also underscore – as I have mentioned in Part II – that certain multi-oceanic States (normally, major maritime powers, such as the US, France and the UK, to name a few), generally enjoy stronger positions and more bargaining power allowing them sometimes to offer trade-offs that are not related to the delimitation per se. That way, they may carry more leverage to obtain the result they look for.

Notes

1 Weil, Prosper (1988), *ibid.*, pp. 155–169 and 173 *et seq*. Another French author has referred to this situation as "laconism", i.e. the translation of the French word "*laconisme*", see: Pancracio, Jean-Paul (2010), *Droit de la mer*, Paris: Dalloz, p. 261.

2 *Separate Opinion of Judges Ruda, Bedjaoui and Jiménez de Aréchaga. Libya/Malta*; which also refers to: Paul Reuter, "Quelques reflexions sur l'équité en droit international", *Revue belge de droit international*, 1980, p. 169 [translation by the Registry]).

3 Jennings, Robert (1981), "What is international law and how do we tell it when we see it?", *Annuaire suisse de droit international*, Vol. 37.

4 Prosper Weil refers to the normative power of the international judge and to the so-called *droit prétorien*; see: Weil, Prosper (1988), *ibid.*, p. 168; see also: Lando, Massimo (2019), *Maritime Delimitation as a Judicial Process*, Cambridge: Cambridge University Press.

5 Weil, *ibid.*, p. 160.

6 *Joint Separate Opinion of Judges Ruda, Bedjaoui and Jiménez de Aréchaga, Continental Shelf (Libyan Arab Jamahiriya/Malta), Judgment, I.C.J. Reports 1985*, p. 90, para. 37.

7 Note that the impact of State practice on the law of maritime delimitation can be political or legal. Due to the scope of this research, I will focus mainly on the legal consequences of State practice; in this regard, see: Churchill, Robin R. (2005), "The Impact of State practice on the jurisdictional framework contained in the LOS Convention", in: Oude Elferink, Alex G. (ed.), *Stability and Change in the Law of the Sea: The Role of the LOS Convention*. Leiden: Martinus Nijhoff, p. 93.

8 In this sense, see *inter alia*: García-Amador, Francisco (1974), *ibid.*; Janis, Mark W. (1975), *ibid.*, Vol. 12, pp. 554–557 and 568; Johnston, Douglas M. And Philipp M. Saunders (1988), "Introduction", in: Johnston, Douglas M. And Philipp M. Saunders (eds.), *Ocean Boundary Making: Regional Issues and Developments*, London (etc.): Croom Helm, pp. 2–3; Remiro Brotóns, Antonio (1993), *ibid.*, p. 118; Vincent, Philippe (2008), *Droit de la mer*, Brussels: Larcier, pp. 91–94 (although this author refers here also to the impact of the Montevideo Declaration and the Santo Domingo Declaration); Pancracio, Jean-Paul (2010), *Droit de la mer*, Paris: Dalloz, pp. 171–174; and Duvic-Paoli, Leslie-Anne (2011), "Régionalisme et droit de la mer: entre renforcement et affaiblissement des normes universelles", *Annuaire du droit de la Mer*, Vol. 16, pp. 22–23.

9 Duvic-Paoli, Leslie-Anne (2011), *ibid.* See also: Focsaneanu, Lazar (1961), "Le droit international maritime de l'Océan Pacifique et de ses mer adjacentes", *AFDI*, Vol. 7, pp. 173–213. Nevertheless, as mentioned earlier in this book, there were differences in the positions of Latin American States.

10 These claims were either in the form of an EEZ or an exclusive fishery zone; although some authors have identified more types, namely: 200-mile territorial sea; modified territorial sea; 200-mile economic resource zone; expanded economic zone; and regional economic zone. See: Alexander, Lewis M. and Robert D. Hodgson (1975), "The Impact of the 200-Mile Economic Zone on the Law of the Sea", *San Diego Law Review*, Vol. 12, p. 571.

11 *Continental Shelf (Libyan Arab Jamahiriya/Malta), Judgment, I.C.J. Reports 1985*, para. 34. See also: *Case concerning filleting within the Gulf of St. Lawrence between Canada and France. Decision of 17 July 1986, RIAA*, Vol. 19, para. 49; see also: ILC, Identification of customary international law, UN Doc. A/73/10, pp. 145–146.

12 See: Churchill (2005), *ibid.*, pp. 95–96.

13 *North Sea Continental Shelf, Judgment, I.C.J. Reports 1969*, pp. 32–33, 47 and 53; and also Akehurst (1977), *ibid.* p. 2. In fact, it has been claimed that State practice taking place between the 1942 Gulf of Paria Treaty and 1958, that is, including the 1945 Truman Proclamations, was "enough" to justify that in 1958 a separate convention addresses the issue of the Continental Shelf; see: Treves, Tullio (1990), *ibid.*, p. 35. See also: Intervention of representative of Argentina, Mr Ruiz Moreno, in the framework of the fourth committee of UNCLOS I, in: *United Nations Conference on the Law of the Sea, Official records*, Vol. VI, pp. 2–3.

14 "Les droits indiqués précédemment ont une très grande valeur s'ils sont établis par un groupe d'États et surtout par les États d'un continent. Les pays de l'Amérique latine, individuellement ou collectivement, ont fixé de grandes étendues de leurs eaux côtières dans des buts déterminés: maintien de leur neutralité, services douaniers, etc., et dernièrement, pour l'exploitation des richesses de leur plateau continental", Opinion

individuelle de M. Alvarez, *Fisheries case, Judgment, I.C.J. Reports 1951*, p. 116, at p. 150. See also, in this regard, Alexander, L.M. and R.D. Hodgson (1975), *ibid.*, p. 569.

15 *Fisheries Jurisdiction* case, see: *I.C.J. Reports 1974*, p. 3, paras. 52 and 54. In this regard, both situations would appear to correspond to the situation of codification of a pre-existing custom. About this and the other two models of relations between codification conventions and customary international law, see: *Military and Paramilitary Activities in and against Nicaragua (Nicaragua v. United States of America), I.C.J. Reports 1986*, para. 177.

16 In this sense: "the extension of fisheries jurisdiction and claimed economic zones out to 200 nautical miles and the rapid advance in the technology of hydrocarbon development on the continental shelf have created a problem of totally new dimensions. These developments have given rise to many new boundaries between opposite and adjacent states which require delimitation and have made many potential boundaries more important to the states concerned"; in: Feldman and Colson (1981), *ibid.*, p. 729; "La réforme du droit de la mer devait rendre ces délimitations [that is, maritime boundaries delimitations concerning coastal fisheries and the surveillance of warships and smuggling], qui portaient généralement sur des eaux de 3 milles de large, insuffisantes et amener les Etats à tracer de façon systématique leurs frontières", "Cette extension des espaces maritimes [the extension caused by the reform of the law of the sea (réforme du droit de la mer)] a eu deux conséquences: elle a accru l'enjeu des délimitation qui portent désormais sur de grandes distances et couvrent des superficies de centaines, voire de milliers de km2; et elle a multiplié les cas où il doit être procédé à une délimitation des eaux relevant de deux Etats dont les côtes se font face"; in: Guillaume, Gilbert (1983), *ibid.*, p. 276–277.

17 "Conduct in connection with treaties" "such as maritime delimitation agreements"; see: ILC, Identification of customary international law, UN Doc. A/73/10, p. 134.

18 Churchill (2005), *ibid.*, p. 95.

19 1970 Mexico/US; 1973 Argentina/Uruguay; 1976 Cuba/Mexico; 1976 Colombia/Panama; 1978 Colombia/Dominican Republic; 1978 Colombia/Haiti; and 1980 Costa Rica/Panama.

20 1978 US/Venezuela; 1978 The Netherlands/Venezuela; 1978 Mexico/US; and 1979 Dominican Republic/Venezuela.

21 1977 Cuba/Haiti.

22 1981 France/Saint Lucia.

23 1980 France/Venezuela; 1981 Brazil/France; and, again, 1981 France/Saint Lucia.

24 In this sense, see for instance Treves, Tullio (1990), *ibid.*, p. 25, where he pointed out that "Les grandes conventions de codification sont ainsi, en même temps, le fruit de la pratique des Etats, un élément de celle-ci et un point de départ d'une nouvelle pratique."

25 *Separate Opinion of Judges Ruda, Bedjaoui and Jiménez de Aréchaga*, in the *Libya/Malta, I.C.J. Reports 1985*, para. 37.

26 *Separate Opinion of Judges Ruda, Bedjaoui and Jiménez de Aréchaga*. Libya/Malta.

27 Status of the Convention on the Law of the Sea is available at DOALOS' website.

28 *Kasikili/Sedudu Island (Botswana/Namibia), Judgment, I.C.J. Reports 1999*, p. 1045, para. 63 and paras. 73–75.

29 One could think, for instance, of the French approach to negotiating its maritime boundaries after the 1977 *Anglo-French* award or, more recently, of negotiations between France and Italy where the 2009 *Black Sea* judgment seems to have shed some light to solve the problem of Italy's determination of straight baselines in the Tuscan Archipelago (Gorgona).

30 Yet one could also argue the contrary when confronted with certain instances where case law seems to disregard State practice. For example: "It is generally acknowledged

that the concept of the single maritime boundary does not have its origin in the Convention but is squarely based on State practice and the law as developed by international courts and tribunals. That is why the Tribunal *is to be guided* by the case law as developed by international courts and tribunals in this matter" (emphasis added); see: *Guyana/Suriname Arbitration, Award of 17 September 2007 ILM*, Vol. 47, para. 334. See also: the Arbitral Tribunal's consideration of the 1990 Trinidad and Tobago/ Venezuela treaty, in *Barbados/Trinidad and Tobago, Award of 11 April 2006, RIAA*, Vol. 27, paras. 346–347. In the *Nicaragua* v. *Honduras* case, the examples of State practice in support of the Parties' claims were advanced; see: *I.C.J. Pleadings, Maritime Delimitation between Nicaragua and Honduras in the Caribbean Sea* (*Nicaragua* v. *Honduras*). Nicaragua's first round of oral argument (Counsel: Ian Brownlie), 6 March 2007 (CR 2007/02), pp. 14–17, paras. 20–35; and also: *I.C.J. Pleadings, Maritime Delimitation between Nicaragua and Honduras in the Caribbean Sea* (*Nicaragua* v. *Honduras*). Honduras' first round of oral argument (Counsel: David Colson), 15 March 2007 (CR 2007/10), p. 17, para. 99.

31 In fact, this was pleaded in the *Nicaragua* v. *Honduras* case, see: *I.C.J. Pleadings, Maritime Delimitation between Nicaragua and Honduras in the Caribbean Sea* (*Nicaragua* v. *Honduras*). Honduras' first round of oral argument (Counsel: David Colson), 15 March 2007 (CR 2007/09), pp. 46–48, paras. 28–34. David Colson referred not only to the 1970 Mexico/US treaty, but also to the 2000 China/Vietnam and to the 2002 Angola/Namibia treaties.

32 *Case concerning the Delimitation of Maritime Areas between Canada and France* (*St. Pierre et Miquelon*), *Award of 10 June 1992, RIAA*, Vol. 21, pp. 265–341.

General Conclusion

Having carried out research on the under-examined question of the relationship between State practice and the law of maritime delimitation in Latin America and the Caribbean, it seems possible to claim that since 1942 a direct relationship developed progressively between the practice of Latin American and Caribbean coastal States and the law of maritime delimitation.

Let us recall that the contribution of Latin America and the Caribbean to the modern law of the sea, although not always acknowledged, has no parallel. It is composed of a number of unilateral claims that followed the 1945 Truman Proclamation on the Continental Shelf, especially those made by Chile and Peru, as well as jointly by the signatory States of the 1952 Santiago Declaration on the Maritime Zone, the 1970 Montevideo and Lima Declarations, and the 1972 Santo Domingo Declaration. The purpose of all of them was not only to extend the jurisdiction of coastal States over the adjacent waters adjacent but also to preserve the resources therein for the benefit of the population and for their economic development.

The practice of States, reflected first in the form of unilateral claims asserting sovereign rights and jurisdiction, and later in the form of bilateral maritime delimitation agreements, was of paramount importance for the expansion of coastal State jurisdiction and sovereign rights (from 12 to 200 nautical miles) that resulted in the United Nations Convention on the Law of the Sea. Hence the relationship consists of a sharp increase in the need to establish maritime boundaries as a consequence of the expansion of coastal State jurisdiction and sovereign rights. Put differently, it might be argued that the need to establish maritime boundaries, with its rules on delimitation, is a result of State practice in Latin America and the Caribbean.

As regards unilateral practice, the crystallisation of the institution of the exclusive economic zone before the adoption of the 1982 Law of the Sea Convention amounted to the emergence of a new rule of customary international law subsequent to the conclusion of a treaty (i.e. 1958 Geneva Convention on the High Seas) that replaced it and eventually gave birth to a new treaty.

Regarding bilateral practice, including during UNCLOS III, some of the delimitation agreements made reference to the equidistance or median line and some to equitable principles. It hence can be asserted that the practice of Latin American

DOI: 10.4324/9781003290452-14

and Caribbean coastal States concerning maritime boundary delimitation had an impact on the provisions of the 1982 Law of the Sea Convention and perhaps on its vagueness. It did so in respect of an area of the law that was not covered by a treaty (i.e. the EEZ) and also in respect of areas of the law addressed by treaties with a similar subject matter (i.e. the Convention on the Territorial Sea and the Convention on the Continental Shelf).

In this regard, the impact of State practice on the law of maritime delimitation can be divided into two: State practice as an element in the formation of customary international law and State practice as an element in treaty interpretation.

As an element in the formation of customary international law, State practice in Latin America and the Caribbean has been unilateral (i.e. claims made by coastal States that paved the way for the extension of maritime areas to 200-nautical-mile zones) and bilateral (i.e. maritime delimitation agreements).

As an element in treaty interpretation, the manner in which States have interpreted UNCLOS provisions, in particular Articles 74 and 83, may have constituted subsequent practice in the application of the treaty within the meaning of Article 31, paragraph 4 of the Vienna Convention on the Law of Treaties.

The law applicable to maritime delimitation, the first version of which was codified in the late 1950s, further developed in the framework of UNCLOS III and even after the adoption of the Convention. During that time, the practice of Latin American and Caribbean States, in the form of 43 maritime delimitation agreements, carried a lot of weight.

Provisions on delimitation were indeed enshrined in the 1982 United Nations Convention on the Law of the Sea. Since then, they have been progressively clarified by maritime boundary case law, which has, in turn, reduced its elements of subjectivity and uncertainty.

As has been noted in this book with the analysis of case law concerning the region, Latin American and Caribbean States have been particularly active in terms of case law production, with a number of maritime delimitation disputes submitted both to the International Court of Justice and to ad hoc arbitral tribunals.

Thus that progressive clarification of the law has also benefited a great deal from the practice of States. In that context, the practice of Latin American and Caribbean coastal States, including in the form of 25 maritime delimitation treaties concluded since the adoption of the Law of the Sea Convention, seems to have been taken into consideration by international courts and tribunals when interpreting UNCLOS' provisions on delimitation and thus settling maritime delimitation disputes.

Indeed, let us recall that one of the most remarkable features of the evolution of the law of the sea has been the dramatic expansion of coastal State jurisdiction and sovereign rights over their adjacent maritime spaces. Latin American and Caribbean States have been the main drivers of that process. As a result, there has been a considerable increase in maritime delimitation disputes. It is thus possible to establish a relationship between the conduct of Latin American and Caribbean coastal States and the development of the law of maritime delimitation. That is a significant contribution by Latin America and the Caribbean to the law of maritime delimitation.

It therefore follows that Latin America and the Caribbean did more than contribute to the development of the modern law of the sea. Latin American and Caribbean States played a decisive role in the consolidation of the law of maritime delimitation.

Annexes

Annex 1 Table of Maritime Delimitation Cases Decided by the International Court of Justice

No. of the Case	*Name of the Case*	*Parties*	*Date of Judgment*
01 and 02	North Sea Continental Shelf	Germany/Denmark and Germany/The Netherlands	20 February 1969
03	Continental Shelf (Tunisia/ Libyan Arab Jamahiriya)	Tunisia/Libya	24 February 1982
04	Delimitation of the Maritime Boundary in the Gulf of Maine Area	Canada/USA	12 October 1984
05	Continental Shelf (Libyan Arab Jamahiriya/Malta)	Libya/Malta	3 June 1985
06	Land, Island and Maritime Frontier Dispute (El Salvador/Honduras: Nicaragua intervening)	El Salvador/Honduras	11 September 1992
07	Maritime Delimitation in the Area between Greenland and Jan Mayen	*Denmark* v. *Norway*	14 June 1993
08	Maritime Delimitation and Territorial Questions between Qatar and Bahrain	*Qatar* v. *Bahrain*	16 March 2001
09	Land and Maritime Boundary between Cameroon and Nigeria (*Cameroon* v. *Nigeria*: Equatorial Guinea intervening)	*Cameroon* v. *Nigeria*	10 October 2002
10	Territorial and Maritime Dispute between Nicaragua and Honduras in the Caribbean Sea	*Nicaragua* v. *Honduras*	8 October 2007

(*Continued*)

Annex 1 (Continued)

No. of the Case	*Name of the Case*	*Parties*	*Date of Judgment*
11	Maritime Delimitation in the Black Sea (*Romania* v. *Ukraine*)	*Romania* v. *Ukraine*	3 February 2009
12	Territorial and Maritime Dispute (*Nicaragua* v. *Colombia*)	*Nicaragua* v. *Colombia*	19 November 2012
13	Maritime Dispute (*Peru* v. *Chile*)	*Peru* v. *Chile*	27 January 2014
14	Maritime Delimitation in the Caribbean Sea and the Pacific Ocean (*Costa Rica* v. *Nicaragua*) and Land Boundary in the Northern Part of Isla Portillos (*Costa Rica* v. *Nicaragua*)	*Costa Rica* v. *Nicaragua*	2 February 2018
15	Maritime Delimitation in the Indian Ocean	*Somalia* v. *Kenya*	12 October 2021

Annex 2 Table of Maritime Delimitation Agreements in Latin America and the Caribbean (before the Adoption of UNCLOS)

No.	*Year*	*Parties*	*Method of Maritime Delimitation*	*Datum/Chart*	*DSP*
01	1942	UK (Trinidad and Tobago)/ Venezuela	Composite delimitation	No	Art. 9
02	1970	Mexico/US	Simplified equidistance	No	No
03	1972	Brazil/Uruguay	Perpendicular to the general direction of the coast	No	No
04	1973	Argentina/Uruguay	Modified equidistance	No	Art. 87
05	1975	Colombia/Ecuador	Parallels and meridians	No	No
06	1976	Cuba/Mexico	Simplified and modified equidistance	No	No
07	1976	Colombia/Panama	Composite delimitation	No	No
08	1977	Cuba/Haiti	Simplified and modified equidistance	US Defense Mapping Agency, No. 26010 1970, rev. 1975	Art. 9
09	1978	Colombia/ Dominican Republic	Simplified equidistance	Nautical chart No. 25000 of US Defense Mapping Agency	Art. VI

No.	Year	Parties	Method of Maritime Delimitation	Datum/Chart	DSP
10	1978	Colombia/Haiti	Modified equidistance	Nautical chart No. 25000, 1975	Art. 5
11	1978	US (Puerto Rico and US Virgin Islands)/ Venezuela	Modified equidistance	NAD 27 and 1866 Clarke's ellipsoid + chart	Art. 5
12	1978	The Netherlands/ Venezuela	Composite delimitation	1956 Provisional South American datum and NAD 27 + US nautical chart 25000 (ed. 1977)	Art.12
13	1978	Mexico/US	Simplified equidistance	NAD 27	No
14	1979	Dominican Republic/ Venezuela	Modified equidistance	NAD 27 and 1866 Clarke's ellipsoid	Art. 6
15	1980	Costa Rica/Panama	Perpendicular to the general direction of the coast	No	No
16	1980	France (Martinique and Guadeloupe)/ Venezuela	Parallels and meridians	French chart 6332	Art. IV
17	1981	Brazil/France (French Guyana)	Modified equidistance	Corrego Alegre (Brazilian system) and Brazilian chart 110 (1979)	Art. 2
18	1981	France (Martinique)/ Saint Lucia	Simplified equidistance	French National Geographic Institute for Martinique (1953)	Art. 4

Annex 3 Table of Maritime Delimitation Agreements in Latin America and the Caribbean (after the Adoption of UNCLOS)

No.	Year	Parties	Method of Maritime Delimitation	Datum/Chart	DSP
19	1984	Chile/Argentina	Composite delimitation	No	
20	1984	Colombia/Costa Rica	Simplified and modified equidistance	No	No
21	1986	Colombia/Honduras	Parallels and meridians	Nautical chart 28000 (US Defense Mapping Agency)	Art. IV
22	1987	Dominica/France (Guadeloupe and Marie-Galante and Martinique)	Composite delimitation	French National Geographic Institute for Martinique (1953)	Art. 3

(*Continued*)

Annex 3 (Continued)

No.	*Year*	*Parties*	*Method of Maritime Delimitation*	*Datum/Chart*	*DSP*
23	1990	Trinidad and Tobago/ Venezuela	Simplified and modified equidistance	1956 Provisional South American datum (International ellipsoid 1924)	Art. X
24	1993	UK (British Virgin Islands)/US (Puerto Rico and US Virgin Islands)	Simplified equidistance	NAD 83	No
25	1993	UK (Anguilla)/US (US Virgin Islands)	Simplified equidistance	NAD 83	No
26	1993	Colombia/Jamaica	Modified equidistance	WGS 84 and US Defense Mapping Agency chart 402	Art. 7
27	1994	Cuba/Jamaica	Strict equidistance	NAD 27 and Clarke's ellipsoid 1866	Art. 7
28	1996	France (Guadeloupe)/ UK (Montserrat)	Simplified and modified equidistance	WGS 84	No
29	1996	France (Saint Martin and Saint Barthélemy)/UK (Anguilla)	Simplified and modified equidistance	WGS 84	No
30	1996	Dominican Republic/ UK (Turks and Caicos Islands)	Coastal length comparison	NAD 83	No
31	2000	Mexico/US	Simplified equidistance	NAD 83 and ITRF 92	Art. 8
32	2001	Honduras/UK (Cayman Islands)	Composite delimitation	WGS 84	No
33	2005	Honduras/Mexico	Simplified equidistance	For 5 out of 6 points: WGS 84. For the other point: NAD 27	Art. V
34	2009	Barbados/France (Guadeloupe and Martinique)	Strict equidistance	WGS 84	
35	2010	Grenada/Trinidad and Tobago	Composite delimitation	WGS 84	Art. IX
36	2011	Ecuador/Peru	Parallels and meridians	WGS 84	No
37	2011	Bahamas/Cuba	Strict equidistance	WGS 84	No
38	2012	Cuba/Honduras	Simplified equidistance	WGS 84	
39	2014	Costa Rica/Ecuador	Equidistance	WGS 84	

No.	*Year*	*Parties*	*Method of Maritime Delimitation*	*Datum/Chart*	*DSP*
40	2016	France/The Netherlands (Saint Martin)	Equidistance	WGS 84	
41	2017	France (French Guyana)/Suriname	Straight equidistance	WGS 84	
42	2017	France/Antigua and Barbuda	Equidistance	WGS 84	
43	2021	UK (Anguilla)/ Antigua and Barbuda	Equitable solution	WGS 84	

Sources

I. Table of Cases

A. CACJ

- *The Republic of El Salvador* v. *The Republic of Nicaragua* (Opinion and Decision of the Central American Court of Justice, 9 March 1917), *AJIL*, Vol. 11, p. 674.

B. PCIJ

- Railway Traffic between Lithuania and Poland, Advisory Opinion, 1931, P.C.I.J., Series A/B, No. 40, p. 116.
- Delimitation of the Territorial Waters between the Island of Castellorizo and the Coasts of Anatolia, Order of 26 January 1933, P.C.I.J., Series A/B, No. 51, p. 4.

C. ICJ

Maritime Delimitation Cases

- North Sea Continental Shelf, Judgment, I.C.J. Reports 1969, p. 3.
- Aegean Sea Continental Shelf, Judgment, I.C.J. Reports 1978, p. 3.
- Continental Shelf (Tunisia/Libyan Arab Jamahiriya), Judgment, I.C.J. Reports 1982, p. 18.
- Delimitation of the Maritime Boundary in the Gulf of Maine Area, Judgment, I.C.J. Reports 1984, p. 246.
- Continental Shelf (Libyan Arab Jamahiriya/Malta), Judgment, I.C.J. Reports 1985, p. 13.
- Land and Maritime Boundary between Cameroon and Nigeria, Preliminary Objections, Judgment, I.C.J. Reports 1988, p. 275.
- Maritime Delimitation in the Area between Greenland and Jan Mayen, Judgment, I.C.J. Reports 1993, p. 38.

- Maritime Delimitation and Territorial Questions between Qatar and Bahrain, Jurisdiction and Admissibility, Judgment, I.C.J. Reports 1994, p. 112.
- Maritime Delimitation and Territorial Questions between Qatar and Bahrain, Jurisdiction and Admissibility, Judgment, I.C.J. Reports 1995, p. 6.
- Maritime Delimitation between Guinea-Bissau and Senegal, Order of 8 November 1995, I.C.J. Reports 1995, p. 423.
- Maritime Delimitation and Territorial Questions between Qatar and Bahrain, Merits, Judgment, I.C.J. Reports 2001, p. 40.
- Land and Maritime Boundary between Cameroon and Nigeria (*Cameroon* v. *Nigeria*: Equatorial Guinea intervening), Judgment, I.C.J. Reports 2002, p. 303.
- Territorial and Maritime Dispute between Nicaragua and Honduras in the Caribbean Sea (*Nicaragua* v. *Honduras*), Judgment, I.C.J. Reports 2007, p. 659.
- Territorial and Maritime Dispute (*Nicaragua* v. *Colombia*), Preliminary Objections, I.C.J. Reports 2007, p. 832.
- Maritime Delimitation in the Black Sea (*Romania* v. *Ukraine*), Judgment, I.C.J. Reports 2009.
- Territorial and Maritime Dispute (*Nicaragua* v. *Colombia*), Merits, I.C.J. Reports 2012.
- Maritime Dispute (*Peru* v. *Chile*), Judgment, I.C.J. Reports 2014.
- Maritime Delimitation in the Caribbean Sea and the Pacific Ocean (*Costa Rica* v. *Nicaragua*) and Land Boundary in the Northern Part of Isla Portillos (*Costa Rica* v. *Nicaragua*), Judgment, I.C.J. Reports 2018.
- Maritime Delimitation in the Indian Ocean (*Somalia* v. *Kenya*), Judgment, I.C.J. Reports 2021.

Other Cases Before the ICJ

- Corfu Channel, Merits, Judgment, I.C.J. Reports 1949, p. 4.
- Fisheries, Judgment, I.C.J. Reports 1951, p. 116.
- Nottebohm, Second Phase, Judgment, I.C.J. Reports 1955, p. 4.
- Arbitral Award Made by the King of Spain on 23 December 1906, Judgment, I.C.J. Reports 1960.
- Frontier Dispute, Judgment, I.C.J. Reports 1986, p. 554.
- Land, Island and Maritime Frontier Dispute (El Salvador/Honduras: Nicaragua intervening), Judgment, I.C.J. Reports 1992, p. 351.
- Sovereignty over Pulau Ligitan and Pulau Sipadan (Indonesia/Malaysia), Judgment, I.C.J. Reports 2002, p. 625.
- Dispute regarding Navigational and Related Rights (*Costa Rica* v. *Nicaragua*), Judgment, I.C.J. Reports 2009, p. 213.
- Alleged Violations of Sovereign Rights and Maritime Spaces in the Caribbean Sea (*Nicaragua* v. *Colombia*), Judgment, 21 April 2022.

D. ITLOS

- M/V "SAIGA" (No. 2) (*Saint Vincent and the Grenadines* v. *Guinea*), Judgment, ITLOS Reports 1999.
- Delimitation of the Maritime Boundary in the Bay of Bengal (Bangladesh/Myanmar), Judgment, ITLOS Reports 2012, p. 4.
- Delimitation of the Maritime Boundary in the Atlantic Ocean (Ghana/Côte d'Ivoire), Judgment, ITLOS Reports 2017, p. 14.
- Dispute concerning Delimitation of the Maritime Boundary between Mauritius and Maldives in the Indian Ocean (Mauritius/Maldives), Preliminary Objections, Judgment, ITLOS Reports 2021.

E. ECJ

- *Western Sahara Campaign UK* v. *Commissioners for Her Majesty's Revenue and Customs, Secretary of State for Environment, Food and Rural Affairs*, ECJ (Grand Chamber), 27 February 2018.

F. Arbitral Awards

Maritime Delimitation Awards

- Decision of the Permanent Court of Arbitration in the Matter of the Maritime Boundary Dispute between Norway and Sweden, *AJIL*, Vol. 4, 1910, pp. 226–236.
- Case concerning the Delimitation of the Continental Shelf between the United Kingdom of Great Britain and Northern Ireland, and the French Republic, *RIAA*, Vol. 18, pp. 3–413.
- Case concerning the Boundary Dispute between Dubai and Sharjah (Emirate of Dubai v. Emirate of Sharjah), award of 19 October 1981, *ILR*, Vol. 91, p. 543.
- Case concerning the Delimitation of the Maritime Boundary between Guinea and Guinea-Bissau (*Republic of Guinea* v. *Republic of Guinea-Bissau*), *ILR*, Vol. 77, p. 635.
- Affaire de la délimitation de la frontière maritime entre la Guinée-Bissau et le Sénégal. Sentence du 31 juillet 1989, *RIAA*, Vol. 20, p. 121.
- Case concerning the Delimitation of Maritime Areas between Canada and France (St. Pierre and Miquelon), Award of 10 June 1992, *RIAA*, Vol. 21, pp. 265–341.
- Eritrea/Yemen Arbitration Tribunal. Award in Phase Two of the Proceedings (Maritime Delimitation), Award of 17 December 1999, *ILR*, Vol. 119, p. 417.
- Arbitration between Newfoundland and Labrador and Nova Scotia concerning Portions of the Limits of their Offshore Areas as Defined in the Canada-Nova Scotia Offshore Petroleum Resources Accord Implementation Act and the Canada-Newfoundland Atlantic Accord Implementation Act. Award in

the First Phase, 17 May 2001; Award in the Second Phase, 26 March 2002, *ILR*, Vol. 128, pp. 425–581.
- Arbitral Tribunal Constituted Pursuant to Article 287, and in Accordance with Annex VII, of the United Nations Convention on the Law of the Sea in the Matter of an Arbitration between Barbados and the Republic of Trinidad and Tobago, Award of 11 April 2006.
- Arbitral Tribunal Constituted Pursuant to Article 287, and in Accordance with Annex VII, of the United Nations Convention on the Law of the Sea in the Matter of an Arbitration between Guyana and Suriname, Award of 17 September 2007.
- Arbitration between the Government of the Republic of Croatia and the Government of the Republic of Slovenia, Final Award, 29 June 2017.

Other Relevant Awards

- Arbitral Award Relating to the Issue of Control and Sovereignty over Aves Island, Raised between Venezuela and the Kingdom of the Netherlands. Decision of 30 June 1865, *RIAA*, Vol. 28, pp. 115–124.
- North Atlantic Coast Fisheries Case (Great Britain, United States), 7 September 1910, Grounds for the Dissent to the Award on Question V by Dr Luis M. Drago, *RIAA*, Vol. 21, pp. 167–226.
- Affaires de frontières Colombo-vénézuéliennes (Colombie contre Vénézuéla), 24 March 1922, *RIAA*, Vol. 1, pp. 223–298.
- Arbitral Award on the Subject of the Difference Relative to the Sovereignty over Clipperton Island, Decision Rendered at Rome, 28 January 1931, *AJIL*, Vol. 26, pp. 390–394.
- Petroleum Development (Trucial Coast) Ltd. and Sheikh of Abu Dhabi, August 1951, 18 *ILR* 144, at p. 155.
- Dispute between Argentina and Chile concerning the Beagle Channel, 18 February 1977, *RIAA*, Vol. 21, pp. 53–264.
- Case concerning Filleting within the Gulf of St. Lawrence between Canada and France. Decision of 17 July 1986, *RIAA*, Vol. 19, pp. 225–296.
- Eritrea/Yemen Arbitration Tribunal. Award in Phase One of the Proceedings (Territorial Sovereignty and Scope of Dispute), Award of 9 October 1998, *ILR*, Vol. 114, p. 1.

G. Annex VII Arbitrations

- The Southern Bluefin Tuna cases (*Australia/New Zealand* v. *Japan*), available at *ILM* 39 (2000): pp. 1359–1401.
- The Mox Plant case (*Ireland* v. *United Kingdom*), available at *ILM* 42 (2003): pp. 1187–1199.
- The Land Reclamation case (*Malaysia* v. *Singapore*), available at *ILR* 126 (2005): pp. 487–535.

- Arbitral Tribunal Constituted Pursuant to Article 287, and in Accordance with Annex VII, of the United Nations Convention on the Law of the Sea in the Matter of an Arbitration between Barbados and the Republic of Trinidad and Tobago, Award of 11 April 2006.
- Arbitral Tribunal Constituted Pursuant to Article 287, and in Accordance with Annex VII, of the United Nations Convention on the Law of the Sea in the Matter of an Arbitration between Guyana and Suriname, Award of 17 September 2007.
- Bay of Bengal Maritime Boundary Arbitration between Bangladesh and India, Award of 7 July 2014.
- *Republic of Mauritius* v. *The United Kingdom of Great Britain and Northern Ireland*, concerning the Establishment by the UK of a Marine Protected Area around the Chagos Archipelago, Award of 18 March 2015.
- *The Republic of the Philippines* v. *The People's Republic of China*, Award of 12 July 2016.
- The ARA Libertad Arbitration (*Argentina* v. *Ghana*), terminated by a tribunal order of November 2013.
- The Atlanto-Scandian Herring Arbitration (*Denmark in Respect of the Faroe Islands* v. *The European Union*), terminated by a tribunal order of September 2014.
- The Arctic Sunrise Arbitration (*The Netherlands* v. *Russian Federation*), Award of 10 July 2017.
- The Duzgit Integrity Arbitration (*Malta* v. *São Tomé and Príncipe*), Award of 18 December 2019.
- The "Enrica Lexie" Incident (*Italy* v. *India*), still pending.
- Dispute concerning Coastal State Rights in the Black Sea, Sea of Azov, and Kerch Strait (*Ukraine* v. *Russian Federation*), still pending.
- Dispute concerning the Detention of Ukrainian Naval Vessels and Servicemen (*Ukraine* v. *Russian Federation*), still pending.

H. Other Means of Dispute Settlement Concerning Land and Maritime Boundaries

- Conciliation Commission on the Continental Shelf Area between Iceland and Jan Mayen.
- UN *Iraq-Kuwait Boundary Demarcation Commission*, Report of 20 May 1993 (endorsed by Security Council Resolution 833, on 27 May 1993).
- UN Good Offices in Equatorial Guinea/Gabon Corisco Bay Islands.
- UN Good Offices in Guyana/Venezuela.
- OAS Mediation in the Belize/Guatemala Territorial and Maritime Delimitation.
- Lauterpacht, Elihu, Schwebel, Stephen, Rosenne, Shabtai, and Francisco Orrego Vicuña (2001), *Legal Opinion on Guatemala's Territorial Claim to Belize*.
- PCA Case No. 2016–10, In the Matter of the Maritime Boundary between Timor-Leste and Australia before a Conciliation Commission Constituted

under Annex V to the 1982 United Nations Convention on the Law of the Sea between the Democratic Republic of Timor-Leste and the Commonwealth of Australia, 9 May 2018.

II. International Instruments

A. Treaties

- Peace Treaty of Lisbon of 13 February 1668, in: PARRY, Clive (1969), *The Consolidated Treaty Series*, Vol. 10, Dobbs Ferry: Ocean, p. 425.
- Provisional Treaty of Lisbon of 7 May 1681, in: PARRY, *ibid.*, Vol. 16, p. 81.
- Peace Treaty of Utrecht of 6 February 1715, in: PARRY, *ibid.*, Vol. 29, p. 201.
- Boundary Treaty of Madrid of 13 January 1750, in: PARRY, *ibid.*, Vol. 38, p. 457.
- Treaty of San Ildefonso of 1 October 1777, in: PARRY, *ibid.*, Vol. 46, p. 321.
- Convention of London of 14 July 1786, in: PARRY, *ibid.*, Vol. 50, p. 47.
- Nootka Sound Convention, in: PARRY, *ibid.* Vol. 51, p. 67.
- Treaty between Costa Rica and Nicaragua (1858), *BFSP*, Vol. 48, p. 1049 (Treaty Cañas-Jerez).
- Treaty between Argentina and Chile (1881), DE MARTENS, *Nouveau Recueil général de traités*, 2e Série, t. XII, p. 491.

Treaties That Involve Some Kind of Lines in Water Areas in Latin America and the Caribbean[1]

- Treaty between Mexico and Guatemala (1882), *BFSP*, Vol. 73, p. 273.
- Treaty between Great Britain and Mexico with Respect to the Boundary between Mexico and British Honduras (1893), *BFSP*, Vol. 85, pp. 58–60.
- Act between Honduras and Nicaragua concerning the Gulf of Fonseca (1900), *BFSP*, Vol. 92, p. 227.

Other Treaties Outside the Region Constituting Early Attempts at Delimiting the Seas

- Peace Treaty of Fredrikshamn between Sweden and Russia (1809), *BFSP*, Vol. 1, p. 338.
- Convention between Great Britain and Russia on a Demarcation Line between Their Possessions (1825), *BFSP*, Vol. 12, p. 38.
- Convention between France and Great Britain for the Delimitation of Oyster Fisheries in the Granville Bay (1839), *BFSP*, Vol. 27, p. 983.
- Treaty between Great Britain and the United States for the Settlement of the Oregon Boundary (1846), *BFSP*, Vol. 34, p. 14.
- Treaty of Vienna concerning the Boundary between Denmark and Germany in the Little Belt (1864), *BFSP*, Vol. 54, p. 522.
- Convention between the United States and Russia in Connection with the Purchase of Alaska (1867), in: PARRY, *ibid.*, Vol. 134, p. 331.

- Declaration for the Delimitation of Jurisdictions of France and Spain Dividing the Bay of Figuier (1879), Ministère des Affaires Etrangères, *Traités et conventions en vigueur entre la France et les puissances étrangères*, Vol. 2, 1919, p. 141.
- Convention between France and Italy on the Determination of Fisheries Zones in Corsica and Sardinia (1908), *BFSP*, Vol. 101, p. 1059.
- Treaty of Passamaquoddy Bay Which Established the Territorial Sea Boundary Between Maine and New Brunswick (1910), *BFSP*, Vol. 102, p. 37.
- Convention between Finland and Norway concerning the Frontier between the Province of Finmark and the Territory of Petsamo (1924), *BFSP*, Vol. 120, p. 341.
- Straits Settlement and Johore Territorial Waters Agreement (1927), *BFSP*, Vol. 70, p. 314.
- Convention between Italy and Turkey Settling the Sovereignty over Certain Islets of the Anatolian Coast (1932), *BFSP*, Vol. 135, p. 629.
- Declaration between Denmark and Sweden concerning the Boundary of Territorial Waters in the Sound (1932), *LNTS*, Vol. 127, p. 57.

Multilateral Treaties

- Convention on the Continental Shelf, 29 April 1958, *UNTS*, Vol. 499, p. 312.
- Convention on the High Seas, CHS, 29 April 1958, *UNTS*, Vol. 450, p. 11.
- Optional Protocol of Signature concerning the Compulsory Settlement of Disputes, 29 April 1958, *ibid.*, p. 169.
- Convention on the Territorial Sea and the Contiguous Zone, 29 April 1958, *UNTS*, Vol. 516, p. 206.
- Convention on Fishing and Conservation of the Living Resources of the High Seas, 29 April 1958, *UNTS*, Vol. 559, p. 285.
- Optional Protocol of Signature concerning the Compulsory Settlement of Disputes, OPSD (Signature: 29 April 1958; entry into force: 30 September 1962), *UNTS*, Vol. 450, p. 169.
- American Treaty on Pacific Settlement (Pact of Bogotá), 30 April 1948 (entered into force on 6 May 1949), *UNTS*, Vol. 30, pp. 84–116.
- United Nations Convention on the Law of the Sea, Montego Bay, 10 December 1982, 21 *ILM*, Vol. 21, p. 1261.
- Vienna Convention on Succession of States in Respect of Treaties, *UNTS*, Vol. 1946, p. 3.

B. Maritime Boundary Agreements (1942–2021)

1. Treaty between His Majesty, in Respect of the United Kingdom and Venezuela.
2. Treaty to Resolve Pending Boundary Differences and Maintain the Rio Grande and Colorado River as the International Boundary between the United States of America and the United Mexican States (Signature: 23 November 1970; entry into force: 18 April 1972).

3. Agreement between the Government of Brazil and the Government of Uruguay Relating to the Maritime Delimitation between Brazil and Uruguay (Signature: 21 July 1972; entry into force: 12 June 1975).
4. Treaty between Uruguay and Argentina concerning the Río de la Plata and the Corresponding Maritime Boundary (Signature: 19 November 1973; entry into force: 12 February 1974).
5. Agreement concerning Delimitation of Marine and Submarine Areas and Maritime Co-operation between the Republics of Colombia and Ecuador (Signature: 23 August 1975; entry into force: 22 December 1975).
6. Exchange of Notes Constituting an Agreement on the Delimitation of the Exclusive Economic Zone of Mexico in the Bordering Area with Cuban Waters (Signature: 26 July 1976; entry into force: 26 July 1976).
7. Treaty on the Delimitation of Marine and Submarine Areas and Related Matters between the Republic of Panama and the Republic of Colombia (Signature: 20 November 1976; entry into force: 30 November 1977).
8. Agreement between the Republic of Haiti and the Republic of Cuba regarding the Delimitation of the Maritime Boundaries between the Two States (Signature: 27 October 1977; entry into force: 6 January 1978).
9. Agreement on Delimitation of Marine and Submarine Areas and Maritime Cooperation between the Republic of Colombia and the Dominican Republic (Signature: 13 January 1978; entry into force: 15 February 1979).
10. Agreement on Delimitation of the Maritime Boundaries between the Republic of Colombia and the Republic of Haiti (Signature: 17 February 1978; entry into force: 16 February 1979).
11. Maritime Boundary Treaty between the United States of America and the Republic of Venezuela (Signature 28 March 1978; entry into force 24 November 1980).
12. Boundary Delimitation Treaty between the Republic of Venezuela and the Kingdom of the Netherlands (Signature: 31 March 1978; entry into force: 15 December 1978).
13. Treaty on Maritime Boundaries between the United Mexican States and the United States of America (Caribbean Sea and Pacific Ocean) (Signature: 4 May 1978; entry into force: 13 November 1997).
14. Treaty on the Delimitation of Marine and Submarine Areas between the Republic of Venezuela and the Dominican Republic (Signature: 3 March 1979; entry into force: 15 January 1982).
15. Treaty concerning Delimitation of Marine Areas and Maritime Cooperation between the Republic of Costa Rica and the Republic of Panama (Signature: 2 February 1980; entry into force: 11 February 1982).
16. Delimitation Treaty between the Government of the French Republic (Martinique and Guadeloupe) and the Government of the Republic of Venezuela (Signature: 17 July 1980; entry into force: 28 January 1983).
17. Agreement between the Government of Brazil and the Government of France Relating to the Maritime Delimitation between Brazil and French Guyana (Signature: 30 January 1981; entry into force: 19 October 1983).

18. Convention on Delimitation between the Government of the French Republic (Martinique) and the Government of Saint Lucia (Signature: 4 March 1981; entry into force: 4 March 1981).
19. Treaty of Peace and Friendship between Chile and Argentina (Signature: 29 November 1994; entry into force: 2 May 1985).
20. Treaty on the Delimitation of Marine and Submarine Areas and Maritime Cooperation between the Republic of Colombia and the Republic of Costa Rica, Additional to the Treaty Signed at San José on 17 March 1977 (Signature: 6 April 1984; entry into force: 20 February 2001).
21. Treaty concerning Maritime Delimitation between the Republic of Colombia and the Republic of Honduras (Signature: 2 August 1986; entry into force: 20 December 1999).
22. Agreement on Maritime Delimitation between the Government of the French Republic and the Government of Dominica (Signature: 7 September 1987; entry into force: 23 December 1988).
23. Treaty between the Republic of Trinidad and Tobago and the Republic of Venezuela on the Delimitation of Marine and Submarine Areas (Signature: 18 April 1990; entry into force: 23 July 1991).
24. Agreement between the Government of the United Kingdom of Great Britain and Northern Ireland and the Government of the United States of America on the Delimitation in the Caribbean of a Maritime Boundary between Puerto Rico/US Virgin Islands and the British Virgin Islands (Signature: 5 November 1993; entry into force: 1 June 1995).
25. Treaty between the Government of the United Kingdom of Great Britain and Northern Ireland and the Government of the United States of America on the Delimitation in the Caribbean of a Maritime Boundary between US Virgin Islands and Anguilla (Signature: 5 November 1993; entry into force: 1 June 1995).
26. Treaty on Maritime Delimitation between Jamaica and the Republic of Colombia (Signature: 12 November 1993; entry into force: 14 March 1994).
27. Agreement between the Government of Jamaica and the Government of Republic of Cuba on the Delimitation of the Maritime Boundary between the two States (Signature: 18 February 1994; entry into force: 18 July 1995).
28. Agreement on Maritime Delimitation between the Government of the French Republic and the Government of the United Kingdom of Great Britain and Northern Ireland concerning Guadeloupe and Montserrat (Signature: 27 June 1996; entry into force 15 January 1997).
29. Agreement on Maritime Delimitation between the Government of the French Republic and the Government of the United Kingdom of Great Britain and Northern Ireland concerning Saint Martin and Saint Barthélemy (Signature: 27 June 1996; entry into force: 15 January 1997).
30. Agreement between the Government of the Dominican Republic and the Government of the United Kingdom of Great Britain and Northern Ireland regarding the Delimitation of the Maritime Limit between the Dominican Republic and the Turks and Caicos Islands (Signature: 2 August 1996).

31. Treaty between the Government of the United States of America and the Government of the United Mexican States on the Delimitation of the Continental Shelf in the Western Gulf of Mexico beyond 200 Nautical Miles (Signature: 9 June 2000; entry into force: 17 January 2001).
32. Treaty between the Government of the Republic of Honduras and the Government of the United Kingdom of Great Britain and Northern Ireland concerning the Delimitation of the Maritime Areas between the Cayman Islands and the Republic of Honduras (Signature: 4 December 2001; entry into force: 1 March 2002).
33. Maritime Delimitation Treaty between the Government of the United Mexican States and the Government of the Republic of Honduras (Signature: 18 April 2005; entry into force: 30 November 2006).
34. Agreement between the Government of the French Republic and the Government of Barbados on the Delimitation of the Maritime Space between France and Barbados (Signature: 15 October 2009).
35. Treaty between the Republic of Trinidad and Tobago and Grenada on the Delimitation of Marine and Submarine Areas (Signature: 21 April 2010).
36. Agreement by Exchange of Notes of Identical Content between the Republic of Peru and the Republic of Ecuador of 2 May 2011.
37. Agreement between the Commonwealth of the Bahamas and the Republic of Cuba for the Delimiting Line between their Maritime Zones (Signature: 3 October 2011; entry into force: 9 March 2012).
38. Agreement between Cuba and Honduras on Maritime Delimitation (Signature: August 2012).
39. Agreement between the Government of Costa Rica and the Government of Ecuador Relating to the Delimitation of the Maritime Areas between Costa Rica and Ecuador.
40. Agreement between the French Republic and the Government of the Kingdom of the Netherlands concerning the Maritime Delimitation in the Caribbean Region (Signature: 6 April 2016).
41. Agreement between the French Republic and the Government of Suriname (Signature: 8 November 2017).
42. Agreement between the French Republic and the Government of Antigua and Barbuda on the Delimitation of Maritime Spaces between France and Antigua and Barbuda in the Caribbean Region (Signature: 15 March 2017).
43. Agreement between the United Kingdom and Antigua and Barbuda (Signature: 27 July 2021).

III. Relevant National Legislation

Argentina

- Declaration Proclaiming Sovereignty over the Epicontinental Sea and the Continental Shelf, 9 October 1946. English text available at *AJIL*, Vol. 41, No. 1.

Brazil

- Brazil: Circular Note No. 43 of 1914, that sanctioned a three-nautical-mile neutrality zone; and Law Decree No. 794 of 1938, (Fishing Code), that considered a 12-nautical-mile zone for fisheries.[2]

Chile

- Presidential Declaration concerning Continental Shelf, 23 June 1947. English text available at *UNLS, ibid.*, Vol. I (ST/LEG/SER.B/1), pp. 6–8.
- Civil Code of 1855, Article 593.[3] Similar provisions can be found in a Supreme Decree of June 1941 concerning the Rules for Maritime, River and Lake Police.[4]

Colombia

- Law No. 14 of 1923, where the territorial sea is to be understood to extend up to 12 nautical miles;[5] and Customs Law No. 79 of 1931 that, however, established a 20-kilometre jurisdiction zone.[6]

Costa Rica

- Decree-Law No. 803, concerning Continental and Insular Shelf, 2 November 1949, "La Gaceta," Vol. 71, No. 249 (5 November 1949), p. 2046; in *UNLS*, ST/LEG/SER.B/1, 1951, pp. 9–10.

Cuba

- Code for Social Defense of 1936; and Organic Law of the Army and Navy, approved by Law Decree No. 7 of 1942.

Ecuador

- Civil Code of 1857.[7]

El Salvador

- Decree No. 1961 of 25 October 1955 (Maritime Hunting and Fishing Act); in *UNLS*, ST/LEG/SER.B/6, 1956, pp. 490–492.
- 1933 Navigation and Maritime Act, whereby the national domain included a maritime zone of one maritime league (three nautical miles).[8]

Guatemala

- Law of 10 June 1934, that claimed a 12-nautical-mile territorial sea; and Decree No. 2393 of 1940 that established that no belligerent submarine could enter into those territorial waters.[9]

Honduras

- Congressional Decree No. 102, Amending the Political Constitution, 7 March 1950, "La Gaceta: Diario Oficial de la República de Honduras", Vol. 75, No. 14055 (16 March 1950), p. 2; in *UNLS, ibid.*, pp. 11–12.

Mexico

- Presidential Declaration with Respect to Continental Shelf, 29 October 1945. English text available at *UNLS: Laws and Regulations on the Regime of the High Seas*, 1951, Vol. I, (ST/LEG/SER.B/1), pp. 13–14.
- General Law of National Patrimony of 1941, that established that the territorial sea extended for 16,668 metres (nine nautical miles) offshore.[10]

Peru

- Supreme Decree of 13 November 1934 on the Regulation on Visits and Stay of Warships and Military Aircraft in Peruvian Ports and Peruvian Territorial Waters in Times of Peace, which established a three-nautical-mile extension for then called territorial waters.
- Supreme Decree No. 781, concerning Submerged Continental or Insular Shelf, 1 August 1947. English text available at *UNLS, ibid.*, Vol. I (ST/LEG/SER.B/1), pp. 16–19.

US

- Presidential Proclamation No. 2667 concerning the Policy of the United States with Respect to the Natural Resources of the Subsoil and Sea Bed of the Continental Shelf, 28 September 1945, in *UNLS, National Legislation and Treaties Relating to the Law of the Sea*, ST/LEG/SER.B/1, pp. 38–40.
- Proclamation No. 2668, Policy of the United States with Respect to Coastal Fisheries in Certain Areas of the High Seas, 28 September 1945.

Notes

1 This list does not include the 1858 Treaty between Costa Rica and Nicaragua (which, following the Latin American practice, is also known as Treaty Cañas-Jerez, see: *BFSP*, Vol. 48, p. 1049), because it established that the bays in the Pacific Ocean and the Caribbean, at the end of the land boundary of both States, were common (condominium).

2 United Nations (1957), *UNLS, Laws and Regulations on the Regime of the Territorial Sea*, Vol. 2, ST/LEG/SER. B/6.

3 United Nations (1957), *UNLS, Laws and Regulations on the Regime of the Territorial Sea*, Vol. 2, ST/LEG/SER. B/6, p. 4.

4 Official Journal of Chile, 27 August 1941.

5 United Nations (1957), *UNLS, Laws and Regulations on the Regime of the Territorial Sea*, Vol. 2, ST/LEG/SER. B/6.

6 Available at Lex base Colombia.

7 CPPS (1974), *Legislación Marítima y Pesquera vigente y otros documentos referentes al Derecho del Mar – Ecuador*, Santiago, pp. 117–118.

8 United Nations (1957), *UNLS, Laws and Regulations on the Regime of the Territorial Sea*, Vol. 2, ST/LEG/SER. B/6.
9 United Nations (1957), *UNLS, Laws and Regulations on the Regime of the Territorial Sea*, Vol. 2, ST/LEG/SER. B/6.
10 García Robles (1959), *ibid.*, p. 407.

IV. Select Bibliography

1. Collective Works

Allain, J.-C., Guillen, P., Soutou, G.-H., Theis, L. and M. Vaïsse (2005), *Histoire de la diplomatie française. II. De 1815 à nos jours*, Paris: Perrin.

Bardonnet, D. and M. Virally (eds.) (1983), *Le nouveau droit international de la mer*, Paris: Pedone.

Buzan, B. and O. Waever (2003), *Regions and Powers: The Structure of International Security*, Cambridge: Cambridge University Press.

Calvert, P. (ed.) (2004), *Border and Territorial Disputes of the World*, London: Harper, 553 pp.

Carré, F. and A. de Séguin (1998), *Mexique, Golfe, Caraïbes: une méditerranée américaine*, Paris: PUF, 249 pp.

Charney, J. and L. Alexander (eds.) (1993), *International Maritime Boundaries*, Vols. I, II, Leiden: Martinus Nijhoff.

Charney, J. and L. Alexander (eds.) (1998), *International Maritime Boundaries*, Vol. III, Leiden: Martinus Nijhoff.

Charney, J. and R. Smith (eds.) (2002), *International Maritime Boundaries*, Vol. IV, Leiden: Martinus Nijhoff.

Churchill, R. and V. Lowe (1999), *The Law of the Sea*, Manchester: Manchester University Press.

Colson, D. and R. Smith (eds.) (2005), *International Maritime Boundaries*, Vol. V, Leiden: Martinus Nijhoff.

Colson, D. and R. Smith (eds.) (2011), *International Maritime Boundaries*, Vol. VI, Leiden: Brill.

Cook, P. and C. Carleton (2000), *Continental Shelf Limits: The Scientific and Legal Interface*, Oxford: Oxford University Press, 363 pp.

Dupuy, R.-J. and D. Vignes (eds.) (1985), *Traité du nouveau droit de la mer*, Paris: Economica.

Elferink, A., Henriksen, T. and S. V. Busch (eds.) (2018), *Maritime Boundary Delimitation: The Case Law. Is it consistent and predictable*? Cambridge: Cambridge University Press.

Fietta, S. and R. Cleverly (2016), *A Practitioner's Guide to Maritime Boundary Delimitation*, Oxford: Oxford University Press, 432 pp.

Freestone, D., Barnes, R., and D. Ong. (eds.) (2006). *The Law of the Sea: Progress and Prospects*, Oxford: Oxford University Press.

Girot, P. O. (ed.), *World Boundaries. The Americas*, Vol. IV, London: Routledge, 202 pp.

Johnston, D. M. and P. M. Saunders (eds.) (1988), *Ocean Boundary Making: Regional Issues and Developments*, London: Croom Helm, 356 pp.

Kapoor, D. C. and A. J. Kerr (1986), *A Guide to Maritime Boundary Delimitation*, Toronto: Carswell.

Lagoni, R. and D. Vignes (eds.) (2006), *Maritime Delimitation*, Leiden: Martinus Nijhoff, 241 pp.
Lathrop, C. (ed.) (2016), *International Maritime Boundaries*, Vol. VII, Leiden: Brill.
Lathrop, C. (ed.) (2020), *International Maritime Boundaries*, Vol. VIII, Leiden: Brill.
Lucchini and Voelckel (1996), *Droit de la mer* (tome 2), Vol. 1, Paris: Pedone.
McDougal, M. S. and W. T. Burke (1962), *The Public Order of the Oceans: A Contemporary International Law of the Sea*, New Haven, CT: Yale University Press.
Nordquist, M. (ed.). *United Nations Convention on the Law of the Sea, 1982. A Commentary*, Vol. 1, The Hague: Martinus Nijhoff.
Ortolland, D. and J.-P. Pirat (2010), *Atlas géopolitique des espaces maritimes*, Paris: Technip.
Prescott, V. and C. Schofield (2005), *The Maritime Political Boundaries of the World*, Leiden: Martinus Nijhoff, 666 pp.
Prolss, A. (ed.) (2017), *United Nations Convention on the Law of the Sea: A Commentary*, Munich: Beck-Hart-Nomos.
Roach, J. A. and R. W. Smith (2012), *Excessive Maritime Claims*, 3rd ed., Leiden: Martinus Nijhoff.
Rothwell, D. R. et al. (eds.) (2015), *The Oxford Handbook of the Law of the Sea*, Oxford: Oxford University Press.
Rothwell, D. R. and T. Stephens (2016), *The International Law of the Sea*, London: Hart.
Sobenes, E. and B. Samson (2018), *Nicaragua Before the International Court of Justice: Impacts on International Law*, New York: Springer, 435 pp.
Vidas, D. (ed.) (2010), *Law, Technology and Science for Oceans in Globalisation*, Leiden: Martinus Nijhoff.

2. Works and Courses

Agüero, M. (2001), *Consideraciones para la delimitación marítima del Perú*, Lima: Fondo editorial del Congreso.
Anderson, D. (2006), *Modern Law of the Sea. Selected Essays*, Leiden: Martinus Nijhoff.
Antunes, N. (2003), *Towards the Conceptualization of Maritime Delimitation. Legal and Technical Aspects of a Political Process*, Leiden: Martinus Nijhoff, 684 pp.
Barton, J. R. (1997), *A Political Geography of Latin America*, London: Routledge, 243 pp.
Benton, L. (2010), *A Search for Sovereignty: Law and Geography in European Empires, 1400–1900*, New York: Cambridge University Press, 358 pp.
Bernhardt, R. (1987), "Custom and Treaty in the Law of the Sea", *Recueil des cours*, Tome 205, pp. 250–330.
Bernstein, I. (1974), *Delimitation of International Boundaries*, Tel Aviv: University Press, 291 pp.
Bouchez, L. (1964), *The Regime of Bays in International Law*, Leiden: Sythoff, 330 pp.
Brown, E. (1994), *The International Law of the Sea. Introductory Manual*, Aldershot: Dartmouth, 494 pp.
Caminos, H. (1987), "The Legal Regime of Straits in the 1982 United Nations Convention on the Law of the Sea", *Recueil des cours*, Tome 205, pp. 11–245.
Chaunu, P. (1949), *Histoire de l'Amérique Latine*, Paris: Presses universitaires de France.
Dabène, O. (2012), *Atlas de l'Amérique latine. Le continent de toutes les révolutions*, Paris: Autrement, 96 pp.
D'Amato, A. (1971), "The Concept of Custom in International Law", *American Journal of International Law*, Vol. 63, pp. 211–223.

De Visscher, P. (1972), "Cours général de droit international public", *Recueil des cours*, tome 136.

Dundas, C. W. (1991), *Practical Steps in Negotiating Maritime Boundary Agreements: A Guide to Small States*, London: Commonwealth Fund for Technical Assistance, Technical Assistance Group, 282 pp.

García-Amador, F. V. (1956), *La Utilización y Conservación de la Riquezas del Mar*, La Habana, Cuba: Lex.

García-Amador, F. V. (1976), *América Latina y el derecho del mar*, Santiago de Chile: Editorial Universitaria, 197 pp.

García Robles, A. (1959), *La Conferencia de Ginebra y la Anchura del Mar Territorial*, Mexico: Fondo de Cultura Económica.

Gidel, G. (1934), *Le droit international public de la mer. Le temps de paix*, tome III, Paris: Duchemin.

Ireland, G. (1938), *Boundaries, Possessions and Conflicts in South America*, Cambridge, MA: Harvard University Press.

Jagota, S. (1985), *Maritime Boundary*, Dordrecht: Martinus Nijhoff, 388 pp.

Jessup, P. C. (1927), *The Law of Territorial Waters and National Jurisdiction*, New York: G.A. Jennings, 548 pp.

Johnston, D. M. (1988), *The Theory and History of Ocean Boundary-Making*, Kingston, ON: McGill Queen's University Press.

Jones, S. (1945), *Boundary-Making. A Handbook for Statesmen, Treaty Editors and Boundary Commissioners*, Washington, DC: Carnegie Endowment for International Peace, 268 pp.

Kamga, M. (2006), *Délimitation maritime sur la côte atlantique africaine*, Brussels: Bruylant, 317 pp.

Kolb, R. (2003), *Case Law on Equitable Maritime Delimitation/Jurisprudence sur les delimitations maritimes selon l'équité. Digest and Commentaries/Répertoire et commentaires*. The Hague: Martinus Nijhoff, 575pp.

Labrecque, G. (2004), *Les frontières maritimes internationales. Géopolitique de la délimitation en mer*, Paris: L'Harmattan.

Labrecque, G. (2011), *Les différends territoriaux en Amérique Latine: Jurisprudence de la Cour internationale de justice*, Paris: L'Harmattan.

Lando, M. (2019), *Maritime Delimitation as a Judicial Process*, Cambridge: Cambridge University Press, 432 pp.

Levy, J. P. (1983), *La Conférence des Nations Unies sur le droit de la mer. Histoire d'une négociation singulière*, Paris: Pedone.

Marchant, A. (1944), *Boundaries in the Latin American Republics*, Washington DC: US Government Printing Office.

Mendelson, M. (1998), "The Formation of Customary International Law", *Recueil des Cours de l'Académie de droit international de La Haye*, Tome 272.

O'Connell, D. P. (1994). *The International Law of the Sea*, Vol. I. Oxford: Oxford University Press.

Oda, S. (1969), "International Law of the Resources of the Sea", *Recueil des Cours de l'Académie de droit international de La Haye*, Tome 127, pp. 355–484.

Oude Elferink, A. G. (ed.) (2005), *Stability and Change in the Law of the Sea: The Role of the LOS Convention*. Leiden: Martinus Nijhoff, 250 pp.

Pancracio, J.-P. (2010), *Droit de la mer*, Paris: Dalloz, 520 pp.

Rémy, P.-J. (2001) *Trésors et secrets du Quai d'Orsay. Une histoire inédite de la diplomatie française*, Paris: JC Lattès.

Rodriguez Cuadros, M. (2012), *Derecho Internacional de la Delimitación Marítima*, Lima: Fondo Editorial UTP.

Riesenfeld, S. A. (1942), *Protection of Coastal Fisheries under International Law*, Washington, DC: Carnegie Endowment for International Peace.

Rosenne, S. (1972), *League of Nations Committee of Experts for the Progressive Codification of International Law 1925–1928*, Vol. 2, New York: Ocean.

Scovazzi, T. (2000), "The Evolution of International Law of the Sea: New Issues, New Challenges", *Recueil des Cours de l'Académie de droit international de La Haye*, Vol. 286, pp. 43–243.

Scovazzi, T. (2004/2005), "Maritime Delimitations in the Mediterranean Sea", In *Cursos Euromediterráneos Bancaja de Derecho Internacional*, Vol. VIII/IX, Tirant lo blanch, pp. 351–504.

Smith, H. A. (1942), *The Law and Custom of the Sea*, London: Stevens & Sons.

Symmons, C. (2008), *Historic Waters in the Law of the Sea. A Modern Re-Appraisal*, Leiden: Martinus Nijhoff.

Tanaka, Y. (2019), *Predictability and Flexibility in the Law of Maritime Delimitation*, Oxford: Hart.

Treves, T. (1990), "Codification du droit international et pratique des Etats dans le droit de la mer", *Recueil des Cours de l'Académie de droit international de La Haye*, Vol. 223.

Ulloa, A. (1957), *Derecho Internacional Público*, Vol. I, Madrid: Ediciones Iberoamericanas.

Vargas, J. A. (1981), *Contribuciones de la América Latina al derecho del mar*, Mexico: UNAM, 138 pp.

Vargas, J. A. (2011), *Mexico and the Law of the Sea. Contributions and Compromises*. Leiden: Martinus Nijhoff.

Vargas Carreño, E. (1973), *América Latina y el Derecho del Mar*, Mexico: Fondo de Cultura Económica, 167 pp.

Verzijl, J. H. W. (1973), *International Law in a Historical Perspective*, Leiden: Martinus Nijhoff, 861 pp.

Vincent, P. (2008), *Droit de la mer*, Brussels: Larcier, 292 pp.

Weil, P. (1988), *Perspectives du droit de la délimitation maritime*, Paris: Pedone.

Weil, P. (1989), *The Law of Maritime Delimitation – Reflections*, Cambridge: Cambridge Grotius.

Yann-huei, S. and K. Zou (2014), *Major Law and Policy Issues in the South China Sea. European and American Perspectives*, London: Routledge, 326 pp.

Zacklin, R. (ed.) (1974), *The Changing Law of the Sea. Western Hemisphere Perspectives*, Leiden: Sjithoff.

3. Articles, and Contributions to Collective Works

Abello, R. (2003), "Eaux et baies historiques en droit international", *Estudios Sociales y Jurídicos*, Vol. 5, Issue 1, pp. 33–76.

Aguilar, A. (1992), "The Latin American Contribution to the Modern Law of the Sea", *Netherlands International Law Review*, Vol. 39, pp. 63–88.

Akehurst, M. (1974–75), "The Hierarchy of the Sources of International Law" (1974–75), *BYIL*, Vol. 47, pp. 273–285.

Akehurst, M. (1977), "Custom as a Source of International Law", *BYIL*, Vol. 47, pp. 1–53.

Alexander, L. M. (1958), "Samuel Whittemore Bogs: An appreciation", *Annals of the Association of American Geographers*, Vol. 48, Issue 3, pp. 237–244.

Alexander, L. M. and R. D. Hodgson (1975), "The Impact of the 200-Mile Economic Zone on the Law of the Sea", *San Diego Law Review*, Vol. 12.

Amerasinghe, H. S., "The Third United Nations Conference on the Law of the Sea", in: Nordquist, M. (ed.). *United Nations Convention on the Law of the Sea, 1982. A Commentary*, Vol. 1, The Hague: Martinus Nijhoff, pp. 1–10.

Anderson, D. (2005), "Developments in Maritime Boundary Law and Practice", in: Colson, D. A. and R. W. Smith (eds.), *International Maritime Boundaries*, Vol. V, Leiden: Martinus Nijhoff, pp. 3197–3204.

Anderson, D. (2006), "Negotiating Maritime Boundary Agreements", in: Anderson, D. (ed.), *Modern Law of the Sea. Selected Essays*, Leiden: Martinus Nijhoff, pp. 417–435.

Antunes, N. (2005), "Some Thoughts on the Technical Input in Maritime Delimitation", in: Colson, D. A. and R. W. Smith (eds.), *International Maritime Boundaries*, Vol. V, pp. 3377–3398.

Bancroft, F. (1896), "The French in Mexico and the Monroe Doctrine", *Political Science Quarterly*, No. 11.

Bardonnet, D. (1989), "Frontières terrestres et frontières maritimes", *AFDI*, Vol. 35, pp. 1–64.

Beer-Gabel, J. (1992), "Variations sur la notion de frontière maritime", in: INDEMER (ed.), *Droit de la mer. Etudes dédiées au Doyen Claude-Albert Colliard*, Paris: Pedone, pp. 11–35.

Beer-Gabel, J. (2004), "Les accords conclus en matière de délimitation maritime", in: INDEMER (ed.), *Le processus de délimitation maritime. Etude d'un cas fictive*, Monaco: Pedone.

Borchard, E. (1946), "Resources of the Continental Shelf", *AJIL*, Vol. 40, pp. 53–70.

Caflisch, L. (1981), "Les zones maritimes sous juridiction nationale, leurs limites et leur délimitation", *RGDIP*, 1981, pp.

Caflisch, L. (1991), "The Delimitation of Marine Spaces between States with Opposite or Adjacent Coasts", in: Dupuy, R. J. and D. Vignes (eds.), *A Handbook on the New Law of the Sea*, Dordrecht: Martinus Nijhoff, pp. 425–99.

Carleton, C. (1994), "The British Virgin Islands/Puerto Rico and US Virgin Islands – Anguilla/US Virgin Islands, *IJMCL*, Vol. 9, Issue 2, pp. 253–260.

Carleton, C. (2006), "Maritime Delimitation in Complex Island Situations: A Case Study on the Caribbean Sea", in: Lagoni, R. and D. Vignes (eds.), *Maritime Delimitation*, Leiden: Martinus Nijhoff.

Carleton, C. and C. Schofield (2002), "Developments in the Technical Determination of Marine Space: Delimitation, Dispute Resolution, Geographical Information Systems and the Role of the Technical Expert", in: IBRU (ed.), *Maritime Briefing*, Vol. 3, No. 4, pp. 7–30.

Cazala, J. (2008), "Retour sur les méthodes de délimitation juridictionnelle d'espaces maritimes mises en oeuvre dans quelques affaires récentes", *AFDI*, Vol. 54, pp. 411–427.

Charney, J. (1993), "Introduction", in: Charney, J. and L. Alexander (eds.), *International Maritime Boundaries*, Vol. I. Dordrecht: Martinus Nijhoff.

Chinkin, C. (1995), "Dispute Resolution and the Law of the Sea: Regional Problems and Prospects", in: Crawford, J. and D. Rothwell (eds.), *The Law of the Sea in the Asian Pacific Region*, Dordrecht: Martinus Nijhoff, pp. 237–262.

Couffignal, G., "La politique étrangère de la France vis-à-vis de l'Amérique Latine", in: Couffignal, G. (ed.), *Amérique latine. L'Amérique latine est bien partie*, Paris: IHEAL.

Davenport, T. (2012), "Southeast Asian approaches to maritime delimitation", *AsianSIL Working Paper*, 2012/7.

Dawson, F. (1998), "The evacuation of the Mosquito Shore and the English who stayed behind, 1786–1800", *Americas*, Vol. 55, pp. 63–89.

Dean, A. H. (1958). "The Geneva Conference on the Law of the Sea: What was Accomplished", *AJIL*, Vol. 52, pp. 607–628.

Dean, A. H. (1960). "The Second Geneva Conference on the Law of the Sea: The Fight for Freedom of the Seas", *AJIL*, Vol. 54, pp. 751–789.

De la Colina, R. (1974), "Evolución del Derecho del Mar en América: Contribución latinoamericana", in: Secretaría de Relaciones Exteriores de Mexico (ed.), *México y el régimen del mar*, Mexico: Tlatelolco, pp. 37–80.

De La Fayette, L. (2000), "The M/V 'Saiga' (No. 2) Case (St. Vincent and the Grenadines v. Guinea), Judgment", *ICLQ*, Vol. 49, pp. 467–476.

De Soto, A. (1973), "The Latin American View of the Law of the Sea", *India Quarterly*, Vol. 29, pp. 126–137.

De Yturriaga, J. A., "Orígen, desarrollo y resultados de la III Conferencia de las Naciones Unidas sobre el Derecho del Mar", in: *Tendencias y perspectivas actuales del Derecho del Mar. Cuadernos de la Escuela Diplomática, España*, Vol. 32, Madrid: Ministerio de Asuntos Exteriores y de Cooperación de España, pp. 13–38.

Dundas, C. W. (2005-A), "Middle American and Caribbean Maritime Boundaries", in: Colson, D. A. and R. W. Smith (eds.), *International Maritime Boundaries*, Vol. V, Leiden: Brill/Nijhoff, pp. 3405–3423.

Dundas, C. W. (2005-B) "Barbados-Guyana", in: Colson, David A. and Robert W. Smith, *International Maritime Boundaries*, Vol. V, Leiden: Brill/Nijhoff, pp. 3578–3597.

Dupuy, R. J. (1984), "Politiques nationales et système juridique issu de la troisième Conférence", SFDI, *colloque de Rouen*, pp. 249–275.

Duvic-Paoli, L.-A. (2011), "Régionalisme et droit de la mer: entre renforcement et affaiblissement des normes universelles", *Annuaire du droit de la de Mer*, Vol. 16.

Evans, H. (1974), "The Nootka Sound Controversy in Anglo-French Diplomacy – 1790", *Journal of Modern History*, Vol. 46, pp. 609–640.

Evans, M. (2006). "Maritime Boundary Delimitation: Where Do We Go From Here?", in: Freestone et al. (eds.). *The Law of the Sea: Progress and Prospects*, Oxford: Oxford University Press.

Feldman, M. B. and D. Colson (1981), "The Maritime Boundaries of the United States", *AJIL*, Vol. 75, pp. 729–763.

Focsaneanu, L. (1961), "Le droit international maritime de l'Océan Pacifique et de ses mer adjacentes", *AFDI*, Vol. 7, pp. 173–213.

Freestone, D. (2012), "The Law of the Sea Convention at 30: Successes, Challenges, and New Agendas", *IJMCL*, Vol. 27, pp. 675–682.

Galindo, R. (1976), "Contribución de América Latina a la Conferencia de Caracas", in: Vargas, J. A. and E. V. Carreño (eds.), *Derecho del mar: una vision latinoamericana*, Mexico: Editorial Jus, pp. 53–77.

Galindo, R. (1979), "Latin America's influence and role in the Third Conference on the Law of the Sea", *Ocean Development and International Law*, Vol. 7, pp. 65–87.

García-Amador, F. V. (1974), "The Latin American contribution to the development of the law of the sea", *AJIL*, Vol. 68, pp. 33–50.

García-Corrochano, L. (2018), "La jurisprudencia internacional sobre delimitación marítima", in: Gutiérrez Castillo, V. (eds.), *América Latina y el derecho del mar. Liber amicorum Alfredo Martínez Moreno*, Jaén: Tirant lo Blanch.

Girot, P. O. (1994), "The Interoceanic canal and boundaries in Central America. The case of the San Juan River", in: Girot, P. O. (ed.), *World Boundaries. The Americas*, Vol. IV, London: Routledge, pp. 84–109.

Gross Espiell, H. (1975), "Le Traité relatif au Rio de la Plata et à sa façade maritime", *AFDI*, Vol. 21, pp. 241–249.

Guillaume, G. (1983), "Les accords de délimitation maritime passés par la France", Colloque de Rouen.

Hamon, G., Arico, S. and C. Monagle (2009), "Marine genetic resources: A review of scientific and commercial interest", *Marine Policy*, Vol. 33, pp. 183–194.

Hollick, A. L. (1977), "The Origins of 200-Mile Offshore Zones", *AJIL*, Vol. 71, pp. 494–500.

Horna, A. V. (2007), "Apuntes acerca del Tribunal Internacional del Derecho del Mar: ¿Hamburgo v. La Haya?", *Agenda Internacional*, No. 25 pp. 131–148.

Horna, A. V. (2009), "Maritime Dispute (Peru v. Chile): Background and Preliminary Thoughts." *Ocean Yearbook*, Vol. 23, pp. 193–229.

Horna, A. V. (2013), "Procedural Aspects Concerning Jurisdiction and Admissibility in Cases of Maritime Delimitation Before the ICJ", in: Boschiero, N. et al (eds.), *International Courts and the Development of International Law. Essays in Honour of Tullio Treves*, The Hague: Asser, pp. 165–178.

Horna, A. V. (2022), "Del mar del Norte al mar Caribe: 50 años de delimitación marítima en la jurisprudencia internacional", *Revista Advocatus*, Vol. 42, pp. 91–100.

Hossain, K. (1980), "Equitable Solutions in the International Law of the Sea: Some Problems", in: Hossain, K. (ed.), *Legal Aspects of the New International Economic Order*, London: Frances Pinter.

Hutchinson, D. N. (1985), "The Seaward Limit to the Continental Shelf Jurisdiction in Customary International Law", *BYIL*, Vol. 56, pp. 111–188.

Janis, M. W. (1975), "The Roles of Regional Law of the Sea", *San Diego Law Review*, Vol. 12, pp. 553–568.

Jennings, R. (1969), "The Limits of Continental Shelf Jurisdiction: Some Possible Implications of the North Sea Case Judgment", *ICLQ*, Vol. 18, pp. 819–832.

Jennings, R. (1986), "Equity and Equitable Principles," *Annuaire suisse de droit international*, Vol. 42, 1986, pp. 27–38.

Jiménez de Aréchaga, E. (1993), "Charney and Alexander", *International Maritime Boundaries*, Vol. I, pp. 757–776.

Kiss, A. (1985). "The Common Heritage of Mankind: Utopia or Reality?", *International Journal*, Vol 40.

Koh, T., "A Constitution for the Oceans", in: Nordquist, M. (ed.). *United Nations Convention on the Law of the Sea, 1982. A Commentary*, Vol. 1, The Hague: Martinus Nijhoff, pp. 11–16.

Kohen, M. (2009), "L'uti possidetis iuris et les espaces maritimes", *Liber amicorum Jean-Pierre Cot. Le procès international*, Brussels: Bruylant, pp. 155–170.

Kopela, S. (2009), "2007 Archipelagic Legislation of the Dominican Republic: An assessment", *IJMCL*, Vol. 24, pp. 501–533.

Kunz, J. (1946), "Guatemala vs. Great Britain: in Re Belice", *AJIL*, Vol. 40, pp. 383–390.

Kwiatkowska, B. (1988), "Equitable Maritime Boundary Delimitation – A Legal Perspective", *International Journal of Estuarine and Coastal Law*, Vol. 3, 287–304.

Kwiatkowska, B. (1993), "Brazil's 1993 Law . . ." *IJMCL*, Vol. 8, pp. 497–506.

Kwiatkowska, B.(2001), "The Law of the Sea Related Cases in the International Court of Justice during the Presidency of Judge Stephen M. Schwebel (1997–2000)", *IJMCL*, Vol. 16, pp. 1–40.

Kwiatkowska, B. (2007), "The 2006 *Barbados/Trinidad and Tobago* Award: A Landmark in Compulsory and Equitable Maritime Boundary Delimitation", *IJMCL*, Vol. 22, pp. 7–60.

Laveissiere, J. (1985), "Les Iles et la Détermination des Frontières Maritimes", in: Constantopoulos, D. (ed.), *National and International Boundaries*, Vol. XV, Thessaloniki: Institute of Public International law and International Relations of Thessaloniki, pp. 79–99.

Legault, L. and B. Hankey (1993), "Method, Oppositeness and Adjacency, and Proportionality in Maritime Boundary Delimitation", in: Charney and Alexander (eds.), *International Maritime Boundaries*, Vol. I, pp. 203–241.

Lodge, M. (2012), "The Common Heritage of Mankind", *IJMCL*, Vol. 27, pp. 733–742.

López Contreras, C. (2011), "Colson, David A. and Robert W. Smith", *International Maritime Boundaries*, Vol. VI, pp. 4202–4212.

Lowe, V. (1981), "The Development of the Concept of the Contiguous Zone", *BYIL*, Vol. 52, pp. 109–169.

Lucchini, L. (2006), "La Délimitation des Frontières Maritimes dans la Jurisprudence Internationale: Vue d'Ensemble", in: Lagoni, R. and D. Vignes (eds.), *Maritime Delimitation*, Leiden: Martinus Nijhoff.

Magnússon, B. M. (2013), "Outer Continental Shelf Boundary Agreements", *ICLQ*, pp. 345–372.

Martin, L. and Y. Parkhomenko (2018), "The Territorial and Maritime Dispute (Nicaragua v. Colombia) and Its Implications for Future Maritime Delimitations in the Caribbean Sea and Elsewhere", in: Sobenes, E. and B. Samson (eds.), *Nicaragua Before the International Court of Justice. Impacts on International Law*, Springer, pp. 113–139.

McLaughlin, R. G. (2008), "Hydrocarbon Development in the Ultra-Deepwater Boundary Region of the Gulf of Mexico: Time to Reexamine a Comprehensive U.S.-Mexico Cooperation Agreement", *Ocean Development and International Law*, Vol. 39, pp. 1–31.

Meese, R. (2005), "Le traité du 18 avril 2005 entre le Honduras et les Etats-Unis du Mexique sur la délimitation maritime", *Annuaire du droit de la mer*, Vol. 10, pp. 237–243.

Molenaar, E. (2003), "Netherlands Antilles and Aruba", *IJMCL*, Vol. 18, pp. 127–144.

Morales Paul, I. (1974), "Venezuela: The Country in the Caribbean", in: Zacklin, R. (ed.), *The Changing Law of the Sea. Western Hemisphere Perspectives*, Leiden: Sjithoff, pp. 125–131.

Nelson, D. (1988), "Delimitation of maritime boundaries in the Caribbean", in: Johnston, D. M. and P. M. Saunders (eds.), *Ocean Boundary Making: Regional issues and Developments*, London: Croom Helm, pp. 142–203.

Nelson, D. (2002), "The Continental Shelf: Interplay of Law and Science", in: Ando, N. et al (eds.), *Liber Amicorum Judge Shigeru Oda*, The Hague: Kluwer Law International, pp. 1235–1253.

Oxman, B. H. (1982), "The Third United Nations Conference on the Law of the Sea: The Tenth Session (1981)", *AJIL*, Vol. 76, pp. 1–23.

Oxman, B. H. (2006), "The Territorial Temptation: A Siren Song at Sea", *AJIL*, Vol. 100, pp. 830–851.

Pfirter de Armas, F. (1974), "Argentina and the Law of the Sea", in: Zacklin, R. (ed.), *The Changing Law of the Sea. Western Hemisphere Perspectives*, Leiden: Sjithoff, pp. 169–187.

Pulvenis, J. F. (1980), "La mer des caraïbes", *Revue générale de droit international public*, No. 1, pp. 310–327.

Quéneudec, J. P. (1988), "Chronique du Droit de la Mer", *AFDI*, Vol. 34, pp. 726–734.

Quéneudec, J. P. (2005), "Unité et diversité des espaces maritimes", *Questions internationales*, No. 14, pp. 20–27.

Ratner, S. (1996), "Drawing a Better Line: Uti Possidetis and the Borders of New States", *AJIL*, Vol. 90, pp. 590–624.

Reeves, J. S. (1930), "The Codification of the Law of Territorial Waters", *AJIL*, Vol. 24, pp. 486–499.

Remiro Brotons, A. (1993), "Problemas de fronteras en Iberoamérica: la delimitación de espacios marinos", in: Mangas, A. (ed.), *La Escuela de Salamanca y el Derecho Internacional en América: del pasado al futuro*, Salamanca: Anuário de Direito Público.

Rosenne, S. (1986), "UNCLOS III – The Montreux (Riphagen) Compromise", in: Bos, A. and H. Siblesz (eds.), *Realism in Law-Making: Essays on International Law in Honour of Willem Riphagen*, Dordrecht: Martinus Nijhoff.

Sanchez-Rodríguez, L. (2004), "*L'uti possidetis*: application à la délimitation maritime", in: Colloque internationale: *Le processus de délimitation maritime. Etude d'un cas fictif*, Paris: Pedone, pp. 303–315.

Scovazzi, T. (2010), "The Seabed Beyond the Limits of National Jurisdiction: General and Institutional Aspects", in: Molenaar, E. and A. O. Elferink (eds.), *The International Legal Regime of Areas Beyond National Jurisdiction. Current and Future Developments*, Leiden: Martinus Nijhoff, pp. 44–60.

Shi, J. (2010), "Maritime Delimitation in the Jurisprudence of the International Court of Justice", *Chinese Journal of International Law*, Vol. 9, pp. 271–291.

Skaggs, J. M. (1994), *The Great Guano Rush: Entrepreneurs and American Overseas Expansion*, New York: St. Martin's Press, 352 pp.

Song, Y.-h. (2013), "Survey of Declarations or Statements Made by the Parties to the Law of the Sea Convention: 30 Years after Adoption", *IJMCL*, Vol. 28, pp. 5–59.

Stevenson, J. R. and B. H. Oxman (1974), "The Preparations for the Law of the Sea Conference", *AJIL*, Vol. 68, pp. 1–32.

Stevenson, J. R. and B. H. Oxman (1975), "The Third United Nations Conference on the Law of the Sea: The 1974 Caracas Session", *AJIL*, Vol. 69, pp. 1–30.

Stevenson, J. R. and B. H. Oxman (1975), "The Third United Nations Conference on the Law of the Sea: The 1975 Geneva Session", *AJIL*, Vol. 69, pp. 763–797.

Tanaka, Y. (2001), "Reflections on the Concept of Proportionality in the Law of Maritime Delimitation", *IJMCL*, Vol. 16, pp. 433–463.

Treves, T. (2008), "The 1958 Geneva Conventions on the Law of the Sea", *United Nations Audiovisual Library of International Law*.

Ulloa, A. (1957), "Régimen Jurídico del Mar", *RPDI*, Vol. XVII, (51), pp. 5–81.

Voelckel, M. (1979), "Aperçu de quelques problems techniques concernant la détermination des frontières maritimes", *AFDI*, Vol. 25, pp. 693–711.

Weisseberg, G. (1969), "The Maltese proposal on the sea-bed and ocean floor – Its fate in two cities", *ICLQ*, Vol. 42.

Whittemore Boggs, S. (1930), "Delimitation of the Territorial Sea. The Method of Delimitation Proposed by the Delegation of the United States at The Hague Conference for the Codification of International Law", *AJIL*, Vol. 24, pp. 541–555.

Whittemore Boggs, S. (1951), "Delimitation of Seaward Areas under National Jurisdiction", *AJIL*, Vol. 45, pp. 240–266.

Young, R. (1948), "Recent Developments with Respect to the Continental Shelf", *AJIL*, Vol. 42, pp. 849–857.

Zacklin, R. (1974), "Latin America and the Development of the Law of the Sea", in: Zacklin, R. (ed.), *The Changing Law of the Sea. Western Hemisphere Perspectives*, Leiden: Sjithoff, pp. 59–78.

4. Sources From the US Department of State

Limits in the Seas No. 11 – Continental Shelf Boundary: Trinidad and Tobago–Venezuela, Issued by the Geographer.

Limits in the Seas No. 64, Continental Shelf Boundary: Argentina–Uruguay. US Department of State, Issued by the Geographer, 24 October 1975.

Limits in the Seas No. 79, Maritime Boundaries: Colombia–Panama. US Department of State, Issued by the Geographer, 3 November 1978.

Limits in the Seas No. 84, Maritime Boundaries: Colombia–Panama. US Department of State, Issued by the Geographer, 1979.

Limits in the Seas No. 91, Maritime Boundary: United States–Venezuela. US Department of State, 21 February 1990.

Limits in the Seas No. 97, Maritime Boundaries: Costa Rica–Panama. US Department of State, Issued by the Geographer, 6 December 1982

Limits in the Seas No. 104, Maritime Boundary: Cuba–Mexico. US Department State, Issued by the Geographer, 10 September 1985.

Limits in the Seas No. 115, United States–United Kingdom Maritime Boundaries in the Caribbean. US Department of State, 11 April 1994.

Limits in the Seas No. 124, Straight Baseline Claim: Honduras. US Department of State, 28 June 2001.

Limits in the Seas No. 125, Jamaica's Maritime Claims and Boundaries. US Department of State, 5 February 2004.

Limits in the Seas No. 128, The Bahamas: Archipelagic and other Maritime Claims and Boundaries. US Department of State, 31 January 2014.

Limits in the Seas No. 130, Dominican Republic: Archipelagic and other Maritime Claims and Boundaries. US Department of State, 31 January 2014.

Limits in the Seas No. 131, Trinidad and Tobago: Archipelagic and other Maritime Claims and Boundaries. US Department of State, 31 January 2014.

Limits in the Seas No. 133, Antigua and Barbuda: Archipelagic and other Maritime Claims and Boundaries. US Department of State, 28 March 2014.

Limits in the Seas No. 135, Grenada: Archipelagic and other Maritime Claims and Boundaries. US Department of State, 28 March 2014.

Limits in the Seas No. 144, Saint Vincent and the Grenadines: Archipelagic and other Maritime Claims and Boundaries. US Department of State, 28 October 2019.

Other Documents

Statement of Judge Rosalyn Higgins, President of the International Court of Justice, on the occasion of the tenth anniversary of the International Tribunal for the Law of the Sea, 29 September 2006.

Statement by H.E. Judge Peter Tomka, President of the International Court of Justice, at the High-Level Meeting on the Rule of Law, 24 September 2012.

Statement by H.E. Ban Ki-moon, Secretary-General of the United Nations, 67th Session of the United Nations General Assembly, 10 December 2012.

Statement by H.E. Judge Shunji Yanai, President of the International Tribunal for the Law of the Sea, at the Plenary of the Sixty-seventh session of the United Nations General Assembly on the occasion of the commemoration of the thirtieth anniversary of the opening for signature of the 1982 United Nations Convention on the Law of the Sea, New York, 10 December 2012.

Speech by H.E. Judge Joan E. Donoghue, President of the International Court of Justice, on the occasion of the Seventy-Sixth session of the United Nations General Assembly, 28 October 2021.

Statement by H.E. Judge Albert Hoffmann, President of the International Tribunal for the Law of the Sea on Agenda item 78(a) "oceans and the law of the sea" for the plenary of the seventy-sixth session of the United Nations General Assembly, New York, 9 December 2021.

Index

Page numbers followed by "n" indicate a note on the corresponding page.

For Product Safety Concerns and Information please contact our EU representative GPSR@taylorandfrancis.com Taylor & Francis Verlag GmbH, Kaufingerstraße 24, 80331 München, Germany